The Murphys
of
Rathcore Rectory

Julia Turner

 FriesenPress

Suite 300 - 990 Fort St
Victoria, BC, V8V 3K2
Canada

www.friesenpress.com

ISBN
978-1-5255-7404-7 (Hardcover)
978-1-5255-7405-4 (Paperback)
978-1-5255-7406-1 (eBook)

1. HISTORY, EUROPE, IRELAND

Distributed to the trade by The Ingram Book Company

Old Furniture

Thomas Hardy
(1840-1928)

I know not how it may be with others
Who sit amid relics of householdry
That date from the days of their mother's mothers
But well I know how it is with me
Continually.

I see the hands of the generations
That owned each shiny familiar thing
In play on its knobs and indentations,
And with its ancient fashioning
Still dallying

Hands behind hands, growing paler and paler,
As in a mirror a candle-flame
Shows images of itself, each frailer
As it recedes, though the eye may frame
Its shape the same.

[...]

Well, well. It is best to be up and doing,
The world has no use for us today
Who eyes things thus – no aim pursuing!
He should not continue in this stay
But sink away.

CONTENTS

MAPS

Map 1: General map of Ireland showing key places mentioned throughout the text.

Map 2: Map of Beara Peninsula, showing key places mentioned in Chapters 2, 3, 5, & 6.

Map 3: Map of places mentioned in Chapter 7.

Map 4: Map of churches mentioned in Chapter 8 and beyond.

Map 5: Map of Ireland explaining the J. E. H. Murphy's family's connection with Achill Island.

Map 6: Map of Achill Island showing places mentioned in Chapter 21.

Map 7: Map showing movements of Leo's Siege Battery in WWI as described in Chapter 24.

Map 8: Map of southwest Ireland showing places mentioned in Chapter 29.

Map 9: Map of Australia showing places mentioned in Chapter 29.

ACKNOWLEDGEMENTS

Special thanks to my two editors, **Linda Menzies** and **Margaret Growcott**. They edit in very different ways: **Linda** reviewing through digitised material and **Margaret** working with hard copies. **Linda** will re-write awkward grammar, sentence structure, and reorganise paragraph contents, while **Margaret** will write on the page *Haven't a clue what you're trying to say* or *Who and Where IS that?* or *NOW you tell me – I needed to know that two pages ago*. Written works need to be scrubbed clean and polished, and between them **Linda** and **Margaret** have the text sparkling. Thank you both for grasping this project so willingly and with such energy and enthusiasm, good humour, and encouragement.

My brother **Robin Wormell**, blessed with an excellent memory, remembers who said what, when, where, and why it was said. He has read through many of the chapters and his critiques have been invaluable, always checking I have caught the essence of the subject.

I am indebted to all those relatives who went before, leaving valuable resources:

- my mother **Daphne (Wallace) Wormell**, daughter of Eva

- my aunt **Valentine (Wallace) Urie**, daughter of Eva

- my first cousin once removed **Geordie Hallowes**, son of Olive

- my first cousin once removed **Harry Murphy**, son of Charlie

- my first cousin once removed **Willie Murphy**, son of Edwy

- my great-uncle **Charlie Murphy**, son of James, who was such a great family raconteur, and who was one of the first to write annual Christmas letters sent to most continents, keeping family connected.

- my aunt **Dorothy (Wallace) Short**, daughter of Eva

I am grateful to those relatives who have provided further material:

Susan Murphy, graphic designer, wife of Edward Murphy, son of Charlie, who spent a year or so developing the circular family tree, which shows so clearly how we are all connected.

Noelle Murphy, wife of Harry Murphy, who cared for and delivered a tape recording she and Harry had made with members of the Peard family in the 1980s.

Veda Hallowes, wife of Geordie, mentioned above, who gathered, saved and passed on a suitcase of photos and material of the Murphys.

Clive Murphy, son of Leo, who provided insights into his father's life.

Royse Murphy, son of Harry, grandson of Charlie. **Royse** has inherited items from the Murphys in Ardgroom, collected and treasured by his grandfather and father, pictures of which he has shared generously. He is also a prodigious internet searcher, willingly and quickly passing along his finds.

Jan Veneto, descended from Catherine Doherty, sister of James, sought out relatives in the Templenoe/Capparoe areas west of Kenmare, and on finding the Doherty Cottage had the foresight to leave with a neighbour there a photograph of herself and two sisters. Only two weeks later, Aunt Val Urie and I knocked on the same neighbour's door, were shown the photo, and so discovered our American relatives.

Jaclyn Hines, descended from Edward Murphy, brother of James, connections with whom were made through the perseverance of Royse Murphy. He uncovered our Australian relatives. **Jaclyn** greatly assisted with information on Edward Murphy, brother of James, and also with results of her Murphy genealogical research.

Margaret (Lennon) Wynne and David Wynne, for all their advice and encouragement, and also their expertise about the development of the Irish railway system.

My brother **Stephen and his wife Valerie** for driving me around before I had an Irish car, accompanying with interest and asking questions I had not yet thought about! We visited the Malahide Golf Club and the Archives in Skerries, and were given a great welcome in both places.

A special thank you to my niece **Joanna Wormell** for her good cheer and support through many years of effort.

I thank the Board of Trinity College, for the conservation, cataloguing and accessibility of material connected to Professor J. E. H. Murphy.

To all those who read material and advised on content I am most grateful:

Dr Susan Parkes, Fellow Emeritus (Education) of Trinity College, Dublin, who read and then advised on Chapter 2 *Eamon*, the most challenging chapter to write. Thanks to her suggestions, the chapter has finally settled, having gone through many drafts.

Mike Murphy of Ardgroom and of New Jersey, USA, whose comments pointed the way forward and saved hours of research.

Maureen Goodbody, who advised on presentation of material in Olive's chapter. Maureen knew of almost every House in Meath mentioned in the chapter, and perhaps every person and their connections and customs in Meath described.

Róisín Nee of Renvyle Peninsula for her expertise with the Irish language. **Róisín**'s interest in making correct translations and her care with colloquial phraseology and usage has created an authentic flavour in dialogue produced around Mary Murphy, mother of James.

Helen Faherty of Rusheenduff, Renvyle Peninsula, who very early on in the writing of the life of James, translated pages in Irish found on the internet, and then typed out the English, with explanations.

Ian Coombes, Principal, Bandon Grammar School, who gave advice on the schooling of James in Bandon, Co. Cork.

Paul and Charmian Arbuckle of Ardgroom for their contributions regarding the early life of James, explanations of the geography around Ardgroom, and last but not least, for their hospitality.

To my son **Dr Derek Turner** of the Faculty of Earth Sciences, Douglas College in Vancouver, who so willingly and cheerfully said, *'I'm ready when you are'* whenever I brought the word *maps* into our conversations, a heartfelt thank you. A professional cartographer amongst other skills and a father of a newborn, he has no free time, but somehow finds enough to create marvellous maps for his mother. And thanks to Derek's wife **Jill Evers** who supports and facilitates these endeavours.

To my son **Craig Turner** and his wife **Birte**, both always ready to answer questions about internet issues and electronics. With five children, they still manage to explain references in German, providing translations.

For their willingness to contribute to the manuscript text, a huge thank you to **Richard Wormell** in London, and thanks also to his wife **Pauline Lyle-Smith** for assisting in interviewing an ex-student of Dr Cyril Murphy, and for helping with photographs and sourcing material on the life of Edward Murphy in Australia. **Pauline** also secured RAF Records for Fred Murphy. And **Richard** and **Pauline** have read my books!

To Wallace Cousins **Brenda Gundersen**, **John Leyland**, and **Kerry Wallace**, grateful thanks.

For cheerful support provided during research, I am grateful to:

The UK National Archives, where personal record files of Frederick Murphy, Geraldine Murphy, and Leo Murphy may be found.

Dáire Rooney, Assistant Librarian and those who work with her in the Manuscripts and Archive Research Library, Trinity College, Dublin.

National Library of Ireland for material about *The Pallas Commission*.

Paul Keogh and the Clifden Library in County Galway, who provided resources so quickly and readily.

Áine Hyland, Emeritus Professor of Education and former Vice-President of University College Cork, Ireland, who assisted Val Urie and myself in the 1990s in discovering items connected to James held by UCC.

Marc O'Hare and **Caroline McCarthy** of the Bere Island Heritage Centre, Ballinakilla, Bere Island, Beara, West Cork, for their research around the Eamon Murphy family.

Tom French, Honorary Secretary, Meath Archaeological & Historical Society, for information on the fate of the Rathcore Rectory, later Rathcore Glebe.

Stuart Hadaway who organised research into RAF records of Fred Murphy.

Lesley van Hoey Smith of Renvyle, Co. Galway, who spent a day pouring over records and maps. Together we created a hand-drawn diagram of the movements of Leo's Siege Battery during the Battle of the Somme, which guided Derek in developing his creation, *Map 7*.

Without the support and encouragement of the **good people of the Renvyle Peninsula**, I may well have given up the writing and taken to life-on-a-beach instead. I'm indebted to them all, and if I miss someone, apologies! **Rose and Joe Conneely** of **Sunnymeade**, **Eamon Grennan and Rachel Kitzinger** of **Áit Éile**, and **Mary and Eugene Barry** of **Rusheenduff**, all of whom kindly provided places to stay where I could write. **Sunnymeade** became a *home away from home*, Rose and Joe became close friends. The enriching friendship of **Mary Donnelly**, next-door neighbour in Rusheenduff, was the highlight of my stay there. Mary and her dogs walked many miles beside me, listening endlessly to 'Murphy Chatter', making suggestions which propelled the book along. To the **Connemara Book Club Members**, and to **John Douglas** and **Lesley van Hoey Smith**, **Róisín Nee**, **Sean Coyne** and **Tegolin Knowland** of the inspiring **Curlew Theatre Company**, **Genealogist Shonagh Love** and to the **Members of the Clifden Writers' Group**, deepest thanks.

...Not in vain
Hath God appointed me for many years
A witness, teaching me the art of letters;
A day will come when some laborious monk
Will bring to light my zealous, nameless toil,
Kindle, as I, his lamp, and from the parchment
Shaking the dust of ages, will transcribe
My chronicles.

Alexander Pushkin, 1825

INTRODUCTION

It's a long journey from Eamon in a stone cottage built into the side of a hill on Bere Island in West Cork, to Olive in Carnalway Glebe House in County Kildare, or to Leo at the Battle of the Somme in World War I. It took over two hundred years and four generations from the Island cottage to the participation of the Murphy tandem bicycle in the Dalkey Bike Ride of 2018, and the changes occurring in that period were enormous. Most individuals made it through by cherishing and nurturing their loyalty to their relatives, and by doing so with optimism and a large amount of goodwill towards each other. Some were best friends.

In 1974, Daphne Wormell, granddaughter of James, wrote:

> What a century and a quarter of change it has been, with our cars and domestic gadgets, TV and radio communications, digital technologies, advances in medicine, telephones of all types and the ability to fly around the world.

Mary Murphy, née Hartnett, was the good Irish name of the mother of James. Surely, the name *Mary Murphy* is one of the most common in Ireland. A query of the name on the splendid new Irish genealogy site *irishgenealogy.ie* might produce over 10 000 results. Researching common names takes great patience and perseverance, done with the hope that answers will be discovered.

There are further obstacles, especially round the transcription of names from records. For example I have seen Mary *Ryan* written as Mary *Ahern*. *Hartnett* has been written as *Harnett*, as *Hornett*, as *Hortnett* and even as *Hodnett*. Inaccurate spellings arise when a name is spoken to a recorder in an unfamiliar dialect, or with a strong accent. Here is what Riobard O'Dwyer has written about the name *Hartnett*:[1]

> According to a Jesuit Priest in a Spanish College, the Hodnetts originally lived in Bantry and had sailing ships doing business with France and Spain during the Penal times. The Hodnetts were caught

---

1   Riobard O'Dwyer, *Who Were My Ancestors?* (Bere Island Parish, 1976), 97.

smuggling Priests back from Spain. Their ships and property were confiscated. There were three Hodnett brothers. Of the three, one went to Allihies and another went to North Kerry. The Priest didn't know what became of the third. ... The name Hodnett changed locally to Hartnett over the years.

Strange to say, there is an 1863 baptism record of a *Jerry Murphy* in the same parish where James's parents Edward, sometimes called Eamon, even Edmond, and his wife Mary Hartnett were living, and Jerry's parents are listed as Edmond Murphy and Mary Hodnett. This is a fine example of a record from which one has to walk away, but about which one is never certain of connections without further time-consuming investigations and research.

The origin of a name also makes a difference. Most Irish know the name *Doherty* originates in Donegal, and if found in southwest Ireland as in our family, ancestors will have travelled in the past, southwards along what is known today as *The Wild Atlantic Way*.

A record recently checked, and shown below, is not included in the chapters of this book. How can it be proved to be the baptism of Edward Murphy (*Eamon* in Chapter 2) other than trying to follow the parents named, which so far has brought nothing to light? But this is the only record of a birth[2] of an Edward Murphy in Munster in 1810. It may well be the correct record. I have frequently wondered if Eamon Murphy came from a Murphy family not rooted in the Beara Peninsula.

On page 359 of the church baptism register of St. Finbar's Church, Cork South Parish, Cork and Ross (RC), 11 February 1810:[3]

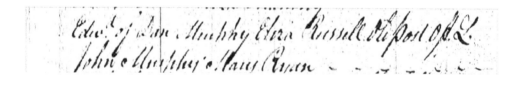

Edwd of Dan. Murphy   Eliza Russell   Old Post Off. L.

John Murphy   and   Mary Ryan.

---

2   **Birth/Baptism:** Babies were baptised/christened very soon after birth. Many died shortly after birth, and the souls of all babies had to be saved through baptism early on.

3   Is this record difficult to read? It has been deliberately left unenhanced to illustrate the difficulty in deciphering many records.

That is:

11 February 1810: Edward Murphy, son of Dan Murphy and Eliza Russell of Old Post Office Lane. Witnessed by John Murphy and Mary Ryan

At some point, a researcher has to stop the online searching, has to say, 'I've done enough', and has to collate material and write it out. New material appears on sites regularly, and will continue for many years and perhaps another generation will find reason to change and contribute further. Family history is never finite. There is no reason for hesitation in interpretation and in writing when based only on what is currently known and understood.

Some families come from a tradition of not registering life events with a church or in Civil Records. In the 1800s, the inhabitants of Bere Island, and beyond, might ask: *Why on earth would any records need to be kept?* – when everyone seemed to know everything about everyone else. The record centres were so far away. *Who on earth would be interested in the likes of us?* – except perhaps a rent collector or a law enforcer? Through the years, many records were burnt or otherwise destroyed. Bere Island was far from Castletownbere, from Kenmare, from Tralee, from Dublin, and even the work of a conscientious record keeper could be lost long before those fires were lit. Many churches managed to hold onto records, but their value depends on the diligence and on the legibility of the writing of the local rectors or priests down through the years. If records of personal information were known about families being held, some were removed by those not wanting to have connections identified.

Seeking further, I travelled to Bere Island on the *Murphy Ferry*, stayed in a B and B run by a *Murphy* family and mailed postcards in a *Murphy* shop in Rerrin, where the postmistress was *Mary Murphy*. West Cork, and Kerry next door to the north, may be described as *Murphy Country*. Yes, there are other names there too, but certainly *Murphys* settled in the area. Many were not closely related. To separate one Murphy family from another, one may be helped by other family historians, and it was Mike Murphy, historian of the other Murphy family in Ardgroom, who stated he knew of our Murphys, and there was no connection between the two. He saved me many research hours.

The later chapters on the Lennons and especially on the Rathcore Murphy children have been written from material gathered over the years. The value of personal papers and letters was recognised by families. These were passed down generation to generation, stored in boxes and trunks in attics or in basements or in garden sheds. I spent several years filing and cataloguing this resource, filling a total of thirteen filing cabinets before completing the task. But long before I had inherited it all, I was out and about with a cassette tape recorder. Family reunions were first held in the 1980s, and during preparations, other family members, and even friends, interviewed and passed along the recordings. All of these I transcribed. Valentine Wallace, not so handy with a tape machine, took notes for hours of her mother Eva, James's eldest daughter, talking when bedridden, and directly afterwards Val filled in any gaps left when hand-writing had not been able to keep up with the spoken word.

Once the individual Murphy files had been established, the contents of each were digitised. My brother, Robin Wormell, visited where I was living at the time, in Renvyle, Connemara, staying in the Sunnymeade BnB, in Tully. As he ate a delicious full Irish breakfast each morning, I read out to him the digitised files, at that time about eleven in all. His comments and memories helped bring the Rathcore Murphy chapters into focus for writing, which in turn went on for many months afterwards.

Although I was the one to write this book, it has been in the writing for genera-tions. I was lucky enough to be the first to come along with sufficient computer skills. As a relative said, *All the facts were there. They just needed to be pulled together.*

Many of those so full of enthusiasm, encouragement and interest in the project have died along the way, and I myself am conscious of how the years are passing by and time is running out.

I dedicate this book to those no longer with us, but who left their work and thoughts behind, and whose spirit of enquiry runs through every page.

Burnt Norton

T. S. Eliot (1888–1965)

Time present and time past
Are both perhaps present in time future,
And time future contained in time past.
If all time is eternally present
All time is unredeemable.
What might have been is an abstraction
Remaining a perpetual possibility
Only in a world of speculation.
What might have been and what has been
Point to one end, which is always present.
Footfalls echo in the memory
Down the passage which we did not take
Towards the door we never opened
Into the rose-garden. My words echo
Thus, in your mind.(*1935*)

(Reproduced here by kind permission from "Collected Poems 1909-1962", published by Faber and Faber Ltd.)

JAMES EDWARD
HARNETT MURPHY

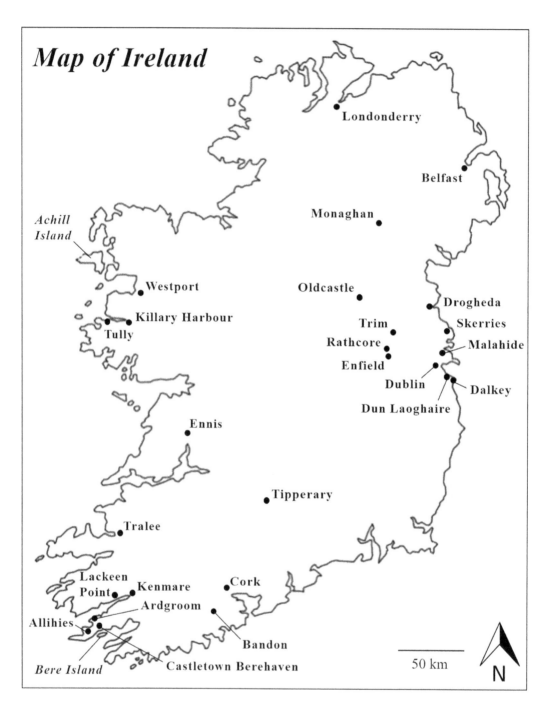

Map 1

JAMES'S CHILDHOOD FAMILY TREE

(with credit to Janet Venito, Valentine Urie, Royse Murphy, Jaclyn Hine and Eva Murphy)

MARY HARNETT (October 13, 1827–May19, 1916)   m.   **EAMONN (EDWARD) MURPHY** (1810–August 25, 1882)

| **John** Edward (1845–October 29, 1880) | **Nora** (1846–) | **Catherine** (1848–) m. March 8, 1871 Dennis Doherty | **James** E. H. (1850–1919) m. January 3, 1883 Emmeline Annie Lennon | **Maria** (1855–c.1896) m. Robert Stabler (widower, Liverpool) | **Edward** Harnett (1858–1926) m. October 22, 1884 Agnes McKenzie (div) | **Nancy** (1860–) | **Michael** (1862/3-) |

1.
THE GOV'NOR.
REVEREND MURPHY.

MURPHY!

I was snatching a few moments to read quietly by my mother's fireplace in Dublin. She suddenly burst into the room. Her feet thumped along the floor as she rushed forward towards my chair. She was clutching a photograph, her fingers bending it, creasing it in her intensity. She declared if I, her daughter, didn't take it out of the house when I left, she would burn it. Destroy it. She was eyeing the fireplace.

I took the photo. The year was 2000. I had been handed a commission.

The photo was of The Gov'nor! Reverend Murphy. Reverend James Edward Harnett Murphy.

He had been dead eighty-one years, and his granddaughter Daphne, my mother, was in a state. Etched on her face were those remote memories of her own mother Eva, homesick and sitting on the side of her young daughter Daphne's bed late at night, in the dark in Canada, recollecting her Rathcore childhood. Poor Daphne! Wasn't she trying to block the nightmares she was still having about her grandfather? Over eighty years old she was, and her fear was fierce, even though she had never met him. Wasn't a favourite expression of hers: *The sins of the fathers will be visited on their children and their grandchildren*? At that moment, as the photo changed hands, the sins were raining down on her. Some of them splashed my way too.

One of Murphy's grandsons stated, 'The man had a towering temper.' Uncontrollable it was, many times brutal, harming everyone and everything around him. And didn't Murphy's son Charlie, many years later show the palms of his hands to my brother. 'See these scars? See these lumps, these bumps? That's where my father beat me with the edge of a ruler. Desperate, he was, to fill me with the conjugation of Latin verbs.'

1

Then there was the time when Murphy and his wife, Emmeline Annie, had planned to go to the train station to catch the train up to Dublin, thirty miles away. Going shopping they were, for some new clothes for the next baby due in a few months. They set out in the horse-drawn buggy down the avenue from the rectory. They were late leaving, and he in a rage already. He whipped the horse, and the poor animal reared up near the rectory's Gate Lodge, where they should have been turning right. But already the reins were mixed up, all caught around the tresses, and the horse was rearing again, swinging to the left. Out tumbled Himself, falling right on his head.

The good people living in the Gate Lodge came out to help. The horse was calmed. Storming, his head sore, Murphy climbed up again into the buggy, and galloped the horse back up the avenue, shouting and fuming and whipping the horse all the way. When that baby was born, the youngest of his ten children, she had spina bifida – 'all the fault of his wife and her delaying the Dublin journey, keeping him and the horse waiting, and causing all the distress, which harmed their baby.'

After the birth he took his wife, Emmeline Annie, a favourite daughter of her father in the big house over the way, and didn't Murphy throw her up on the dining-room table. And he beat her. Yes, he beat her hard. He was determined the devil should be exorcised, whipped out of her. Their daughter Eva, twelve at the time, later said he used the horsewhip. His descendants still shudder at the thought of it, the sound of it ringing in their ears, thinking of his children hiding in their bedrooms where their mother had sent them, to stay out of the way until morning.

All the older children were beaten at various times. The eldest son was so terrified of his father, he would hide behind the living room couch at the sound of his voice. Don't forget the horsewhip beating of Charlie, the very same son that showed his hands' scars to my brother, sixty years later. Why Charlie, the second son, had to be beaten that day is lost to history. When he was eight, his father took the horsewhip to him, and beat him on his bare legs, on his back, on his arms and hands. 'Cut the clothes off him,' Eva said. The boy was brutalised. The whole household could hear the screams and the pleadings. 'Please! Please stop! Please stop! I'll be good! I promise! I'll go away and never bother you again! Please don't hit me anymore!' He got away from his father's clutches, ran outside, swung up on his bike, crying, shaking, sobbing, and he set off towards the road to the village. When Charlie's bike was heard rattling down the avenue, his sisters Eva and Geraldine got out their bikes and the chase was on. Charlie sped through the village, his tears flying off his face, like a water spout behind him. He was intent on leaving home forever. When Eva and Geraldine caught up, and all three were pedalling like crazy, Charlie was sobbing, 'I don't know where to go! I don't know where to go!' They sped through the village, where everyone would have noticed them. *Them three Murphy childern, wild on their bikes they are.* A few miles out along the Dublin Road, they all slowed down. Eva and Geraldine felt they had to turn back, and they watched as Charlie picked up speed again and rode on towards Dublin. Would they, too, 'get it' back home? 'We won't tell,' they had promised Charlie. True to their word, on reaching the rectory, they reported: 'Charlie rode too fast. He went through the village. We don't know where Charlie has gone.' However, they found the storm at home was spent, the household was calm.

But everyone knew Charlie had gone away.

Next day, Murphy boarded the train to Dublin, to check with the uncles who lived up in Dublin. Had Charlie arrived on his bike? Murphy came home alone, he hadn't any word of his eight-year-old son, Charlie. Five days passed.

Charlie had gone to stay with friends of the family about ten miles away. He had then biked over to Hotwell House, a couple of miles from the rectory, where an aunt and uncle lived. They treated his welts and wounds with salve. Charlie begged them not to take him home to the rectory for fear he would break down, and get soft-hearted, and cry over the terrible sores, some of which were infected. On the Saturday, when everyone was at home, his uncle went over to the rectory, and paved the way for Charlie to be welcomed back home.

Murphy was working on creating an English to Irish dictionary. He had one page handwritten out, perfectly, and he left it on his desk. When he returned, there was an ink splat right there, on the page:

> *Was this the ink splat?*
> *Discovered on manuscript:*
> **Ms 2096, Trinity College,**
> **8, Vol 3.**

MS2096, Vol.3, TrinityCollege.[4] This may have been the "ink splat" described above.

Who had done this? No one owned up, so all the children were beaten that time, both girls and boys, one after another. Eva was ten years old.

When the middle boy, Fred, reached eighteen, and when his father charged after him yet again with the horsewhip, Fred turned around and wrestled the whip from his father's hands. Fred broke that whip across his knee. More than the whip snapped in two, that day.

---

4   **IE TCD MS 2094-2096a**. Irish-English dictionary (X 3 vols) compiled by Professor James E. H. Murphy, professor of Irish in T.C.D. based on 'An Irish-English Dictionary' by Edward O'Reilly (Dublin 1877) with annotations by Murphy and bound with a very large number of interleavings written by Murphy.

Murphy had a revolver, which he kept in a drawer in his desk. One time he loaded it. Shots were fired, with the study door closed. No one knew if he had shot himself. All went silent. It turned out he had been shooting at the wall, 'To frighten us,' said Eva.

Many years later, when Cyril, the youngest son, was entertaining Fred and his wife for dinner, the conversation turned to their father. 'Fine man!' commented Cyril. 'An awful bugger,' replied Fred. Fred's remark was not well received. By the time Cyril was growing up, his father's rages had mostly abated. Cyril knew nothing of the background of his older brother's childhood.

Eva was the eldest girl, and close to her mother, Emmeline Annie. She would shake with fear when on an evening, with the servants gone home, a wife beating would take place. Finally, her mother told her to go outside if she ever heard the noises again. Out into the dark, out where she couldn't hear. She liked to hide in the henhouse, amidst her own hens, all bred and reared by herself. The gentle clucking was a comfort to the frightened girl. Eva used to sell the eggs her hens laid, which provided her with a bit of pocket money.

Eva was in her early twenties, and one day her father returned home, late, from Dublin. He was tired, cold, and hungry. He unhitched the horse, which had a cough from standing in the rain, waiting all day as it had at the station, for the return train from Dublin to pull in. He took the horse into the barn and went to get the bran to feed it. The bin was empty. His temper flared, and, banging open the back door, he charged into the house, muddy boots and all. He was roaring, 'Where's Eva? Where is she? Come down here at once.' No bran left, all used on her hens. 'Those hens have to go!' For the first time, Eva stood up to him. 'It's your fault the bran has run out! The horse had it all. There has been no bran in that bin for days. Nothing to do with my chickens! Not my fault!' He insisted the hens would have to go. With clenched fists, Eva shouted back: 'If they go, I go!'

And that was it.

First light the next morning, Eva took a small bag, tied it to her bike, rode quietly down the rectory avenue, and never again returned to the house. It was now her turn to ride along the Dublin Road, about thirty miles into the city where she could safely live with relatives. She arranged for her hens to be shipped to her. A couple of times, desperately homesick for her mother, through a message written to a neighbour she would manage to meet her mother in the evening 'out behind a haystack closest to the hawthorn bush in the back.' She would sleep that night under the hedge, and slip away at dawn. One Christmas, Eva felt brave. She cycled up the Rathcore Rectory avenue, and knocked on her family's front door. Her father, the minister, locked and bolted the door against his eldest daughter that Christmas Day.

Eva saw her father only one more time, when she was in her late twenties. Having decided to emigrate to Canada, she was catching the train at Amiens Street Station to take her up to Belfast, where she and her friend, Florrie, were to join up and together travel on board a liner for Montreal. Murphy appeared on the station platform, clutching a Bible as a present for Eva. She carried that Bible with her, deep in her bag, but the thought of it brought on tears, and she wept all the way from Dublin to County Down. Her children in Canada remembered the book well, sitting as it did high up on a shelf, looking down on them through all the years. In reality, the Bible was ostracised up there on that shelf, never touched, left unopened, and only referred to as 'that awful book given to Mum by her father.' Or was it 'that book given to Mum by her awful father?'

These horrors were not spoken of. An occasional whisper, that was all. The first major indicator to Murphy's great-grandchildren, that stories of him caused nightmares, was his place on the printed family tree, prepared for a family reunion in 1983. No birth date, and only the year of his death – on a tree where six generations were shown with almost all dates and places given in full detail. No one had wanted to research Murphy, to create records of him, to introduce him into conversations. His presence was to be minimised, hardly noticed, except for his final date, the day he died.

Murphy had been like a dark, threatening cloud, looming, distorting, discolouring everything. Even when far away, and even when dead, his threatening presence permeated the generations. Seeking to understand him, to bring his own experiences forward and to recognise how our forebears overcame their fears, thriving in spite of them, might help lay his ghost and his misdeeds to rest.

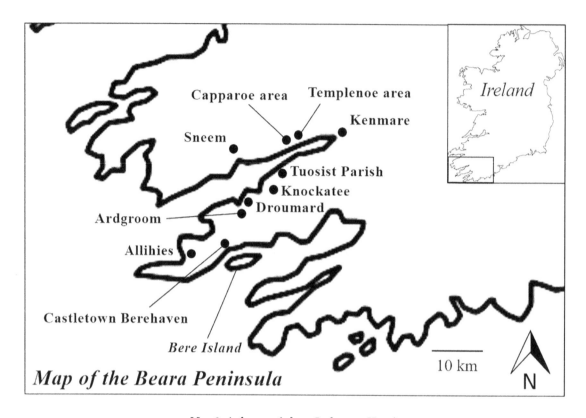

Map 2: Ardgroom: 'where Cork meets Kerry'

2.
EAMON

Several years ago, a resident of Bere Island said of the mid-1800s:

> 'Beatings? Everyone in this area was beating or being beaten back then. It was going on in every household and in every school. That was the way of it. Yes, beatings were all around, everywhere.'

> *'Ah, let it be. It is what it is.'*

Even today, in any society, beatings and bullying can be a part of family life. The tradition may come down through personal experience. An aggressor seeks control of family members, justifying violent acts by persuading himself, or herself, that he or she knows best. To imprint the corrected behaviour, pain or threatening abuse were the most successful methods – they were swift: both could be used together, and they bore fruit. School masters believed these techniques to be the correct methods to raise and teach a child, or to train a woman to be a submissive wife.

In 2019, a friend who wanted to be identified only as *Rose*, stated:

> 'I dreaded every Friday morning at school. That was the day we were heard our spelling. Every Friday we had a spelling test: ten Irish words and ten English words. You had to get at least twelve spellings correct out of the twenty. Failing to do this, for every two missed spellings you got a slap with a bamboo cane on the palm of a hand.

> 'I am dyslexic and no matter how hard I tried, every Friday when I was in the Master's classroom, I was sent to the Headmaster's Office, where I was beaten on the palm of my right hand. He would tell me, 'You'll amount to nothing.'

> 'A couple of years ago I encountered the same Headmaster when I was out walking on the road. I said, 'Hello! I'll never forget you! You

walloped me every Friday morning my whole school life.' He replied, 'I never beat anyone!' Until that day, I had never felt any animosity towards the man, but after our conversation, I felt as though he had beaten me again.'

James Murphy grew up in a similar environment. His father was a school master, a husband and a father. There can be no doubt James received beatings and witnessed many more. He was a quick learner and had a good memory. We have all heard: *What worked when I was young – look at me! – will do as well today.* But, in his case, the lessons learnt by James were compounded by his wicked temper, which could flare up suddenly, almost wildly, causing him to strike out blindly and uncontrollably. Add into this mix the beliefs and superstitions he would have heard as part of his heritage. James would have believed a deformed baby was a child of the devil, inherited through the mother's womb, and, for the sake of his wife's sanity and health, his duty was to beat the devil out of her.

Not until 1982 was corporal punishment abolished in Irish Schools.

What of Eamon, father of James? A major characteristic of Eamon was how he frequently altered his name, both his first and last names. Early on, he referred to himself as *Eamon O'Grady Murphy.*[5] When James was born in 1850, Eamon was already Edmund Murphy, but here is a copy of a record made on July 16, 1848, on the occasion of the baptism of Eamon's first son John,[6] witnessed by Honora Cotter. Although this baptism was held on the same day as that of Eamon's second child, Catherine, the named being referenced in the far right-hand column as *Cath Murphy* may be the signature of an aunt or cousin:

**16   John Bap[tised] Cath[olic]   Edmundi Murphy Grady Sch[ool] Mas[ter]
          et Maria Harnett   Honora Cotter, Village**

IRE_PRS_MICROFILM 04282-04_0187

In West Cork, Murphy Country, the name *Murphy Grady* would have been used to distinguish one family of Murphys from another. The Grady/O'Grady name might

---

5   ***O'Grady Murphy:*** This is how Eamon was registered as being a school teacher on Bere Island. [Information provided by the Bere Island Heritage Centre.]

6   ***John:*** the eldest son of Eamon and Mary, was born in 1845, as written on his tombstone. He may have been baptized originally as a Protestant, or may not have been baptised previously, at all.

have been Eamon's mother's maiden name, or indeed, it may go further back, to one of his distant forebears. The O'Grady Murphy name, or the Murphy Grady name would have identified a family and set them apart from all other Murphys. Everyone in the village would have known where they lived, and their cottage home could have been pointed out with ease to enquiring strangers.

It is likely *Eamon a Ċnoc*, that is, *Eamon on the Hill*, or *Eamon from the Hill*, even *Eamon from Knockatee,* lived on a hillside not far from Rerrin on Bere Island. With the Island full of Murphys, some with the very same first and last names as our Eamon Murphy, *Eamon a Ċnoc* would have quickly identified him.[7] Speaking in Irish, a villager might have asked: *Is it Eamon a Ċnoc ye're after? Isn't he up there, above them fields, up on that hill? That's where ye'll find him.* Possibly, before his time on Bere Island, Eamon may have stayed or may have even grown up on Knockatee, a hillside area on the north of the Beara Peninsula.

As time went by, Eamon would sign his name on documents as *Edwin*, or *Edmond*, or finally, as *Edward*. Almost a steady change from the Irish *Eamon* to the strongly English *Edward*. His reasons will become apparent as this tale unfolds.

Unfortunately, records of Eamon prior to the mid-1800s have not been found. Today, Eamon's origins are uncertain, although he was born in 1810, and the birth record of *Edward Murphy* in Cork City, as explained in the Introduction, may indeed be his.

When Eamon was fifteen, in 1825, an inquiry into the education of students whether Protestant or Catholic, whether paid or voluntary, was conducted in every parish throughout Ireland. This was before the state-funded National School System had been introduced, and at the time, funding for the one school on Bere Island was being provided by Protestants in Castletown Berehaven. When the inquiry recommended Protestant and Catholic students should be educated together, this would have been Eamon's experience as a pupil, wherever he was receiving his education. However, the inquiry also advised that during religious instruction, Catholic and Protestant students should be separated. To provide for this and, at the same time, to prevent the local parish priest from entering the school, each school should try to have two teachers, one from each religion.

Such recommendations became a part of the National School System, which was set up in 1831. Meanwhile, Eamon now twenty-one, had likely been recognised for his qualities and was working alongside an experienced teacher in a monitorial system, a cheap but efficient technique where a teacher directed senior students who in turn

---

7   ***Eamon a Ċnoc:*** Not to be confused with the rebel hero, Éamonn an Chnoic, also "Ned of the Hill", whose real name was Éamonn Ó Riain, who lived 1670–1724, and about whom many songs have been written.

taught junior pupils. There was no formal teacher-training until later in the 1830s, but many teachers were well-educated, having possibly travelled to the Continent, and these were respected and admired in rural society. If Eamon did indeed take this route, he would have travelled on foot, as most of these young men did, staying without charge in education centres, cathedral schools and continental monasteries along the way. Other minimal funding, such as ferry fares for the journeys, were granted for free, or would have been supplied by the Catholic Church in the hope that most youths would return to their homeland and become priests. In later years, Eamon would teach his eldest son Latin, and he would read Latin from the Bible fluently, and he may have learnt these skills on the Continent. The subjects Eamon would have been taught as a school pupil in southwest Ireland, would have been English, Arithmetic (Numeracy), and Social and Moral Values.

Late in the 1830s, the Protestant Church of Ireland Rector for Bere Island was Rev Thomas O'Grady, a son of the brother of the first Viscount Guillamore. It is possible Eamon was a distant cousin of the minister. Rev Thomas O'Grady was based in Castletown Berehaven, on the mainland. He was responsible for the welfare of his parishioners on Bere Island, and he needed a teacher. If Eamon was indeed a relative, he would have been a Protestant, or possibly one of his parents had been a Protestant. But his education had been a Catholic experience. He was perfect for the teaching job, with an understanding of religious requirements on both sides. He was a fluent Irish speaker, able to communicate with the pupils. The number of students on Bere Island was low, hardly justifying two teachers, and the requirements for schools under the new system would take years to be established in the far reaches of County Cork. Possibly Eamon was encouraged to take the job as a result of influence from the O'Grady family. Perhaps he was also facilitated by the parish priest, and undertook to instruct at a basic level in reading, writing, and arithmetic, as well as providing religious education.

By the 1840s, our Eamon Murphy was living in West Cork, on Bere Island. He was teaching there, in a simple, thatched, rough stone-walled structure, under conditions, as described in *Bere Island School Folklore Collection, 1937*, held at the Bere Island Heritage Centre:

> Páirc Sgoile got its name because there was an old school there long ago. This school is situated on the High Road. This is the oldest road in Berehaven. This school is the first school built in Bere Island by the Board of Education. It was the only school in the Island.

Síle Sullivan, p. 10

Until schools at Lawrence Cove and at Ballinakilla were built, there was a one-storied school. It was mixed, with two playgrounds, one for the boys and one for the girls. The students they had not any desks or seats. They had a fireplace built with stones and there was no chimney, but the smoke managed to get out some way through the door and windows. There was a very small attendance at that time; some of the scholars would not go to school because there were no guards.

Mary C. Sullivan, p. 10

Today, the High Road may be driven, with care. There are several stone structures along the way on the slightly more sheltered eastern hillsides, and perhaps one of these was the site of the early school, or possibly, some stones used for today's small enclosures may have come from the early school building.

It is thought Eamon taught in a Hedge School, a clandestine school which continued to offer education even after the Penal Laws forbidding education of Catholics had been relaxed sixty years earlier, in 1782. In Eamon's time, Hedge Schools were Catholic Pay Schools, 'in which the masters receive some small stipend from the children who attend them: schools set up on private speculation; schools that receive no Aid, either from the State or from any Society … The Masters received 1d [one penny] a week or so from the children; sometimes more and sometimes less.'[8]

Bere Island was an isolated community in the first half of the nineteenth century. Although Eamon's time teaching there would have been late in the 1830s to the early 1850s, changes in education were slow to arrive and then to be implemented on the Island. It would have been necessary for most children to catch up to a basic level and for their parents to be supportive of their children's learning as well as to fully support the teacher, in spite of not having been schooled themselves. Most children would have been encouraged to attend, regardless of age. The situation posed a challenge for all involved. Eventually, Eamon's salary would have been £15 per annum, likely paid to him out of a pledge of local finance by the Church of Ireland parish in Castletown Berehaven. Rector O'Grady would have seen to it.

By 1845, Eamon would have realised there were soon to be two National Schools built on Bere Island – ominous clouds of change threatened on the horizon. Teachers were to be trained, schools and teachers were to be inspected, and the running of the schools was to be divided between a central board and a local school management team. Perhaps he did not want books and their contents to be controlled by a board? The books used in

8   Antonia McManus. *The Irish Hedge School and its Books, 1695-1831* (Four Courts Press, 2004), 72.

Hedge Schools were chapbooks,[9] but new official textbooks were being prepared. Maybe he did not approve of new regulations stating instruction was to be given in English, and Irish was not to be taught or used at all. Pupils were to deny their Irish heritage. We know Eamon was soon to leave his school, his pupils, his house, and the Island.

Eamon's children had a deep-rooted respect for their father. *A fine man* they said when they thought of him in later years. The following extract from the Report for 1835 by the Board of National Education indicated the image of a teacher the Board wished to see promoted:[10]

> 'Living in friendly habits with the people, not greatly elevated above them, but so provided for as to be able to maintain a respectable station, trained to good habits, identified in interest with the State, and therefore anxious to promote a spirit of obedience to lawful society.'

Eamon would have lived up to these expectations. When Eamon a Ċnoc left Bere Island, he got along well on the mainland, as did his growing family. They now settled into a home in Droumard, Ardgroom, living closer to Eamon's wife's family on the Beara Peninsula.

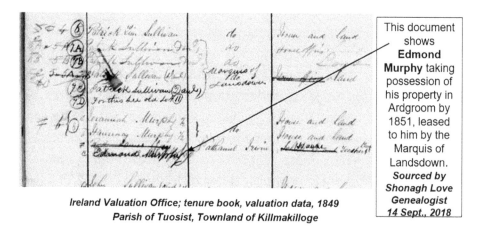

This document shows **Edmond Murphy** taking possession of his property in Ardgroom by 1851, leased to him by the Marquis of Landsdown. *Sourced by Shonagh Love Genealogist 14 Sept., 2018*

Ireland Valuation Office; tenure book, valuation data, 1849
Parish of Tuosist, Townland of Killmakilloge

Latterly, Eamon used the anglicised version of his name, *Edward*. A record of Edward's marriage to Mary Hartnett, of their marriage which officially took place in 1859, is a Roman Catholic Church record.[11] Here, recognition is given to *Edward*, not

---

9   ***Chapbooks:*** Chapbooks were small booklets, cheap to make and cheap to buy, offering an affordable form of literature for all ages. They covered a range of subjects from fairy tales and ghost stories to news of politics, crime, or disaster. Initially 1 penny, later 6 pence, about 300 000 were produced in Irish presses annually.

10   Coolahan, John, "The Daring First Decade of the Board of National Education, 1831-1841," *The Irish Journal of Education / Iris Eireannach an Oideachais 17,* no. 1 (Summer, 1983), 35-54.

11   ***1859 Marriage Record:*** Why they were married in 1859 is unknown. This may have been a requirement by church or state officials before providing papers for children's records.

Eamon, but Mary's maiden name is given as *Hartnett*, despite all other records of her later in life having the middle 't' dropped, and recorded as *Harnett*.

22nd *Edward Murphy to Mary Hartnett*
Witness: John Coakley & Honora Hartnett

The name *Edward* is sprinkled through his descendants, not least through the Murphys of Rathcore Rectory:

> James himself carried the second name of *Edward*, and third name of *Harnett*.

> James named his eldest son, born on 17th March, 1884, *Edward Patrick Harnett*, always known as *Edwy*, who in turn called <u>his</u> eldest son *James Edward*, known as *Jimmy*.

> Charlie, the second son of James, the only one of the Rathcore Murphys to travel to meet relatives in Kerry, named <u>his</u> second son Herbert *Edward Harnett*, who was always known as *Edward Murphy*.

Today, Eamon's descendants are at least six generations down, but it is still possible to glean something of the man, and the following from Goldsmith describes how many of us feel about our ancestor:

> Yet he was kind, or if severe in aught,
> The love he bore to learning was in fault;
> The village all declared how much he knew;
> 'Twas certain he could write, and cypher too;
> Lands he could measure, terms and tides presage,
> And ev'n the story ran that he could gauge.
> [...]
> While words of learned length and thundering sound,
> Amazed the gazing rustics ranged around;
> And still they gazed, and still the wonder grew,
> That one small head could carry all he knew.
>
> Oliver Goldsmith, *The Deserted Village (1770)*

3.
FAMILY BEGINNINGS

In 1827, Mary Hartnett was born to Stephen and Honora Hartnett, in Allihies, a copper mining town on the western shores of the Beara Peninsula. Honora's maiden name had been Kelly and that is all we know of Mary's Hartnett family. There were some other Hartnetts in the area, but not many, and connections have not been found. 'Stephen' was not a common name in rural Ireland, and one record states 'Stevie [Hartnett] got killed in a threshing accident at home.'[12] If this refers to Mary's father, it would explain why Mary's mother, Honora, is always considered to be from the Tuosist area, moving there, having left Allihies when suddenly widowed. Mary would have accompanied her mother.

Mary had a strong Roman Catholic faith, which would hold her in good stead up ahead. She was a native Irish speaker. She must have had ties to the O'Sullivans, or Sullivans, a prominent Kerry family who were traditional chiefs of the area. O'Sullivans appear on several documents related to Mary's activities – as godparents to her children and the witness signature at her death. But they may well have been her only relatives who could sign papers correctly, as Mary was illiterate, like so many around her.

When Eamon was thirty-five and Mary eighteen years old, their first child was born, in 1845. Apparently, Eamon and Mary had not yet married, and would not do so until February 22, 1859. Both were Catholic. Both spoke Irish. The baby was named John Edward, a strong English Protestant name. A Catholic Irish speaker would more likely have named a son Séan Eamon. And perhaps John was the name of Eamon's father, or of a benefactor?

As explanation, there are two possible scenarios: 1) Mary was pregnant by someone other than Eamon, and Eamon kindly undertook to care for her and the baby. In return, Eamon insisted on naming the child. OR 2) Eamon himself was the father,

---

12   Riobard O'Dwyer, considered by many to be the most informative source for the Beara Peninsula, wrote *Who Were My Ancestors? Genealogy (Family Trees) of the Allihies (Copper Mines) Parish, County Cork, Ireland.* (Coominches, Allihies: Riobard O'Dwyer, 1988).

and possibly no priest could be found who would marry them, then and there, Mary being pregnant and single. In fact, it is likely no priest was informed of the out-of-wedlock pregnancy, as the fear of Mary being forcibly removed to a special home for young, single, pregnant girls, or even to a Magdalene Laundry, was very real. Although we know from his gravestone's inscription that John was born in 1845, he was not baptised until three years later.

Becoming the wife of a schoolteacher, an educated man, would have caused a sensation! But then 1845 would have been a tough time on Bere Island. The population was over 2 100 in 1841, and due to the Great Famine, dropped in 1851 by 700 to just over 1 400. On average, seventy people were dying daily in an area of about 11 square miles. Times were changing. As the number of students declined, and for other previously described reasons, there was no longer a teaching job for Eamon. Understandably, the couple couldn't withstand the desperate hunger and suffering all around them. Maybe they had difficulty finding supplies to feed their blossoming family. Eamon and Mary were considering leaving the Island about this time.

Ministers and teachers would often socialise together, both groups being well-educated. No doubt, they would invite each other for a visit and a meal. As happens all over the globe on such occasions, the men would gather outside, or even inside an outbuilding, and the women would cook and chat together in the kitchen, surrounded by the children who would grow up remembering those as the best times of their childhoods. In this fashion, surely Eamon and Mary would occasionally socialise with Rev Thomas O'Grady and his family, and also with Rev Thomas's curate, the well-respected Rev John Halahan. These two ministers were based in Castletown Berehaven, and Bere Island was part of their parish. The Murphy family would have passed through there, travelling over to the mainland to find some supplies, or walking farther on, to the northern shore of the Beara Peninsula to visit Mary's family, now settled in the Lehud, Bunnau, and Lauragh areas in Tuosist Parish.[13] Even when living with Eamon on Bere Island, Mary would travel over to her family to give birth in one of the homes belonging to a relative, where she felt properly cared for and safe, and where a family member, or a neighbour, was a successful midwife.

In February 1846, James O'Grady died, aged eight years. He was a son of Rev Thomas O'Grady. *Berehaven Records*, held at the Bere Island Heritage Centre, tell us three days later Rev Thomas's daughter died, aged seven years. In February 1846, Mary would have been six months pregnant with her second baby. By 1846, deaths

---

13   ***Tuosist:*** the name Tuosist comes from the Irish Tuath Ó Síosta, meaning the 'territory of Ó Síosta' – a tribe named Ó Síosta must have lived here. "Tuosist," Logainm.ie, Government of Ireland, 2020, https://www.logainm.ie/. Translated by Róisín Nee of Renvyle Peninsula.

and births were on all sides. The Great Famine was taking hold. Even if Mary or her mother was well-versed in local herbal remedies, fevers and infections were not well understood. Children infected each other.

Following what would become her usual pattern, before giving birth Mary travelled off the Island and headed north to Tuosist Parish. On May 21, 1846, Eamon and Mary's second child, named Honora after her grandmother, and called Nora by her family, was born. She was baptised in the Roman Catholic Church of Lauragh, in the parish of Tuosist. The family was listed as living in Lehud, Tuosist, but this address might have been provided by the priest, who would have known Mary and possibly her young son, John, had been staying at that time with relatives in the Lehud area.

We do not hear of Nora after her baptism, and she might have died young. The health of the eldest child, John, was never good. Conditions on Bere Island had become untenable, causing the family to further prepare to move off the Island. But, where to?

Meanwhile, north of Castletown Berehaven, up through the gap between the Slieve Miskish Mountains and the Caha Mountains, and then along the northern coastline of the Beara Peninsula, lies the village of Ardgroom.[14] Here the minister was Rev Michael Fitzgerald, who lived with his family in the rectory there. Either Eamon met up with Rev Michael, or Rev Michael sent word to Castletown Berehaven. The message for Eamon would have described the half acre of available land out his way, across the little bay from the Rectory Glebe. Possibly, one of the group of ministers put in a word either with Lord Bantry, who owned all the land in these parts, or perhaps with Lord Lansdown himself, or maybe with the Lord's rent collector, about a dependable and available tenant. That's how business got done in those days, and it is still the preferred way today. *It's all about who ye know, and who ye are.*

In January 1848, William Hodges, a scripture reader in the Ardgroom area for many years, died. Scripture readers read improving passages from the Bible to any gathering of the poor, such as those found at soup kitchens and in night shelters.

A widespread practice amongst those running soup kitchens during the Famine was that in exchange for receiving food, recipients would be asked to convert from Papism to Protestantism, to sign away their souls from the Roman Catholic faith to the Protestant one, before they took the soup. People who converted like this, for food for themselves and their families, were known as *soupers* in some parts, and as *jumpers* in others.

---

14   *Ardgroom:* the name refers to two hills dhá dhroim – Droim ard (big hill) and Droim beag (little hill). There are two drumlins – Drom Árd and Drom Beag, on opposite sides of Ardgroom Harbour. Dhá Dhrom > á Dhrom > Ardgroom. "Ardgroom," Logainm.ie, Government of Ireland, 2020, https://www.logainm.ie/. Translated by Róisín Nee of Renvyle Peninsula.

As we have seen, there were many troubles weighing on Eamon and Mary at this time. The population on Bere Island was being devastated, their own children and those of their acquaintances being sickly, even dying. Meanwhile, here was the possibility of obtaining a lease on a piece of land, where he could build a cottage and eventually graze a cow for fresh milk for the young children, as well as rear a calf and fatten a couple of pigs. He was also being pressured to take on the role of scripture reader, which would actually provide a better wage than he received when teaching. A scripture reader was paid from Church funds, or by the Quakers running the soup kitchen in Ardgroom, and these groups offered a wage of £60 per annum, as well as providing a set of half-decent clothing. Eamon was a natural choice for this vacancy, as the readings were in either Latin or English. His teaching experience would have qualified him in both Latin and English. Even so, the truth was Eamon and Mary were poorer than any minister and wife, and they were not far from the horrendous poverty of the congregation to whom a scripture reader would read.

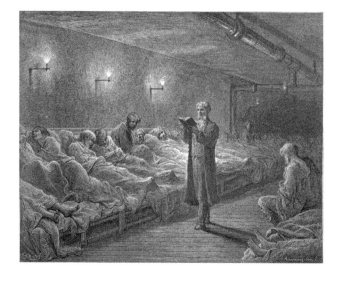

Scripture Reader (Copyright Museum of London)

Still based on the Island, in 1848 Mary gave birth to a daughter, Catherine, and in 1850, a boy, James, over on the mainland. Both were baptised off the Island as Protestants, and also baptised as Catholics on the Island. Perhaps Eamon was covering all bases, but more likely he was himself leaning towards becoming Protestant. With the distress this would have caused Mary and her own family on the mainland, having a baptism within each religion would have eased these tensions.

Eventually, Eamon did become Protestant. He became *a souper*, exchanging his religious commitment from Roman Catholicism to Church of England Protestantism, in exchange for food for his whole family. And unlike most other *jumpers*, Eamon never reverted back, even though his wife continued to worship as a Roman Catholic.

This was Eamon's meal ticket for his family, and the way he could see forward, by helping his children get up and out from the poverty into which they had been born.

Three of his children would emigrate – to North America, to Australia, and to England. Another would pursue education in Ireland, improve his social standing, and provide opportunities for his own children to become well-established.

And along with Eamon's conversion came other changes: the 't' in his wife's maiden name was dropped – more Protestant; the O'Grady/Grady was dropped from Eamon's surname; and the name *Eamon* was changed to *Edmond,* then *Edwin,* eventually settling into the very Protestant, very anglicised *Edward.* In the 1850s, Queen Victoria's heir was also called *Edward.*

It is, therefore, perfectly understandable why the second son of Edward and Mary Murphy should be given the full-blown Protestant, anglicised name of James Edward Harnett Murphy.

'Give Me Three Grains of Corn, Mother.'

Amanda M. Edmond (1824 – 1862)

Give me three grains of corn, Mother,
Only three grains of corn;
It will keep the little life I have
Till the coming of the morn

I am dying of hunger and cold, Mother,
Dying of hunger and cold;
And half the agony of such a death
My lips have never told

It has gnawed like a wolf at my heart, Mother,
A wolf that is fierce for blood;
All the livelong day, and the night beside,
Gnawing for lack of food

I dreamed of bread in my sleep, Mother,
And the sight was heaven to see;
I awoke with an eager, famishing lip,
But you had no bread for me

How could I look to you, Mother,
How could I look to you
For bread to give to your starving boy,
When you were starving too?

For I read the famine in your cheek,
And in your eyes so wild,
And I felt it in your bony hand,
As you laid it on your child

The Queen has lands and gold, Mother,
The Queen has lands and gold,
While you are forced to your empty breast
A skeleton babe to hold

A babe that is dying of want, Mother,
As I am dying now,

With a ghastly look in its sunken eye,
And famine upon its brow

There is many a brave heart here, Mother,
Dying of want and cold,
While only across the Channel, Mother,
Are many that roll in gold;

There are rich and proud men there, Mother,
With wondrous wealth to view,
And the bread they fling to their dogs tonight
Would give life to me and you.

What has poor Ireland done, Mother,
What has poor Ireland done,
That the world looks on, and sees us starve,
Perishing one by one?

Do the men of England care not, Mother,
The great men and the high,
For the suffering sons of Erin's Isle,
Whether they live or die?

Come nearer to my side, Mother,
Come nearer to my side,
And hold me fondly, as you held
My father when he died;

Quick, for I cannot see you, Mother,
My breath is almost gone;
Mother! Dear Mother! Ere I die
Give me three grains of corn.

4.
FAMINE [15]

Aroo from Cork?
I am! Aroo?
Do you eat potatoes?
Indeed I do.
How do you eat dem?
Shkins and all.
Do dey choke you?
Not at all.

Folk rhyme from Cork, over 100 years ago

Potatoes were first cultivated by the Incas, in Peru. In 1589, Sir Walter Raleigh introduced potatoes to Ireland, to supplement diets of dairy, oatcakes, porridge, and seafood.

Ireland had experienced potato crop failures throughout the early 1800s. The Irish knew about hunger, especially those who had been hardest hit, small farmers and the poor. But the potato was resilient, and by the 1840s, it had become the main food source. All that was needed for cultivation was a wooden spade to dig the trenches to provide for drainage followed by the build-up of soil over top of spread out sets of seed potatoes. These beds were so well prepared and tended, they can still be seen today clearly defined in fields and on mountain sides throughout the West of Ireland. They are called *lazy beds*.

Lazy beds visible (l) after a snowfall on a hillside and (r) in a small field, both beside Tully, Co. Galway, 2018

---

15   ***Chapter 4:*** See Appendix 1 for Bibliography

Animals held by a household could be fed on potatoes. A pig, some chickens, and a cow would do well. As the population in the West rose, great pressure was put on the land. The number of farms grew increasingly smaller and began to extend onto marginal land. People discovered potatoes would grow where other crops would not.

Some farmers grew turnips, but for a turnip crop a wide, flat field was required and with the landscape so rocky and little available acreage, most did not attempt it. Reliance on the one crop took hold in spite of the risks involved. The potato did not store well, being inedible if kept for a year or more. However, the potato was cheap to cultivate, was prolific, and if supplemented by the occasional fish or some daily milk, it alone could provide enough nutrition. Seaweed, free and abundant, made excellent fertiliser. The doctor on Achill Island wrote: 'At the time of planting, the roads here are covered with cheerful boys and girls mounted on their ponies going to collect seaweed for their potato beds.'

When today's tourist thinks back over a visit to the West of Ireland, an abiding memory will be the spectacular views out from the coast to the horizon over the Atlantic Ocean. The questions an alert traveller may ask about the Famine are: 'Why was the local farmer not out in his boat, catching free fish to feed his youngsters? Why was a fishing industry not developed?' Back then, the locals were poverty-stricken, there were almost no trees, and not a bit of lumber was available for boat building. Any man fortunate to own fishing tackle and a boat soon sold these or visited the pawnbroker for money for food. The *curragh* was the popular boat – made of a skeleton built of narrow strips of wood covered tightly by hides, or today by canvas, and tarred for waterproofing. These boats are still favoured, powered by outboard motors, but in the 1800s, rowing was the only power source.

Much of the coast along Ireland's western seaboard is riddled with rocks, accompanied in many places by very high cliffs. It is not as though every cottage sits up against a beach! The weather was unreliable, unpredictable, fierce at times, and a curragh filled with fish was extremely difficult to bring safely into shore, especially if a squall blew up. In some areas, fishermen would have had to row many miles out to where the fish were, at the main fishing grounds near the Continental Shelf. The twenty-five-mile row from Castletown Berehaven was hardly worth the risks involved.

If all of these obstacles could have been overcome, and, indeed, a curing station had been built at one time, but difficulties, such as a lack of a dependable fish supply, no viable mode of transport, as well as long, arduous distances to markets, meant baskets of fish were left on the docks. In 1847, there were no railways in the West of Ireland, and no refrigeration. This decided the fate of the curing station, built in the 1840s in Castletown Berehaven by the Quakers, who had also hired a trawler for £45 a month. The trawler gathered the fish from the curraghs in the twenty-five-mile zone, and rushed the haul back to the Castletown Berehaven Station. But this all proved to be unsustainable economically, and the Castletown Berehaven Station closed its doors in 1852.

A potent blight hit the potato crops in North America in the early 1840s, causing loss to growers in the United States and Canada. This new fungal disease crossed the Atlantic, hitting Holland in 1844 and moving through England to Dublin a year later. It would lie dormant and unobserved in slightly infected potatoes, which would then be planted accidentally alongside healthy potatoes. The fungus would grow up from the tubers underground, through young stems and into sprouting leaves. These diseased shoots soon produced spores which could be blown around in all directions, rapidly infecting nearby healthy plants. The fungus thrived in the mild, moist summer weather, and in a flash, it had infected the whole country. Suddenly growers noticed the thriving potato plants, lush and green the day before, had now turned black. Farmers rushed to dig up and save the potato tubers, but already they, too, were black with oozing liquid and giving off an unbearable stink.

Autumn turned into winter, and people were facing trouble, trying to keep themselves going, living off anything available. Some tried to eat even the diseased potatoes, although they knew well that their pig or cow had already died from eating the same. By the beginning of 1846, people were starving. They were exhausted, but they hoped for a renewal of growth and at the very least, some good potatoes to grow up from their lazy beds. But the weather of 1846 was again warm and wet, and the potato blight was worse in this second year.

The Irish were not bread eaters. The larger farms in the country's east had harvested grain crops successfully. These farmers used a good system of crop rotation which included wheat and barley, and they managed well when their potato crop failed. They were already exporting to England and Europe, where there had also been crop failures, and where food prices were now soaring. Grains were fetching a good price for Irish sellers.

When autumn 1846 came, and was followed by winter, the weather turned cold. Snow fell in November, as much as six inches in places. In fact, the winter of 1846–1847 was unusually severe, with continuous frosts and wild winds blowing snow, hail, and sleet. Roads became impassable, and transport came to a standstill. People fainted from exhaustion. The sound of children screaming from pangs of hunger could be heard. Children began to die. Blighted potato beds were scoured again and again for any scraps of edible potatoes. If there were turnip fields, they, too, lay empty and neglected. Small farmers resorted to consuming their seed stock, unable to think beyond immediate basic survival. Nettles and blackberries, and the edible roots and leaves of cabbages, on which people had been eking out an existence, disappeared. There were no farm animals to be seen anywhere.

Bewilderment led to hopelessness and alarm. Thousands of beggars in rags roamed about in hordes. Panic set in, which led to thoughts of flight across the sea. Clothes and bedding were sold for money for food.

Fear hung about.

Sullen, emaciated men with spades, looking for work, were marching on the roads, inspiring terror. Rumours began to spread that people were arming.

When rent could not be paid and landlords grew busy evicting rent evaders, thousands of squatters resorted to living in sod huts on the seashores. Families there were surviving on weeds and seaweed, limpets, mussels, and winkles which lasted for a while. Fearful of encouraging dependence on handouts, Public Works projects were being organised. By December 1846, numbers employed in these relief schemes reached about 500 000. But the weather was so harsh, many such projects had to be shut down.

The Board of Works developed further work projects, but as the numbers applying to participate increased, tens of thousands of starving, discontented, angry men gathered together outside hiring centres. As attempts were made to remove from the works those considered to be ineligible, assassinations followed. An official in charge of controlling relief wrote in December 1846: 'The great evil with which we have to contend is not the physical evil of the famine, but the moral evil of the selfish, perverse and turbulent character of the people.' This was the prevailing attitude amongst those in power, that the *depraved Irish* brought famine on themselves. Authorities also believed if the state had to provide money or free food and clothing to the destitute, trade would be hurt, and the national economy would be ruined.

All works were to be of benefit to the community. Roads were laid out that led from nowhere to nowhere, canals were dug into which no drop of water has ever flowed, and piers were constructed which Atlantic storms soon began to wash away. Towers were constructed for no purpose, and today are referred to as 'follies'.

The Old Famine Road, Killary Harbour, 2018

Through all of this, there was an extraordinary contradiction occurring all over Ireland. There were indeed markets plentifully supplied with meat, bread, and fish. But this was not at all understood by the British Government who insisted the 'resources of the country should be drawn out.' Export at all cost. Statesmen did not understand these 'resources' were completely inaccessible to even those who found work at 8 pence to 10 pence a day. High prices and lack of money had put food out of reach for the general population.

Workhouse at Clifden, Co. Galway (First opened in 1847)
Illustrated London News, 1850.

Workhouses and poorhouses were built, but quickly filled up. And from the day they opened, they were insolvent, dirty, and disorganised.

Small amounts of relief appeared: £14 000 from India where the younger sons of Irish families were serving with the Queen's troops or in the East India Company. Relief committees formed in Leinster, and

Ladies' Work Associations in Ireland and England made clothes and knitted jerseys. Of great importance was the formation of the Central Relief Committee of the generous Society of Friends, the Quakers, in Dublin. And they subscribed to the strictest instructions given that 'no preference should be made in the distribution of relief on the ground of religious persuasion.' The Quakers opened soup kitchens, free for anyone in need, set up initially in Dublin, and followed closely by one in the town of Cork. These became the models for soup distribution all over the country.

The Protestants and the Roman Catholics on the other hand, set out in competition with each other, proselytising and cajoling the starving to abandon their religion if their faith was not 'the proper one'. Hungry people were persuaded to walk away from their traditions, to become *soupers* or *jumpers*, and to join the 'only true faith', the reward being food for their starving family.

In 1847, the scheme of relief by employment was abandoned, in recognition of the failure of the Public Works projects. Expenditure had been enormous, the work hopelessly inefficient, the right people had not been employed, and there had been violence, corruption, and scandals. Now the Works were to stop, and instead, Irish Relief was to be administered on an entirely different principle. Works were closed down, but many of the workers were by now too feeble to work, some soon falling down dead, others fainting, too weak to move. And hand in hand with famine went dropsy as well as scurvy.

Further soup kitchens were now established, finally permitting local Relief Committees an opportunity to provide something of value – good soup accompanied by a piece of bread or a meal cake.

The Soup Kitchen Act was presented in January 1847. New Relief Committees were to be nominated by the Lord Lieutenant (the Queen's representative in Dublin) and the Committees' members were, and still are, referred to as 'the Guardians'. They were charged with the further establishment of soup kitchens, from which soup would be distributed without any work being required in return.

This relief was instead to be paid for out of the local rates, to be collected by the Guardians, or their representatives. What they failed to recognise was that in most places the collection of rates from the poor was impossible. Even before the Famine set in, it had to be calculated that each shilling paid, had cost at least a pound to collect. Now the British Government assumed that when Ireland was famine-stricken and disorganised, a Poor Rate could be collected which would almost certainly be ten to fifty times larger than ever before. The Guardians did their best, struggled to collect the rates. Police and troops were freely used, and additional magistrates appointed. Rate collectors required extra pay, and the guarantee of an armed escort. Some Guardians advanced money out of their own pockets. But huge numbers of tenants were evicted from their mud huts, or stone cabins, many landlords removing roofs or levelling the dwellings as soon as the families had been evicted. This was known as the 'land clearances.'

By March and April, the promised, new soup kitchens were only slowly starting up, due to the fresh burden of rates.

The responsibility of finding food for the soup kitchens rested on the Relief Committees. Much of the soup was not so much soup for the poor, as poor soup. One hundred gallons could be made for £1. Many people suffered from dysentery already, and there were rumours claiming dysentery was from the soup. In West Cork in January 1847, 17 000 pints of soup was distributed daily, but this was only a drop in the bucket.

To add to the general misery, a new terror rose up – that of fevers caused by typhus, or of another type, relapsing fever. The people were filthy. They had sold every stitch that would fetch even a fraction of a penny, they were wearing the same rags, day after day, night after night. Their bedding had long gone, and they slept covered with rags and old coats on mud floors. To heat water to wash themselves or their clothes was out of the question. They were eating their food half – or wholly – raw, because they had no money to buy fuel. If they had access to a suitable bog nearby, no one had energy to cut or gather the turf. All lay down to sleep side by side together, to keep warm on the cabin floor. By day, they stood side by side, packed together, waiting for wages or begging at the soup kitchens.

Hosts of beggars or homeless paupers tramped the roads, drifting from place to place without a fixed destination, filthy, starving, louse-infested, often with the fever actually on them. Whole families lay in fever by the roadside, this fever known as road fever. The odours were intolerable.

Many doctors and clergy tried to help. Physicians and clergy died. Forty-eight doctors in the Province of Munster alone died of fevers. There was evidence of an outbreak of cholera.

Workhouses had disgusting drains, giving off a stench. They tried to build fever sheds, lean-tos against the walls of the Workhouses. Thousands died daily. There were no funeral services, corpses were burnt at night, leaving no trace. Numbers reported were unreliable.

Up till then, to leave Ireland had been regarded as the most terrible of all fates, 'transportation' being the most dreaded of sentences. But now, the people were ter-rified and desperate, and they made their way to ports, only wanting to escape the misery. In a great mass movement, they made their way out of Ireland by the tens of thousands, across the ocean to America or across the sea to Britain. Fever went with them. The journey itself to a new life became a nightmare.

Emigrants left where they had grown up, abandoned all they had known, and carried nothing with them. They had suffered starvation, many carried fever, but they would die if they stayed. They had no choice. Many had been evicted during the land clearances. On arrival in their new country, they lived in cellars and outhouses fit for animals, not unlike the stone cottages or mud cabins they had left behind. They were treated much like animals, too, but by the second or third generations their Irish characteristics of being quick-witted and charming, and having a dogged determination to get ahead, shone through and served them well.

Over a million went directly to the United States, where they felt at home because there the hatred of the British was still very strong. The American War of Independence, 1775–1783, and the War of 1812, both with the British, were still in living memory. Many went by way of Canada, passage to the Canadian Colony offered by British ships, about £21, being cheaper than with foreign ship lines to New York. Once in Canada, a walk across the US border was easy. Even greater numbers emigrated to Great Britain, the relatively short passage across the Irish Sea being about £6.

The years 1846–1847 saw the first ships sailing back and forth across the Atlantic all year round, braving the harsh Atlantic weather. Some landlords even paid steerage for their tenants, happy to see the end of them. Ships were overcrowded, unsanitary, and of old construction. The preferred ports from which to sail were the smaller ones, like Castletown Berehaven, where there were no inspectors. Provisions on board were scanty and there was never enough water. If the ship got through the storms, many of passengers arrived sick, or died before reaching shore. These ships are still referred to as 'the Coffin Ships'.

The photos below show a stark and striking monument in Murrisk, between Westport and Louisburgh in County Mayo. It is an appropriate commemoration of the millions who perished as a result of the Great Famine over one hundred and fifty years ago. Crafted in bronze by John Behan, the dramatic sculpture depicts a 'Coffin Ship' with skeleton bodies in the rigging.

This National Famine Monument was unveiled in 1997 by President Mary Robinson.

In 1847, in the St. Lawrence Seaway, the line of ships waiting for inspection of immigrants for the presence of fever and quarantine selection, was several miles long.

In 1841, the population of Ireland was just over eight million. After the Famine, it had dropped to about six million. 'One million died, another million sailed' is popular belief today. This is only a rough indication. There were no records of deaths, and many must have died unknown. Fever victims found lying dead on the road in West Cork were buried in ditches. Overall, Munster lost about one quarter of its population. Further north, on Achill Island in County Mayo, the population of about seven thousand was halved. In 1911, seventy years later, the country's total population was close to four and a half million.

The British public were more or less uninformed about the Famine in Ireland. Not until *The Illustrated London News* carried images of the poverty, the hopelessness, and the despair of the starving and dying did the English sit up and take notice. The first sketches included scenic views, and showed sturdy people, not emaciated wretches. These were pleasant pictures. But by the end of the 1840s, printed images were harrowing and were accompanied by emotive text. They caused a stir, and politicians were forced to provide some real relief.

L: Ruins of a village in County Galway
R: A house in Ennis, Co. Clare
The Illustrated London News, January 5, 1849, page 4.

Some artists travelled with Queen Victoria when she paid a visit to Ireland, beginning at Cork on August 3 and 4, 1849. They set out to investigate the rumours, and to discover and sketch what was happening in the far west of the region.

Famine left hatred behind. It filled many of the hearts of those who had successfully emigrated, and later those of their descendants, with anger and bitterness. It is estimated £13 million was sent back home to Ireland by emigrants in America between 1848 and 1864, and such generosity continues to some degree up to the present day.

In spite of pressure, no adequate measures of reconstruction were undertaken and a steady drain from the best and the most enterprising continued to leave Ireland for generations, to enrich other countries.

The Famine is not discussed today: 'too sad, too much pain and anger to go into that.'[16] It occurred 170 years ago. *The Great Hunger* was followed by *The Long Silence*. Today, there is no more hunger, disease is under control, but tensions still remain.

In 1885, a cure for the potato blight was discovered. A relatively simple spray of a copper sulphate solution applied to the stalks of potato plants prevents development of the spores. It was discovered too late for many.

Quarantine

Eavan Boland (1944-2020)

In the worst hour of the worst season
of the worst year of a whole people
a man set out from the workhouse with his wife.
He was walking—they were both walking—north.

She was sick with famine fever and could not keep up.
He lifted her and put her on his back.
He walked like that west and west and north.
Until at nightfall under freezing stars they arrived.

In the morning they were both found dead.
Of cold. Of hunger. Of the toxins of a whole history.
But her feet were held against his breastbone.
The last heat of his flesh was his last gift to her.

Let no love poem ever come to this threshold.
There is no place here for the inexact
praise of the easy graces and sensuality of the body.
There is only time for this merciless inventory:

---

16   Patsy Faherty (1942–2018), Rusheenduff, Renvyle, Co. Galway, Ireland, 2016.

Their death together in the winter of 1847.
Also what they suffered. How they lived.
And what there is between a man and woman.
And in which darkness it can best be proved.

[From *New Collected Poems* by Eavan Boland. Copyright © 2008 by Eavan Boland.
In Canada, published by Carcanet.
Printed here by kind permission of Eavan Boland
Eavan wrote, in part, on February 20, 2020:
'You're welcome to use "Quarantine". My own permission is sufficient.
'I wish you so well with the book. Family history matters so much and leads to larger histories.
'This comes with every good wish
'Eavan.']

Lazy beds beside Lough Muck, north-west of Lough Fee, Co. Galway, 2018
The cluster of rocks to the right of the beds may indicate where a dwelling once stood
'the old cottages lie like bones over the open fields'
Taken from 'Place', a poem by Eamon Grennan

5.
CHILDHOOD OF JAMES

The Murphy family moved off Bere Island in the early 1850s. Perhaps members of the church congregation in Ardgroom arranged for a donkey and cart for their use, or possibly they were assisted by their family members with whom Mary had stayed for the birth of her children. But they would have been a nineteenth-century family travelling along the tracks and pathways, carting all their belongings with them, in search of a better way to live, full of hope for a better future; not unlike twenty-first century refugees on the move, shown to us almost daily in the media. The difference for the Murphys would have been they walked alone, as only one family.

The thatched cottage they settled into had the usual floor plan for that period, and had been built by Edward:

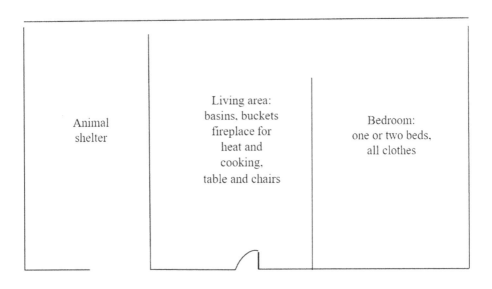

Floor plan for thatched cottage belonging to the Murphy Family

It is thought this structure still stands, in Droumard, about one mile east of Ardgroom. It faces eastwards, its solid backwall built against prevailing west winds. It nestles sideways up against a hillside, one crowned by a *rath*, an earthen ring fort, which is a small, circular, fortified home, likely built during the Bronze Age, sometime before the year 1000 AD.

Left: Front view, facing East, the back wall facing west, fending off stormy weather . Right: Close up of lintel.

It is highly possible these remains, found in Droumard and close by the rath there, were once the backbone of the cottage built by Eamon. They have all the correct attributes. Likely, Eamon used the stone described below for his lintel, and maybe after the description below was published, to preserve the pillar stone, it may have been removed from the cottage and replaced by a series of smaller rocks on either side, and the remaining gap filled in with cement.

W. O'Halloran describes the parish of Killcatherine [*Kilcatherine*] in *Early Irish Antiquities and the History of West Cork*[17] as being 'bold and romantic', rich with many pagan remains, such as stone circles.

He continues:[18]

'Not far to the south of the Dromard [Droumard] fort stands another fort, and hard by is a stone circle consisting of ten standing stones from 7 to 4 feet high, also a pillar stone 8 feet high and 5 wide. Another

17   W. O'Halloran, "Chapter XII: Danish Invasion of Ireland," *Early Irish History and Antiquities, and the History of West Cork* (Dublin: Sealy, Bryers and Walker, 1916), https://www.libraryireland.com/WestCorkHistory/Contents.php

18   W. O'Halloran, "Chapter XII: Danish Invasion of Ireland," *Early Irish History and Antiquities, and the History of West Cork* (Dublin: Sealy, Bryers and Walker, 1916), https://www.libraryireland.com/WestCorkHistory/Eyeries.php

similar stone I was informed was taken by a man named Murphy and used as a lintel.'

View of Droumard Ringfort from Ardgroom Harbour

(Murphy House hidden on far side)

Raths were common in Ireland, and the Droumard Ringfort's diameter of about thirty-five metres would have had an entrance passing through the earthen banks. A true fort. The entranceway would have been closed at night against natural predators such as wolves, as well as human raiders. In James's time, the fort would have been a boy's dream playground.

The cottage walls were built up loosely with rough stones, great care having been taken to fit them as tightly together as possible. The roof was thatched, the floor was earthen throughout, but packed hard like a rock with use. Crawling children could move about easily, but great care had to be taken to keep them away from the open fireplace. Not only would the turf fire give off a good heat, but suspended from hooks above were cooking pots full of boiling liquids, and, permanently sitting on the hob, a soot-blackened kettle of boiling water.

If there was an upper floor, or part of a floor, this is where winter feed, mostly hay, would have been stored, safe from wind and rain.

During a storm, the wind would have howled about the cottage. Wind would creep inside, too – a child would feel it blowing across his face at night. As the storm progressed, rain would blow in under the thatch.

Babies' nappies would have been rags, which also served as monthly menstruation pads. No *Tampax* back then!

There was no running water. It had to be carried from a well, and carefully stowed. Today, small stone or cement outhouse buildings may still be seen outside cottages, where a hole in the ground sufficed at one time. In the 1850s in Ireland, 'they went out to the field up at the back. They cleaned themselves with dock leaves or clumps of grass. You had to be careful where you stepped. When the rain fell, the field was cleaned up.'

This was where James spent his childhood. The language spoken was Irish. His mother could not read, but his father made up for that by *having the English* and by having been trained in Latin. When it came to teaching his son, Edward would have used his cane liberally, as *spare the rod, spoil the child* was the accepted form of punishment for children.

The family lived in poverty. Today we would describe their clothes as rags; the children went barefoot, even as teenagers. The worst of the Famine was over, but food was still scarce, and Mary had to make tough decisions as to the food distribution at mealtimes. Everyone was hungry. Who would get the best, most nutritious part? How much should be assigned to each family member?

And then, the family continued to grow: Maria in 1855, Edward Harnett in 1858, Nancy in 1860, and Michael in 1862. Mary was now thirty-five and had given birth at least eight times. She might have had more children whose records have not yet been discovered. Some on the family tree might have died. The children of James never heard tell of some of their aunts and uncles, and of others, James altered some details.

James would have played with neighbouring children, most of whom were of the same social level, but he would have also spent much of his time with the children of the ministers. With this group, James received education far beyond what the local school could offer. These boys were given lessons by Rev Thomas O'Grady, Rector in Castletown Berehaven, by Rev John Halahan, the Curate who was destined to be promoted to Dean of Ross, by Rev Michael Fitzgerald, who had been 'appointed to convert the people of Ardgroom,'[19] but who was not yet priested although already known as Rev Fitzgerald, and also by his father, ex-schoolteacher Edward Murphy. All of these men were very interested in education, and most were recognised scholars themselves. They were especially keen on researching Irish language issues, and Irish culture, which abounded on the Beara Peninsula and which might explain why they were content to have settled so removed from centres of learning.

The only problem in this exciting, enriched environment for James was that all the ministers' boys came from homes that were much bigger and warmer, and where there were servants. These houses would have had staircases to upper levels, and there would have been plenty of room for instruction of all the children and four tutors. James's home would never have worked in this set-up, and everyone would have been aware of this divide. Likely, Edward took James, and later, son Edward as well, down

---

19   Riobard O'Dwyer, *The Ardgroom Soup* Pot, <riobardodwyer@eircom.net>

to Castletown Berehaven, a good three-hour walk, each way. It is hoped in return for Edward's teaching services, his two boys were given a good meal. Edward, too!

However, James had everything else going for him – he was very bright, he was physically big and strong, he could articulate well (his father thought he should be a lawyer!), and if a remark or even a tease was made, he could deliver a powerful punch with his fist. But, did the ministers' children have shoes? Did each have his own winter coat? James had neither.

From the beginning, James would have had to face his lower social status, knowing the reasons he and his brother Edward were being included in these study sessions. All because their father was a good teacher, was now a Protestant, knew all about the exams the boys must pass with merit, and was fluent in English and Latin. Hard lessons, learnt early.

At the time, the big old house across the little bay close to Droumard belonged to a prominent local family. However, the roof had sprung a leak, and the house had been given to the local rector for use as a rectory. This was where Rev Fitzgerald and his family lived, it is hoped under a sound roof. With a short swim, or a quick rowing of oars, or a punting with a handy pole, the Murphy boys could swiftly cross the small inlet. The Murphy house, tiny in contrast, was crowded. The older children would have been sent outside, every day, rain or shine:

Will ye get on out of it? Ye'll be steppin' on the little ones.

Amac̄ lιb . Is ᴀ5 sιuιl oRᴄᴀ ᴀ beιð ᴄú .

At this time, an older woman was living with the Murphy family. Her name was also Mary Hartnett, and she stayed with them until her death, aged ninety-five in 1871. This would place her in her mid-seventies when James was a young child. This older Mary was not the mother of Edward's wife, who was Honora Kelly, but she could have been a Hartnett aunt, or, perhaps, a cousin. Almost every household would have had an older person living with them, usually a woman, as women lived longer than the men. There were two main reasons for this arrangement. First, it spread around the family the care of the elderly, avoiding committing them to the Workhouses, a dreaded fate. And secondly, having a second adult in the house would be a huge help to the housewife: someone to watch the children when she had to dash over to the well, someone to guard the little children from the fireplace, someone to peel the potatoes. Many of these older women spent their days sitting beside the hearth, trying to keep warm, perhaps riddled with arthritis, only going outside to sit for a short while, when the sun came out.

Oh, Eamon, would ye take them two boys off with ye, this evening? They're a bother.

Ah a Eamon , beir leat an beirt buaċaill sin, um tratnóna .

Is mór an trioblóid an beirt acu .

It is clear when Edward went out, he would take James, at least, with him. Surely James, and sometimes Edward, sat to the side, observing their father, the scripture reader, reading the Bible and noticing how the words were received by his intended listeners. Reading in Latin or translating into English, virtually no one present, except Edward himself, would have understood what was being said. Unintelligible to everyone.

James would never forget these things. He would remember well.

6.
MOTHER MARY, 1862,
DROUMARD IN ARDGROOM

She didn't know it yet. Four of her children would emigrate, would be lost to her. And *their* children, her grandchildren, would hear of her only if stories were told around kitchen tables far, far away. She had heard of the pain of mothers left behind in dark stone cottages, watching their loved ones walking away into the cold light of dawn, striding out never to return, in that too-deliberate way of those who are unsure of themselves.

Everyone knew of mothers who were fearing the worst, yet hoping for the best. Yes. She knew of the letters which sometimes arrived back to childhood homes. Years of wondering and longing would be put away, replaced by sheets of paper scrawled over with pencil scribblings. A mother might be fortunate to hear the news read out by a younger, literate child if there was one, or by the priest when next he called. Or, perhaps someone after Mass on a Sunday would read out the letter to her. There might be a bit of cash in the letter, but usually money came only after some time had passed. There were stories of mothers who had given up all hope, only to open a letter one day, stuffed with US dollars inside, and the letter's handwriting perfect, having been done by a hired writer. One such mother had aged double her years, not having had word, any word, for about ten years. She had thought her loved one had gone down in a coffin ship in a storm. *What use the money now?* she asked, lying sick in her bed all day long. Wasted away she was, no longer hungry for food or for word, hardly able to care for herself, let alone the children left at home.

All that was mostly part of the Great Famine long past, ten, no, fifteen years ago. The fear of the Coffin Ships had left terror amongst those still at home in Ireland, those too scared to take their chance in a boat. Wasn't there always tomorrow, when the weather might be better and when God might suddenly remember them and come down to help their poor souls?

41

Today, Mary Murphy in her mid-thirties, with a babe on her hip and another lying inside on the bed asleep, was standing at her door, watching her fine young son, James, big and strong and robust as he was, striding out down *the boreen*, or *the lane*, as James might be calling it soon. He seemed so sure of himself, as though he was ready to walk all the way to the edge of the world. Perhaps he would fall off? How would she ever know?

Her cottage was up a small rise in the land, and she could watch him walking along for quite a while as he made his way down the lane to the road. Here he turned right towards the village where he would meet up with another student, likely the son of the Protestant clergyman in Ardgroom. The bushes were still green, smelling fresh in the crisp, autumn air, and as his head and shoulders bobbed up and down, she followed his progress, visible here and there above the uneven hedge.

James was her third living child, but he had taken up as much space in the cottage as all the others combined, what with his forceful presence and his lack of patience with the young ones in the family. His temper was quick and sharp, flaring up if challenged. Not with his father, mind you, for Eamon would beat him to keep him in order, on both sides of his hands to put the learning in him, and on his backside and legs for everything else. James would cry and yell out. It wasn't as though Eamon enjoyed this side of being a father. But he agreed with the ministers who held to the old saying: *Spare the rod, spoil the child.*

Eldest son John was sickly, sitting by the fireside or resting on the bed, quiet-like and no bother. Catherine, the second, was the greatest of help, walking around with a crying baby, fetching water, or sweeping out the cottage. Never complained, that girl, and always in good spirits. Then there was James, careful but quick at the outside work and with the animals, helping his father cut and bring in the turf for stacking, and then, lifting and carrying anything heavy. And he had excelled at his lessons, Eamon had told her, not that Mary knew anything about learning. But she could see it in the way James and Eamon would talk by the fire, as they discussed something the ministers had taught that day, or she saw it in the way they walked off down the boreen together, voices echoing over the ditches and up into the few trees here and there.

Now, Eamon would miss his son James. Eamon had gone off earlier, not wanting to appear emotional, having long ago given all the advice he could think of. He knew James was beginning a long, hard trail, would cry himself to sleep some nights and would be too fierce some days, but the boy would do well academically, would grow into himself, and the world was waiting for him with endless possibilities.

Mary knew nothing of the outside world and how it would cause strain and difficulties. She had her own daily trials right here. She watched as James stopped and gave her a big wave, as his father had instructed him to do. And then he was out of sight. He was gone. He was lost to her.

Wiping the salty tears off her face, Mary turned back inside, telling herself, 'Wouldn't James be back for Christmas holidays, a few months away?' And then, inside, there were Catherine and Maria busy washing, drying and stacking the dishes from breakfast, and Edward was building up the fire with turf. This was where she belonged, where her life was. These children needed her. Her heart might ache for a while if she thought of her 'lost son' walking out of her life, making her feel like *a Mother of Sorrows*, but that would slowly fade. Eamon would seem more relaxed, less anxious without James, the arguments and loud discussions being over for now. From today, Eamon would have more time for Edward, teaching him about determination, and the right way to hold to convictions.

James had always shown great affection for his mother. All his life he would send her money which he could ill afford to spare. And he would visit her each year, catching a train at Kingsbridge Station in Dublin, initially travelling to Tralee, where the railway line had been opened in 1853, and later journeying to Kenmare, after a new line was opened from Headford to Kenmare in 1893.[20] James would walk the rest of the way to Droumard or to wherever Mary was living. When she was dying in 1916, he would race down to be with her, but he did not, could not, attend her funeral. Mary had held onto her faith as a Roman Catholic, and James had become a Protestant Minister. There is no headstone for her, James being the one who would have ordered it. He must have wrestled with what to do: add her name, and she a Roman Catholic, to the gravestone he had set up for his father, a Protestant? Give Mary her own gravestone, and he, James, who always dressed as a Protestant Minister, causing scandalous gossip by ordering such a thing in a Catholic stone cutter's yard? James did nothing and Mary lies in an unmarked grave.

But the memory of Mary Murphy lingers on. She is remembered by her descendants today, who live in Ireland, England, Scotland, Germany, the United States, Canada, and Australia. She spoke only Irish, but likely understood much of what was said in English. Her descendants speak English, German, French, some are fluently bilingual, but none speak Irish well.

In the nineteenth century, living with a growing family in a stone cottage in the south-west of Ireland was grim, demanding, and physically wearing. A mother's daily routine would have included ensuring the level of water in the house was maintained, sometimes carrying it in from the well herself, and checking the stack of turf indoors was sufficient to keep the fire going. Eamon would have done most of the physical

---

20   *Railway Lines' History:* Researched by Cousins David Wynne and Margaret Lennon Wynne.

lifting into the cottage, but Mary would have kept a close eye on it all, reliant as she was on fire and water. Daily she was baking Irish soda bread in a large covered pot surrounded by hot ashes. She was skimming cream off the milk from the cow, the milk having been left to settle overnight in a bowl in the coolest part of the cottage. She was culturing buttermilk and churning butter in a primitive butter churn, perhaps made for her by Eamon. If meat was available, she was concerned about keeping it fresh, possibly in an outdoor safe, while meat fat such as bacon grease, was often used on bread instead of butter (and wonderful was the taste of it!). Mary was cooking with pots hanging from hooks suspended over the fire, bits of charcoal falling in from the chimney above, and smoke flavouring everything, as she anxiously watched for the contents to boil which would ensure preservation of any leftovers, overnight. She was washing dishes in a basin on the table, and she was washing clothes in a sort of battle with the elements outside, patiently waiting until better weather came so the wash could be laid around outside to dry. And all this time, she was nursing a babe 'on demand', and dealing with young children, coping with their difficulties.

It is thought thyroid gland malfunction came into the family genome from the Murphys. Thyroid troubles have plagued some descendants, depending on genes inherited. Mary may have carried those genes, not medically understood in her time, and she may have suffered from such symptoms as overwhelming fatigue, emotional distress, breathing difficulties, and increased sensitivity to cold. The usual explanation for these complaints was 'a weak heart'. And, even today, muscle and joint issues can be misdiagnosed, not accredited to a thyroid problem. In Mary's time this would have been labelled as arthritis, from which it is certain she also suffered, having lived and slept in pervading dampness all her life.

After Eamon died in 1882, Mary was to live on for over thirty years. Where she resided for this time has not been uncovered. She died in the Kenmare Hospital, which at that time meant being housed in the cramped women's quarters in the Workhouse. After the death of her husband, it is possible Mary suffered from some kind of break-down, physical, emotional, or both. She might have just given up. Widows were poorly treated at the end of the nineteenth century, and there are examples recorded in other branches of the family, where new widows *lost the place*. Possibly the priest or Mary's daughter Catherine still residing in Capparoe arranged for her to move to Kenmare, where she was placed in the Workhouse. It is thought she died there in May 1916:

No.	Date and place of death:	Name and Surname:	Sex:	Condition: Widow	Rank:	Cause of Death:	Signature: John J. O'Sullivan	Date and signature when registered:
52	1916 May ninth Kenmare Hospital	Mary Murphy [of] Lehud	female	Age: 90 years	Farmer's Widow	Senile Decay Certified	Occupier Kenmare Hospital	May Eleventh. 1916

Image of the Death Record of Mary Murphy, from Civil Records at www.irishgenealogy.ie

Mary may have suffered strokes or other debilitating illnesses requiring full-time care. Just by being placed in the dreaded Workhouse alone might have brought on the *senile decay* listed above.

Not a good ending, but we can hope Mary died not knowing where she was. We are told James reached her to provide comfort before she died, and we can imagine him whispering some words to her in Irish:

A Ṫiarna, breaṫnaiġ uait anuas ó neaṁ ar do ṡeirḃíseaċ, a ḃfuil ár n-urnaiṫe á n-éileaṁ ar a son. Féaċ uirṫi, tar á fiosrú agus tabair faoiseaṁ di .

Aṁarc uirṫi le súile do ṫrócaire; más é do ḋea ṫoil é. Cosain ó ionsaiṫe an namad í agus ó eagla roiṁe, agus coinniġ go slán suaiṁneaċ go deo í trí Íosa Críost ár Ṫiarna, Amen.

Translation into English:

Prayer for the Sick:

Lord, look down from heaven on your servant, for whom we offer this prayer. Watch over her and comfort her. Mercifully look upon her; if it be your will.

Protect her from all her enemies and fear of them, and keep her safe and peaceful forever through Jesus Christ our Lord, Amen

Perhaps James would have thought of a Psalm:

Salm 23:
Is é an Tiarna m'aoire : ní beró aon ní de óít orm .
Cuireann sé féin i mo luí mé i móinéar féir ġlais .
Seolann sé ar imeall uisce an tsóláis mé mar a bfaiġim
suaimneas.
Seolann sé ar ślí na fíréantaċta mé mar ġeall ar a ainm .
fiú dá siúlfainn i ngleann an dorċadais, níor baol liom an t-olc
agus tú faram le do ślat is do baċall ċun sólás a tabairt dom .
Cóiríonn tú bord ċun béile dom i látair mo naimde.
Ungann tú mo ċeann le hola ; tá mo ċupa ag cur tairis.
Leanfaió cineáltas is buanġrá mé gaċ lá de mo śaol ;
i dteaċ an Tiarna a mairfió mé go bráċ na breite .

Translation into English:

Psalm 23:

The Lord is my Shepherd: therefore can I lack nothing.

He shall feed me in a green pasture and lead me forth beside the waters of comfort.

He shall convert my soul and bring me forth in the paths of righteousness, for his Name's sake.

Yea, though I walk through the valley of the shadow of death, I will fear no evil, for thou art with me; thy rod and thy staff comfort me.

Thou shalt prepare a table before me against them that trouble me, thou hast anointed my head with oil, and my cup shall be full.

But thy loving-kindness and mercy shall follow me all the days of my life, and I will dwell in the house of the Lord for ever.

Fill, Fill, Fill a Rún Ó

Come back, come back my love
A song

**A Catholic mother implores her son who became a
Protestant Minister to return to the Catholic Church**

Fill, fill a rún ó
Fill, a rún is ná himigh uaim
Fill orm a cuisle is a stór
Agus cífidh tú an glóir má fillean tú

Fill, fill a rún ó
Fill, a rún is ná himigh uaim
Má filleann tú inniu nó go deo
Fill insan Ord in ar oileadh tú

Diúltaigh tú Peadar is Pól
Mar geall ar an ór is an airgead
Diúltaigh tú Banríon na Glóire
Agus d'iompaigh tú i gcóta an mhinistir

Fill, fill a rún ó
Fill, a rún is ná himigh uaim
Fill orm a cuisle is a stór
Agus cífidh tú an glóir má fillean tú

Come back, come back my love
Come back my love and don't leave me
Return to me my darling and my treasure
And you will see the glory if you come back

Come back, come back my love
Come back my love and don't leave me
If you come back tomorrow or ever
Return to the Order you were trained in

You foresook Peter and Paul
On account of gold and silver
You foresook the Queen of Glory
And you turned to the coat of a minister

Come back, come back my love
Come back my love and don't leave me
Return to me my darling and my treasure
And you will see the glory if you come back

James would have known the following by heart, and would not have had to produce a Protestant prayer book to say the words:

From the Church of England Service of Commendation:

Go forth upon your journey from this world, O Christian Soul. In the name of God the Father, who created you. In the name of Jesus Christ who suffered for you. In the name of the Holy Spirit who strengthens you. In Communion with all the blessed Saints, with the angels and archangels, and all the heavenly host. May your portion this day be in peace and your dwelling in the City of God.

If James could not bring himself to speak this prayer at his mother's bedside, the words would have been in his head as he strode out towards the train station, on his way yet again to return to his other life, the one he had built for himself with his father's blessing.

7.
JAMES ON HIS WAY

How good it felt to be heading out on an adventure! A real one, not an imaginary game. He and his pal, together they made a strong team, and James was certain his friend would be waiting for him by the village bridge. The future might get scary at times, but he felt confident in himself. Across his back was slung the strap of a bag a minister's wife had told him he could have. 'Sure, no one else wants that old thing,' she had said, shoving it quickly at him as she sent him home out the door. His own mother had told him later that the poor woman was probably afraid one of her own sons would claim it back, if she was seen giving it away. But James did not care. He was delighted with it, made as it was of tough worn leather, soft and not too big. There was little he could bring with him, anyway. A pencil handed to him one day by the teacher from his local school. James had spent a whole evening sharpening the wood and graphite to perfection using a small kitchen knife. And a small sheaf of papers with a couple of envelopes his father had said he should have. 'You won't be getting none of that in Bandon now, lad, but they'll make sure there's a stamp on any letter you send us. We'll be wanting to hear you arrived safe and all.' A woman in the village had knitted a large buttoned jacket for him, which he was wearing in the morning chill, but if he got too warm on the walk, he could take it off and stuff it inside the bag. His mother had wrapped up some buttered scones in a piece of worn, brown paper. Those buttermilk scones were his favourite lunch, and they would be washed down with water, as the boys would be drinking out of streams, just as he and his Da used to do, when walking.

Everyone in the village of Ardgroom knew the two students, 'the two scholars' they called them now, who were leaving that morning early in September. Parents and children in every cottage were watching out to catch a glimpse of the boys, walking along, barefoot with few clothes, but a good jacket on each. 'Good luck, lads! Study hard! See ye in December. God bless ye both.'

James and his pal began by climbing up the slope of *Tooreennanma*, which would lead them up into the Caha Mountains. Depending on the weather, and on how well they got along, they could get to Glengarriff the first day, on to Dunmanway the second and reach their destination, Bandon Grammar School on the third. The boys would be doing that walk, each way, a couple of times a year for a number of years yet. They knew if they could get to the road which ran from Castletown Berehaven to Glengarriff, and if they could hitch a ride on a cart, they would get along better and be more rested for the next stage afterwards. Sometimes they would meet up with other students, but usually not till they at least reached Glengarriff.

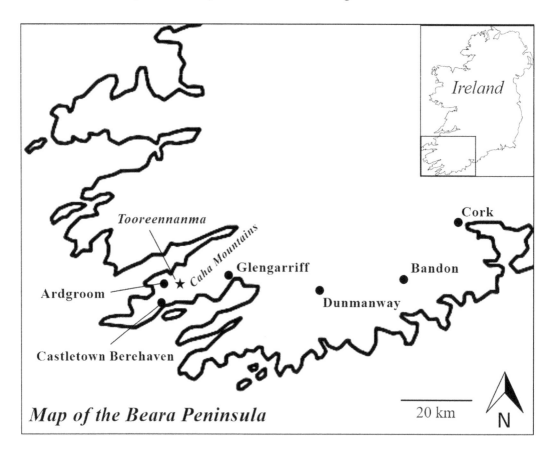

Map 3; Beara Peninsula and the route to Bandon.
The boys walked barefoot all the way, about 75 miles to school,
over a mountain and along gravel roads.

They would receive an open door at any rectory, for the word of their journey would have been passed around at West Cork clergy meetings, and so the boys would have been expected. A good meal and a place to lie down and sleep, all followed in the morning by a big breakfast and a packet of more food for their bags.

Tired and footsore in the true sense of the word, they would stumble into the school at Bandon, which was ready for them. Here they would be washed, provided with proper school clothes, and other items like a facecloth, a toothbrush, and a comb. Most importantly, they would be given a good pair of shoes, good food, and all necessary school supplies.

This is what Eamon had hoped for his boy, drilling him all those years to prepare for the scholarship exam. Eamon had known if James could win a scholarship, doors would open up, open wide to the future. Eamon had handed James the key, and James had unlocked the door.

This was September 1862. James was twelve years old and on his way.

8.
JAMES THE STUDENT

His first language was Irish, but he could speak limited English and he picked up English vocabulary as he went along. Now a student in Bandon, English was what everyone spoke around him, and would do so from here on. But it wasn't language which caused him difficulties, it was his accent. He had a strong brogue, and even today, if one is listening to anyone from West Cork speaking, most will not understand what is being said. The words flow very fast, are almost sung, and great energy goes into the speaking. The dialect is unique. School boys would have jeered at this type of speech, teasing, sneering, and James would have felt the threat to his very core. He had little to fall back on, his parents having no stature of any kind. James had a bad temper, and boys would gather around, to enjoy watching him getting *riled up*. But James could bash tormentors, keeping them at bay. And at Bandon Grammar School, James made a good friend who remained a friend for life. John Quarry Day came from a well-established southern Irish family, the Days, well known in religious and judiciary circles. We do not know how the two boys became such good friends, and surely there were stories, but these have not come down to us.

We know both boys did well at the school. Likely, Day entered Bandon Grammar School as a fee-paying student, and went on to Trinity College, Dublin, in the same way. James paid no fees at either. James was a *sizar student*, which meant he studied as an undergraduate at Trinity College, Dublin, receiving financial help from the College, free Commons (evening meal) every day, but in return having to perform certain menial duties.

This may sound good today, but only if the menial duties could be performed out of sight of peers. However, in James's case, he had to serve other students their dinner in the Dining Hall. It must have been demeaning, degrading, and he would have been taunted by those with posh accents, whether they were of British or of Irish origin. *Here comes our favourite Bogman, Murphy from the County Cork. No wonder our dinner is cold. You're so slow, man. Did you have to dig up the spuds, first? Get going, you culchie.* James would have struggled daily to control his rising temper. These very same students were in his lectures by day. James kept it all bottled up inside.

James and John were studying law, where a student is expected to stand and give his opinion. Not a happy situation, when fellow students could not understand what he was saying, and considered him a joke. And on top of these difficulties, James had no experience whatever in social training, was uncouth, and wore clothes which could make him a laughing stock. Perhaps his hygiene was lacking. A weaker fellow would have crumbled under all of this. James was made of strong stuff, but he never lost the scars. His temper could be dreadful, blinding his judgement. He learnt to use fists, not words, and when he did speak in public, he would shout, apparently unaware this emphasised his accent. Bandon was known to be a Protestant town, and Trinity was a Protestant centre. Not many in the Protestant Establishment liked him, but John Quarry Day held true.

After two years, both James and John recognised there was little future in a career in the legal profession for either of them. Maybe it was because no company would offer either student a position for articling. They both switched their studies to Divinity.

Their careers followed similar patterns:

James E. H. Murphy	John Quarry Day
1850 Born	**1849** Born
About 1863 Student at Bandon Grammar School	**About 1863** Student at Bandon Grammar School
About 1870 Student at Trinity College, Dublin	**About 1869** Student at Trinity College, Dublin
1878 BA and ordained Deacon	**1873** BA
1879 Priest. Curate of Kilmainhamwood with Moybologue	**1877** Ordained Deacon in Cork. Curate of Kilmallock
1881 Rector of Rathcore. Received MA, TCD	**1879** Priest. Curate of Arklow
1882 Rural Dean of Clonard	**1882** Curate in Loughcrew
1889 Appointed Deputy Professor of Irish at Trinity College, Dublin	**1886** Rector in Loughcrew
1896 Appointed Professor of Irish at Trinity College, Dublin	**1889** Rural Dean of Fore
	1897 Received MA, TCD
1901 Member of the Diocesan Council, Diocese of Meath	**1900** Curate-in-Charge of Kilskyre
1903 Member of the General Synod	
1904 Member of the Diocesan Board of Education	

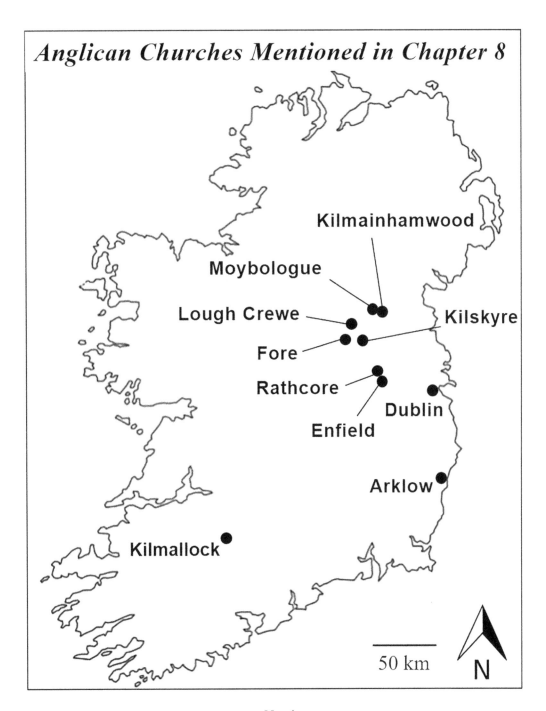

Map 4

Family Tree for the
Four Lennon Girls of Newcastle House

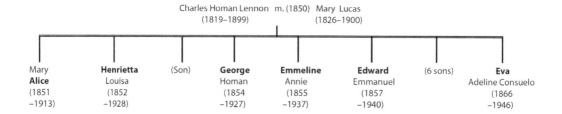

Charles Homan Lennon m. (1850) Mary Lucas
(1819–1899)   (1826–1900)

Mary **Alice** (1851–1913)

Henrietta Louisa (1852–1928)

(Son)

George Homan (1854–1927)

Emmeline Annie (1855–1937)

Edward Emmanuel (1857–1940)

(6 sons)

Eva Adeline Consuelo (1866–1946)

9.
THE FOUR LENNON GIRLS OF NEWCASTLE HOUSE

The Lennon family at Newcastle House in Enfield had twelve children, and of these eight were sons. All but two sons emigrated to the United States, where most of them thrived, married and had families. They supported each other as best they could, and contributed to the communities where they settled.

Of the two sons who remained behind in Ireland, Edward Emmanuel became a medical doctor, as described in Chapter 16, and George bought a farm close to Newcastle House, where he happily continued the Lennon family tradition of successfully farming the land. These farms were in County Meath, one of the most prosperous parts of Ireland, with rich soil and excellent weather. George was well known as a good cattle man. And Charlie had chosen to cycle to his Uncle George, having been beaten by his father as a young lad. And talking of the hospitality of George's home, Hotwell, his nieces would record:

> When we were children we loved Hotwell. We could do no wrong, and we had a wonderful time, always outdoors. They would ply us with food. We would be there for the haymaking. It was absolutely gorgeous.
>
> Hotwell was a splendid home to visit. I can see Uncle George now, in his dinner jacket, and with £2 for us in his pocket. He would say, "Don't tell anybody. This is our secret!" Wasn't that lovely?

There were four girls in the Lennon family living in Newcastle House. They were the daughters of Charles and Mary Lennon, and all were very different, but they kept close all their lives.

Mary (Lucas) Lennon and Charles Lennon, parents of The Four Lennon Girls

These girls were members of the Protestant minority who were either landowners or leased the land from absentee landlords. Their families were relatively prosperous at a time when parts of Ireland were still reeling from the effects of the Famine. Their children often moved freely between the big houses, staying with their first cousins, sometimes for extended periods. Spending so much time together, these children would naturally fall in love as teenagers, and one such couple, first cousins, even married.

The eldest Lennon child was **Mary Alice**, followed by **Henrietta Louisa**. The third and fourth children were sons, but immediately afterwards another girl arrived, **Emmeline Annie**. The growing family now had five children, all in the space of five years. But it wouldn't stop there; six sons followed in the next seven years. Finally, the twelfth child was born, another girl, **Eva Consuelo,** with fifteen years between this new baby and the first born of the family. Thus, the 'Four Lennon Girls' in this chapter, were **Alice, Henrietta, Emmeline Annie**, and **Eva**.

The eldest was known to succeeding generations as *Aunt Alice*. She seems to have been a steady girl, no doubt leaned on by her mother and the house servants, to help with the children at all times. Where she met her husband is not known, but when she was twenty-six and he was twenty-five, she married James Ross and settled in County Monaghan, in Liscarney House. They had three boys – James, Charlie, and Sharman – followed by one girl, Gladys. As we shall see, the three boys' lives were interwoven with those of their relatives in Newcastle House, County Meath. Gladys was born blind, a result of her father having contracted syphilis.

The Ross Family c. 1911 left to right: James, Sharman, Gladys, Charles, Mary Alice (née Lennon)

Henrietta was the second child, the *Wild Girl* of the Lennon family. Even though she lived far from Ireland as an adult, and was removed from Meath society, her actions haunted the Lennons back home, and caused repercussions for many years. Some years before, there had been a teenage cousin staying with the Lennon family in Newcastle House, who had fallen in love with a local charmer, but had been spurned. In despair, she had walked into the canal at the edge of the property and drowned herself. This had traumatised the Lennon family, her sad story becoming part of their family lore.

So when Henrietta was fifteen, she 'fell for this fellow, this Cyril, who just didn't qualify.' Henrietta declared she 'would walk into the Canal and would drown herself unless she could marry her man.' The family refused to allow her marriage to her unfortunate admirer, and afterwards, they watched her every move.

But, 'Aunt Hennie was a terror for the boys. And she had the Lennon charm. What a charming woman she was.' Very soon Henrietta fell in love again, this time with a suitable local fellow, a son of a Church of Ireland clergyman, and, even better, he was a doctor in the Indian Service. In no time, Henrietta was engaged, and then married to Dr Richard Gerald Fitzgerald, Staff Assistant-Surgeon, home on leave from Lahore. She was sixteen, and 'everyone was glad to get her married'. Off went the newlyweds to India, and in six years, four daughters had arrived. The youngest of these was only three weeks old when Dr Fitzgerald died from TB. There was some talk of him 'having been fond of the drink, but it was the T.B. that killed him.'[21]

---

21   *Exploits of Henrietta:* To follow her travels and experiences, and her children, see Appendix 2.

At that point, Henrietta had had enough. 'Shortly after her husband's death, she came home, and she dumped two of her children on one grandmother and two on the other. She sped back to India where she married Tom Maxwell, also in the Service, and she had five further children with him.' It was said that Colonel Maxwell commanded the Regiment and Mrs Maxwell commanded the Colonel.

Henrietta and Richard Fitzgerald with Nurse holding baby, possibly Elsie, c. 1871

The two girls Henrietta left at Newcastle House, in the care of her parents, Mary and Charles Lennon, were Chota and Blackie. When the family discovered that Blackie had contracted TB from her father, Mary Lennon, their grandmother at Newcastle House, could not cope, and Blackie, with Chota in tow, was sent to live with the family of Emmeline Annie, where she thrived. But she had brought TB into the Murphy family, into Rathcore Rectory. Strange to say, Blackie died at fifteen by drowning accidentally in the same canal as her mother had threatened to do many years before.

Henrietta's granddaughter would record: 'Henrietta our Grannie really was a hard woman. She never came home from India and saw those four children. She was there in India for thirty years, before retiring to England. No Christmas presents, birthday presents, letters of any kind, for which I can never forgive her. She was as hard on Tiny and Biny, putting them into a Convent in Belgium, abandoning them there. They didn't get enough to eat, which ruined the health of both.'

Emmeline Annie Lennon

Tom Maxwell and Henrietta retired to Britain, living for a while on a moored boat off the coast of north-east England. They finally settled in Barnstaple, North Devon. Henrietta died there on June 16, 1928, and is buried just south of Barnstaple, in Umberleigh.

The third daughter at Newcastle was **Emmeline Annie**, who was the mother of the Murphy family in Rathcore, as described in the following chapter.

The fourth daughter and final child at Newcastle House

Eva Consuelo

was **Eva Adeline Consuelo**, born in 1866. In 1982, Emmeline Annie's granddaughter Daphne knew Eva Consuelo well, and wrote:

> Emmeline's sister Eva is always known as *Eva Consuelo*, to distinguish her from Emmeline's daughter, Eva Emmeline.
>
> Eva Consuelo was tall and stately with fine features and very formal manners. She never married in spite of her beauty. Someone once said to my mother *Your Aunt Eva was a perfect example of a fine lady - face, voice, manner, and carriage were superb.* She was also reputed to have had a lovely singing voice, and would lead the choir in Rathcore Church, while her sister, Emmeline Annie, played the organ.
>
> After her father's death, Eva Consuelo lived at Newcastle with her mother except for an interlude, when she paid an extensive visit to see her brothers and their families in the U.S.A. When her mother died in 1900 her brother Percy inherited the farm, and Eva moved to be a housekeeper to another brother, Dr Edward Emmanuel Lennon, in his home at 22 Merrion Square, Dublin. There they were most hospitable to any of the family who came to Dublin, and especially to their various nephews and nieces, many of whom were receiving education of one kind or another.
>
> This arrangement came to an end when in 1908 Edward, at the age of fifty-one, married Eileen Metge. Eva Consuelo, like so many other sisters similarly situated had to make other plans. Fortunately, she had become very friendly with a brother and sister called Pentland. She went to live with them at Clifton, 2 Castle Avenue, Clontarf. This *ménage à trois* lasted until the end of the Second World War. When Mollie Pentland and her brother died, Eva continued to live at Clifton until her death at the age of eighty in 1946.
>
> I had tea with her many times when I was a student in Trinity College. She attended our wedding, and I remember her coming to see me in the nursing home when my daughter, Julia, her great grandniece, was born early in 1946.

As descendants of the Newcastle Lennon family spread out across the globe, they tried to keep connected by letter writing. Most letters have not survived. However, in 1951, Chota Peard (née Fitzgerald), daughter of Henrietta and at that time a widow living in Australia, wrote a letter to her first cousin, Eva Wallace (née Murphy), daughter of Emmeline Annie, living at French Creek on Vancouver Island, in Canada. Chota had grown up as part of the Murphy household at Rathcore, she was fifteen years older than Eva Murphy, and in her late teens she had moved to Dublin to live with her Aunt Eva Consuelo. She had then married, and lived in South Africa, moving in 1939 to Australia. In 1951, Chota (Maud Hope Peard) wrote, in part:

> My dearest Eva
>
> You will be surprised to get this from your cousin Chota after all these years... I now write to you having got your address from Elsie a few days ago... she tells me you are living in a "wee shack"[22] on Vancouver Island... you will be surprised to hear I am contemplating a trip to Vancouver Island. Do write to me like a dear and tell me all you can about climate, best time of year to travel, exchange rate of the dollar, and what about churches?... I suppose your "shack" would not hold me also? Or is there another close by? I should love the primitiveness of it. I am just tired of Australia, and England is no place to go to at present... Yrs. M. H. P.

As far as is known, Chota never made it to visit or to live in Canada.

There is information on the internet discussing a family Bible as follows:

> 'My daughter recently purchased a small old Bible in Townsville QLD, and on the back page was written. . .' and here follows written out a list of all of Henrietta's Maxwell children. Likely that Bible had been amongst Chota's possessions at one time.

Liscarney House, Monaghan; Home of Mary Alice (née Lennon) Ross

22   **Wee shack:** Elsie's description of the cottage at French Creek!

10.
EMMELINE ANNIE

EMMELINA on her birth certificate,
EMMA to her family and
EMMELINE ANNIE to her descendants

Emmeline Annie Lennon was born in Newcastle House near Enfield in County Meath, on Christmas Eve, 1855. Living for almost eighty-two years, she died December 22, 1937, upstairs in one of her son's rooms in Fitzwilliam Square in Dublin. For sixty-five of those years, Emmeline Annie had lived almost exclusively in the Enfield area. Years later, her granddaughter Daphne was giving a sermon in Waterford Cathedral:

> I was thinking as I drove here, I am in 1974 at the same stage of my life as was my grandmother Emmeline Annie, in 1900. What a century of change it has been, with our cars and domestic gadgets, TV and radio communication, telephones and flying the Atlantic. But none of these inventions mark my life off from my grandmother's, as does the emancipation of women. What really makes the difference between her life and mine is that, in spite of having a husband and four children, from within my own home I am able to have a life of my own, make my own contacts, do my own thing. And almost as remarkable, when I think of my grandfather James, is that in all this I have the encouragement and active co-operation of my husband. In spite of subterranean grumblings, women continue to expand their activities.

Emmeline Annie's parents in Newcastle House had twelve children, eight boys and four girls. Most of the boys emigrated, most of the girls left, but Emmeline Annie was happy enough to be the one to stay close to home. She seems to have been her father's favourite child. He called her his *Pinkie* because of her lovely *roses and cream complexion*, which stayed with her, even in her eighties. She and her three sisters were carefully coached by their father to walk gracefully. He emphasised the importance of carrying oneself well, of having a straight back and holding one's head up. Each girl was given a china dish to balance on her head as he coached them to walk up and down the stone floor of the long hall at Newcastle.

Emmeline Annie used to reminisce how after dinner at Newcastle, the women left the men to their port and cigars in the dining room, and they, the ladies, entered the *with-drawing room*. Here they would all turn their backs to the roaring open fire and lift up the back of their long skirts, *to have a hate*[23] *on their own while the boys is out.*

Rev James Murphy, the local rector, wanted to marry Emmeline Annie. Her parents were not against it. Rev John Quarry Day, Murphy's great friend from his TCD days, was Rector at Lough Crewe, in the same diocese. They were both bachelors, and when Day visited Murphy shortly after Murphy and Emmeline Annie became engaged, Day complained, *Like to an owl in an ivy bush, a lonesome thing am I.* This saying became a favourite quote for Emmeline Annie.

They were married in secret on January 3, 1883 – she was twenty-seven and he was thirty-three. The sextoness was told to have the church heated, and the service was held early in the morning by Rev Fred Lucas, brother of Emmeline Annie's mother and a minister in the Dublin area. The newlyweds then drove in a horse and trap to Enfield Station, and took the train and boat to London for their two-week honeymoon. The highlight was a visit to the Crystal Palace.

Murphy took the whip to Emmeline Annie very freely, and she left him a couple of times. She began legal proceedings each time, but never followed through to the end. One time, Murphy took a penknife and cut up Emmeline Annie's clothes so she wouldn't be able to go out anywhere. On another occasion, John Quarry Day attended the Rathcore Harvest Service, and he commented to Murphy, 'Mrs Murphy looks very fetching in that hat.' Murphy asked Emmeline Annie, 'Would you let me see the hat you had on last Sunday?' He took the hat and 'cut it to bits'.

Emmeline Annie's religious faith was steady and simple. Her Bible had _passages necessary for salvation_ underlined in red, a "red-letter edition". She played the organ in Rathcore Church for thirty years. Her services are recorded on a memorial plate attached to the organ.

---

23   **Hate:** heat.

The plaque reads:

> In memory of
> **EMMELINE ANNIE MURPHY**
> who over 30 years
> presided at the organ
> in this church
> 1938

Emmeline Annie
(Lennon) Murphy

She was essentially a practical person with little time for interest in politics, literature, or philosophy, but she had a wonderful love of life and a fund of everyday wisdom based on her own deep experience. Two of her favourite sayings were:

What can't be cured must be endured
and
Necessity is the mother of invention

Whenever male members of her household were cogitating how best to fix something, involved as they were in a major discussion, Emmeline Annie would quietly and deftly mend and make do before they could come to a decision. Long before such skills were used by doctors, she put back the tip of her son's finger when it was accidentally cut off. Indeed, she was known in the parish for her nursing skill, and for her care for the sick of all classes and creeds. Perhaps not by chance five of her eight surviving children qualified as doctors. Emmeline Annie did a lot of visiting of the sick and lonely, driving the horse and trap and taking her eldest daughter, Eva with her. Eva always had difficulty remembering the difference between her left and right, and Emmeline Annie would be highly embarrassed if Eva put out her left hand instead of her right hand, to shake hands. What to do?

Eva said:

> Mother was so worried that I would put out my left hand, worried because that was considered the mark of a child not brought up properly. Eventually, I learned to clench my right hand as I climbed into the trap. I would keep it shut, with a handkerchief inside until we arrived at our destination. Then I would know which hand I was to use to shake hands.

One day, the whole family went to Trim for tea. Rev Murphy was probably attending a diocesan meeting with the bishop, Trim being the diocesan centre. The children, all under ten at that time, were at loose ends, so they all climbed up the top towers of Trim Castle and ran around the narrow ledge surrounding the tower's top. No railings, and loose pebbles on the ledge!

Trim Castle

Emmeline Annie was noted for her generous and easy hospitality. Lonely people were invited to stay for Christmas. There is a story of her looking out one lunch hour and seeing a party of five or six members of the Day family walking up the avenue to the rectory. Before she greeted them properly at the front door, she slipped out to the henhouse in the backyard, wrung the neck of a chicken and handed it to her maid to pluck and prepare. A chicken dish was on the table shortly.[24]

Emmeline Annie's sense of humour, her positive attitude to life, and her love of the energy and vitality of young people, are legendary. Even when over seventy, if invited out she would whisper to her hostess, 'Put me in with the young people.' She knew that was where the fun was most likely to be.

Emmeline Annie with her children on the back steps of the Rectory:
L. to R. Charlie, Emmeline Annie holding Leo, the nursemaid, Eva.
Front: Geraldine, Fred [Edwy away]

At the same time, she was proud of being a housewife and a mother. The rectory was a very good Victorian house, with sizeable rooms, but not too large. A well-planned building with a large number of bedrooms. There was a walled garden behind the

---

24   Margaret Lennon-Wynne, *The Lennon Family Irish Heritage Tour,* DJW Consultants, 40 Windsor Road, Dublin, 1998, p.29.

house, which was built several miles west of Enfield, which itself is about thirty miles west of Dublin.

She inspired her daughters, and then her granddaughters who passed it on to many of their own daughters, a love of kith and kin, a deep and lasting interest in the art of home-making, and at the same time, a respect, even admiration for women who can also develop their own talents.

She had been a very good rector's wife, having had an innate medical sense, a natural instinct for caring for the sick. She was much loved amongst the parishioners. When she had to leave Rathcore Rectory after her husband had died, the people of the parish collected money as is usual on these occasions, and they bought her a silver teapot. The teapot would have held three cups, with some difficulty. The family was very disgusted. They labelled the teapot *Labour in Vain* and from that day to this it has been called *Labour in Vain*.

Inscription reads:

*Presented to Mrs. Murphy
on her departure from
Rathcore.
As a small token of affection
from Parishioners and other Friends
1919*

Her brother Edward Emmanuel Lennon became a distinguished doctor in Dublin, and he, in turn, influenced six of Emmeline Annie's children to go into that profession.[25]

Emmeline Annie was a very caring, kind, loving, warm, and generous woman. But her children, by standards of the day, were considered 'wild'. For example, on the train from Enfield to Dublin, the compartments were made of wood, with spaces between. Travelling one day, a Murphy lad reached through and tied a girl's two long plaits of hair around a post.

When her husband died in 1919, Emmeline Annie moved to the house in Skerries, where she lived for about fifteen years. Her children would visit her there, and some lived with her on extended stays. The house backed onto the beach, and all the Murphys loved the sea.

But Emmeline Annie's health was poor, and in the beginning of December 1937, she became quite ill. She had developed allergies, especially to feathers. It so happened that her youngest son, Cyril, was one of the first doctors interested in allergies, and to protect Emmeline Annie from exposure, she had been 'confined to barracks', upstairs

---

25   ***Dr. Edward Lennon:*** See Chapter 16.

in his residence at 44 Fitzwilliam Square in Dublin. Every visitor had to succumb to a major screening before being permitted to see her. Needless to say, after one visit, most guests did not return.

In December 1933, one of her daughters living in England, wrote of her mother Emmeline Annie to a sister:[26]

> I hear Mother is delighted with her life in Dublin and wouldn't go back to live in Skerries for anything. She feels right in the thick of things in Dublin. I feel dreadful living so comparatively close to her, and yet never seeing her.
>
> I don't suppose she'll ever come over to England now. If only my husband could get a job then I might be able to get over for a little bit to see her. She is such a darling to us all. Everybody who meets her loves her.

Emmeline Annie died on December 22, 1937. The cause of death was asthma, described as *dying out of her lungs*. All the relatives came, and the funeral was held down in the country, in Rathcore Church. A few days before she died a poor old countryman, who could hardly walk himself, and who in his seventy-five years had hardly ever left Enfield, somehow managed to hire a car and he came up the thirty miles to Dublin to see her – a tribute indeed.

---

26   From Geraldine in Buckinghamshire, England, to Eva in Calgary, Canada. December 1, 1933.

Emmeline Annie in later years: "true nobleness of character."

11.
REVEREND FREDERICK JOHN LUCAS

UNCLE FRED
February 12, 1833 – April 3, 1921

Playing a central role in the lives of family members, the Reverend Frederick John Lucas was a gentle, thoughtful minister.

Uncle Fred was the brother of Mary (née Lucas) Lennon of Newcastle House. To his sister's married family of Lennons, and with the family of Murphys of his niece, Emmeline Annie, he was the kindly uncle, always willing to assist anywhere and in any way he could. Never married, and not having any children of his own, he apparently enjoyed watching the development of the children and the grandchildren of his sister, Mary. He gave advice where he could, and his door was always open, welcoming to any of them who came to visit him in Dublin

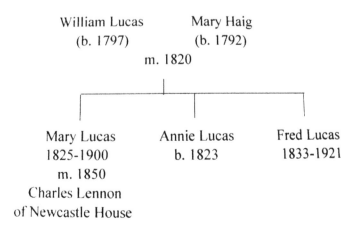

William Lucas   Mary Haig
(b. 1797)   (b. 1792)
                m. 1820

Mary Lucas   Annie Lucas   Fred Lucas
1825-1900   b. 1823   1833-1921
m. 1850
Charles Lennon
of Newcastle House

William, the father of this Lucas family was a perfumier from Clapham Manor, at that time near London, but today a part of the City of London. It is thought Fred's father was Jewish, but he married a Christian. Mary and Annie followed the mother and were baptised as Christians, but the son, Fred, went with the father to the synagogue. At confirmation age, Fred opted in with his sisters on the confirmation certificate. Fred was seventeen. This happened on November 13, 1850, less than four short months after his sister Mary married Charles Lennon, July 30, 1850.

Lucas is a common Irish name, and perhaps the father had Lucas relatives in Dublin. William Lucas moved his family to Dublin from London. They set up a boarding house on Camden Street. Charles Lennon from Newcastle House in County Meath, journeyed to Dublin once a week for the cattle sales. He had property in Dominick Street, and perhaps he would stay there several nights to enjoy the social whirl of the city. This is how a gentleman from rural Enfield met, fell in love and married Mary Lucas, a city girl.

In 1862, when Fred was thirty, he graduated from Trinity College, Dublin, with a BA. He became a deacon in 1862, and was priested in 1863. In 1864, he obtained a Div. Test, an MA in 1871, a BD in 1873, a DD in 1879 – a string of degrees. It is apparent he was a studious man, and did not want the care of a full-time parish. He had a connection with Trinity for many years, and was probably a part-time lecturer in mathematics, which was his main subject, but also, as time went by, he may have lectured in courses in theology. It has been said: 'The Lucases brought brains to the Lennon family.'

Eventually, Fred and his unmarried sister, Annie, set up house at 2, Cliff Terrace in Kingstown, now DunLaoghaire. Over the years, Fred was a minister in a number of parishes in and around Dublin, although his last position from 1876 – 1879 was as Rector of Mountmellick, in Co. Laois. He was Principal at Dalkey College. In 1910 he was a Member of the Royal Society of Antiquaries of Ireland, one of Ireland's premier learned societies, established in 1849 with the aim to 'preserve, examine all ancient monuments and memorials of the arts, manners and customs of the past.' In 1912, he was Senator for Dublin University.

To the families of Lennons and Murphys, the Reverend Fred Lucas was invaluable. He performed one secret marriage, and conducted other marriages by 'special licence'. He baptised many of the younger generations, and was well-loved by them all.

One grand-niece recorded:

> I was at the Dublin Horse Show, all dressed up. Just before I climbed
> up into the Stand to watch the horse-jumping, I met Uncle Fred there.
> He was delighted to see me, and in front of the Stand, which was full
> of so many people I knew, he lifted his top hat and he bent down and
> kissed my hand. Wasn't that lovely? That was Uncle Fred!

It appears several children were named after Uncle Fred. His brother William named
a son *Frederick John Lucas*. His sister Mary named one of her sons *Frederick Albert
Lennon*. And Emmeline Annie Murphy, his niece, named one of her sons *Frederick
John Murphy*. Finally, by happy coincidence, six generations down from Mary Lucas
and her brother Uncle Fred, and through the Murphy family line, a young lad has
been named *Freddy*. No doubt some of Uncle Fred's charm has arrived there through
inherited genes!

12.
JAMES THE FAMILY MAN

One of the students boarding at Rathcore Rectory was Arthur, and he fell in love with Chota Fitzgerald, who was living over at Newcastle House. The pair of them had a secret stone in a ditch under which they hid letters they had written to each other. Under the same stone Emmeline Annie had put a note with the word *Caution*. James found that note, and he kicked up a row, and for a while he forbade his wife from talking to her relatives.

James took in five boarders at a time, all boys. The boarders were clergymens' sons, stockbrokers' sons, solicitors' sons; it was cheaper for them to stay at Rathcore compared with going to boarding school. Some of the boarders were special needs, others had behaviour problems, attacking the Murphy girls or trying to smuggle whiskey into their bedrooms.

Two of these boys later emigrated to Canada, one farming in Alberta. He attended a Farmers' Convention in Calgary. A fire broke out in the hotel when he was asleep and he froze to death in his bed from fire hose water. Another was killed in the Klondike Gold Rush to the Yukon.

John Quarry Day was now at Lough Crew, about thirty-five miles from Rathcore. The two ministers visited each other, back and forth. When Rev Day visited James, the two of them would hide in the bushes beside where two of the Newcastle Lennon girls, Emmeline Annie and Eva Consuelo would be passing on their daily walk. The men would discuss the merits of each girl. Rev Day wanted Rev Murphy to marry Eva, telling him, 'Eva would make the better wife for you, but Emmeline Annie would be more easily moulded.' But James was already in love with Emmeline Annie, and her Lennon family supported this match. Rev Day was heard to say, 'Like to an owl in an ivy bush, a lonely thing am I.'

Emmeline Annie turned twenty-seven on Christmas Eve in 1882, and ten days later on January 3, 1883 she and James were married in Rathcore Church, by Emmeline Annie's uncle, Rev Fred Lucas, brother of her mother.

They were married in secret, very early in the morning. The sextoness was told to have the church heated. The maid at the rectory was told to take the letters announcing the marriage, to the rectory gate at 8:30 a.m., to be ready there for the postman on his rounds, when he would collect them and deliver them to the Post Office.

Why all the secrecy? Was James afraid of an intrusion at the point in the service where the minister asks, 'Does anyone present know any reason why either of these two people should not be married?' Was he concerned someone would step forward and announce James had been baptised originally as a Roman Catholic? A disgrace in the eyes of many Protestants, but not, apparently, in the eyes of Emmeline Annie's parents or in the eyes of Rev Fred Lucas. As for the West Cork Murphy family, James knew he could not invite any of them from Ardgroom. His father had been a Protestant, but he had died, and all the rest were Roman Catholic. Bad news!

Perhaps the ceremony was held secretly because his father had died only four and a half months before, and it might appear disrespectful to be marrying so soon after a death in the family. But, James had another concern, for if he waited he might lose his Emmeline Annie. Even his best friend, John Quarry Day, was eyeing her!

The most likely scenario would be all of these reasons mixed together, once again causing James to struggle and be stressed. And he never fully recovered from his jealousy of his wife appearing attractive. One time, Rev John Quarry Day came over from his parish in Lough Crew to attend the Harvest Thanksgiving Service in Rathcore Church. Afterwards, he commented to James, 'Mrs Murphy looks very fetching in that hat.' Later that week, James asked his wife, 'Would you let me see the hat you had on last Sunday?' He took the hat and cut it to pieces.

The newlyweds drove to Enfield and took the train and boat to London for their two-week honeymoon. The highlight of their trip was a visit to the Crystal Palace. This was Emmeline Annie's only journey out of the County Meath and County Dublin areas.

James had grown used to not mixing in a society that refused to acknowledge him. The Murphys did have contact occasionally with other families, but usually there were rows when they met, and afterwards great effort had to be put into patching up the difficulties. Mostly, the Rathcore household of students and Murphy children and some of the Fitzgerald girls was isolated. However, they all managed to entertain themselves with drama, playing musical instruments, and having good old-fashioned fun, and if some neighbouring children came along on an afternoon, they all made a happy a group, calling themselves *The Balcony Club*:

The Balcony Club. They also played music together as the Balcony Minstrels

James *made a god out of education*. Every Murphy said so, some with a tinge of gratitude, but mostly it was said in disgust. The children all had to be at their desks very early in the morning, studying their Latin verb conjugations. The eldest daughter, Eva, kept watch at the schoolroom door, because the younger ones would fall asleep over their copybooks on the desk tops. There would be a moment or two between the time of hearing his first footfall on the hall floor and him reaching the schoolroom door. *Coming*, she would whisper, loudly, and they would shake each other awake quickly. Too slow, and they would be beaten. Eva dreaded hearing the sounds of it.

During term time, the rectory changed three to four times in a week: James was fulfilling his university duties by being away from home, up in Dublin for a whole day. The strict disciplinarian and hard schoolmaster would leave sufficient school exercises for the younger children still at home, but the lid was off when 'The Guv'nor' was away. The children would jump on their bikes and speed down to the bridge over the Blackwater River for a lark. The railway to Enfield ran alongside the river, so when the train whistle bringing their father home from Dublin was heard, they hid to let the approaching train pass. Hopping back on their bikes, they would be pouring over their books by the time he walked into the schoolroom.

James earned £280 per annum as a rector, as well as having use of the rectory house and grounds. When he became a professor, he earned a further £200 per annum. With this salary, he was able to put six of his children through Trinity College, Dublin, although as a professor's sons, the boys received free residential rooms in number 39, second floor, and were charged no course fees. His daughter Geraldine stayed at the women's residence, Trinity Hall. Some of his children said, 'We all wanted to study Medicine so we would cost our father more money.' But this was mostly 'sour grapes' and the only real cost to the Murphy students at TCD was their food, most of them remembering being starving hungry when studying, and carrying bags of food back to Dublin with them after a weekend visit to their mother's kitchen in Rathcore. Visitors who expected food to be provided were not welcome in the rooms. John Quarry Day occasionally visited the Murphy students in their TCD rooms, but he was resented because he would eat all their marmalade and they without a penny to spare. A Wallace relative arrived over from New Zealand, setting up his bed in a corner of the rooms. He, too, was broke, and he ate them out of house and home. They had to kick him out.

Meanwhile, back in the rectory, James was taking the horsewhip to his wife, very freely. When Emmeline Annie's mother died in 1900, Emmeline Annie had been staying up at Newcastle House for her mother's final days. James was distraught with this absence of his wife. When she returned to the rectory before the funeral service was held, he would not let her even talk to her relatives. This time he took a penknife and cut up all her clothes once again. Emmeline Annie left James several times, staying with her brother George nearby in the same parish, or with her Uncle Fred in Dublin. She even tried suing him, but she could not bring herself to make the charges stick, which would have brought the wife beatings into the public eye. James was terrified his wife would tell the truth, but not enough to control himself further.

Both James and Emmeline Annie knew if the beatings became known, were gossiped about, and were publicly discussed, the future careers of their children might be compromised, even jeopardised.

A rare photograph showing all of the Rathcore Murphy Family. In later photographs, some members are absent, are away at school or university, or have fled from their father:

On the back is written: Granny and Grandpa Murphy with Family
Back left to right: *Grandpa, Eva (with a parasol), Geraldine, Granny, Edwy.*
Front left to right: *Charlie, Cyril, Olive, Leo, Fred.*

13:
RATHCORE MURPHY HOUSES

A. RATHCORE RECTORY

Locally known as 'RA'COR RECTORY'

Rathcore Rectory, Co. Meath 1977

A general description of the Rectory at Rathcore in County Meath was discovered in a scrapbook developed by a granddaughter of James Murphy. The article undated by year, describes the rectory as being up for auction on 20th September, the agents being 'Potterton'. The source of the article is unknown, but the scrapbook is currently held by the Archives of the Church of Ireland in the R.C.B., in Rathgar, Dublin. It explains:

As it is called today, Rathcore Glebe—what a strange mixture it is—quite simply, one house added on to another and much earlier one. The early portion or house—the back one—is, I would say, Queen Anne—but with its original front merged into its addition, it is difficult to judge. The latter and front portion of the house(s) is red-brick.

It sounds horrific; in fact it is charming, a quality due, I think, to the fact that whoever added the two together made no bones about matching them—he or she just didn't try. In the end, the front screens the back—in other words, one house screens the other—and you tend not to notice. Which all goes to prove that what the eye doesn't see . . .

There are three reception—drawing-room, dining-room and study—kitchen, two bathrooms and five bedrooms. There's hardly an indifferent room in it and I found it a house full of charm and possibility. It is for one thing full of light; and secondly there is a sense of space and height throughout.

The grounds are equally nice—there are tall beeches and chestnuts and sycamores; and a court and a few old stone buildings, including a groom's cottage. The outbuildings in fact . . . are mostly brand new . . .

In 1887, *the Meath Diocesan Magazine* ran a series of articles on the history of Rathcore. The series was written by the Rev J. E. H. Murphy AM.[27]

In the February edition, he wrote, in part:

Of the general history of Rathcore, as distinct from its Church history, I find nothing worthy of note between 1431 and the time of the Restoration of Charles II. [Charles II reigned from 1660–1685.] . . . About the Restoration most of the estates in the Parish of Rathcore, as in other Parishes, were confiscated, were transferred from their former owners (who either inherited them from those to whom those lands were granted by our earlier English sovereigns, or "who were placed in possession of the lands by Cromwell's Commissioners"), and given to men who were more deserving of favours at the hands of those then in power.

In the July edition, he continued, in part:

27   *AM:* Anglican Minister.

Hitherto the account given of Rathcore was confined to its <u>general</u> history. I now briefly glance over its <u>ecclesiastical</u> history.

The first Church foundation at Rathcore was established by St. Ultan (Mac-hUi-Conga), Abbot of Clonard, who died A.D. 664; so that Church life has existed at Rathcore at least for more than 1,223 years. St. Ultan's Holy Well, in which he baptised the first converts from paganism at Rathcore, situate about a gun-shot from the Church, still remains, though within the last fifty years it has become almost closed up with accumulations of mud and sledge. This well had been for centuries frequented by invalids, who sought in its waters some miraculous healing qualities; and around it on the "Pattern Days"[28] large assemblies enjoyed themselves "in raal ould Irish style." I cannot accurately ascertain the cause of the discontinuance of the "Patterns", or of the neglect of the Holy Well; but certain local traditions trace its present lack of repute to the fact that it had been polluted by the tenant of an adjoining farm so as to put an end to the constant trespass through his land to it; and explain that, as usually happened in such cases, the said farmer died "within a year-and-a-day"—a fate which so selfish and sacrilegious a creature almost deserved.

It would appear that the good people of Rathcore, soon after the death of the Saint, had their parish Church named "The Church of St. Ultan," after him who had been the first to proclaim the Gospel to them . . .

In the August edition, Rev J. E. H. Murphy continued. He notes in the **1630**s the church is referred to in documents as being the *Church of Rathcower*, but by the **1660**s it is described as the *Chapel of Rathcore: it is a chapel, with the cure of souls, belonging to the Church of Trymm* [modern-day Trim]. In **1693**, the following notice states that *Rathcore is a Chappel of Ease belonging to ye Rectory of Trymm, and valued with it. Chappel ruined since 1641.* Rev Murphy finds an account of Rathcore from **1733** which states: 'The Church is in repair, but not very decent; 'tis shingled, and has a Pulpit, reading-desk, and a few seats. There is a Communion Table which is railed in, but the floor is only common earth. There are 6 Protestant families in y^e Parish, and about 300 Popish.'

---

28   ***Pattern Days:*** Patron saints' anniversaries.

St. Ultan's, Rathcore Church, 1952

Reverend James Murphy became Rector of the parish of Rathcore in 1881. He was thirty-one and a bachelor. As was the custom, each rector was provided with a house by the Church, which was a marvellous bonus, but which could cause problems when the rector retired, or indeed, left his wife as a widow who had to suddenly and immediately vacate her home to make room for an appointed replacement.

The rectory would have been huge for one person. Rev Murphy would have employed at least a housekeeper to clean and wash and cook for him. It would have been expected that he would marry at some time, and have a family. This rectory was a suitable home for such a purpose.

Inside the front door of the house, on either side of the hallway, was a living room to the left and a dining room to the right. The staircase to the upper level was straight up from the back of the hallway. The back half of the rectory housed the nursery downstairs to the right, and another room which served as the schoolroom. Over on the left was a study for James, and in between could be found the kitchen.

The top floor held all the bedrooms. At the back of the rectory there were sheds, animal shelters, and chicken houses. A barn for equipment and for storage of hay, potatoes, oats, and seeds was of a good size.

On the back is written:
The Rectory showing
Mother's room
Drawing-room
School room
Nursery
Recent

On the back is written:
The Rectory
Front view
(recent)

An article describing activities of rectors who had lived in Rathcore Rectory over the years, wrote of the tenure of Rev Murphy:

'Rev. James Edward Harnett Murphy tilled the land, sowed oats, cropped hay annually and kept bloodstock. His five sons helped to work the land, and his wife Emma kept hens.'

Aerial view of Rathcore Rectory

When James died, his wife Emmeline Annie would have had to prepare for the looming crisis: a new replacement rector would be found shortly and he would require the rectory immediately. Fortunately, there had been some foresight, and another house was already in the family's possession in Skerries, a purchase made possible by inheritance money left to Emmeline Annie. The move was made.

After many years, the rectory was sold off by the Church of Ireland, and was given the name of *The Glebe House*. Then, in May 1981, an old-fashioned oil heater caused a fire on the ground floor, and smoke and flames shot upstairs to the roof. Two sleeping men managed to escape, but only five rooms were saved. The Glebe became a ruin, and stands today as a shell of its former self.

Two pictures of the burnt-out Rectory, taken in 1993

From the dining-room window

B. DUNROE

Eldest daughter Eva recorded: 'Soon after the turn of the century, we began to rent a house in Skerries by the sea for the whole month of September.' Then, in 1908, James bought *Dunroe*, in Skerries, a tall house which was one in a row of houses facing onto the stony beach. Eva recorded: 'Most of the year he had it rented, but in the summertime, we spent weeks there. Amiens Street Station[29] was the gateway to Paradise for me. We would be free from Saturday to Monday, every weekend, as he had to return to Rathcore for the Sunday service and to look after his parish.'

Modern view of the back of Dunroe, facing out to the sea.

When James was away, the children would meet together with locals and they got up to all kinds of mischief. They went to nearby Rush, where they tried to wrench the knocker off the door of the convent. Eva's daughter remembered:

> The worst story I heard was that they were coming home one night and they saw a ham hanging out to dry outside a house. It had been cooked, so they took it home to their mother, along with some tale about it being a gift. And when Reverend Murphy went to carve the ham at supper on his return the next day, he remembered some news

29   ***Amiens Street Station:*** Today known as Connolly Train Station. It was the railway station for trains travelling northwards from Dublin.

he had heard, and he commented that there had been a ham stolen from Mrs. Battersby's. He said, "Whoever stole that ham from Mrs. Battersby deserves to come to a bad end."

They were full of high spirits, but it was all too brief. Two of their Skerries friends, young men, were killed in the War.

Emmeline Annie became a widow in her early sixties, and having to leave Rathcore Rectory, she moved to live in *Dunroe* from 1919 to the 1930s, when she sold the house, and moved to live in Dublin with her son, Dr Cyril. For those years in Skerries, her children would live with her, or travel long distances to make extended visits. In 1924, her daughter, Eva accompanied by her four children, travelled from Calgary and the Prairies in Canada, to spend a summer with her mother Emmeline Annie by the sea in Skerries and to show off the grandchildren. Even when in their eighties, the elder grandchildren had vivid memories of Dunroe and Skerries, and of their grand-mother, Emmeline.

View of the sea from the front of Dunroe

Of this view, Eva's eldest daughter recorded: 'I sat on the big rocks and gazed for hours out at the sea. I had never seen the sea from a beach before.' She was seven years old.

Dunroe always was a warm, welcoming place for members of the Rathcore Murphy family, where they gathered happily with their mother, and forgot their father.

14.
JAMES THE MINISTER

James was ordained Deacon in 1878, and was assigned to the parish of Kilmainhamwood with Moybologue, which stretches across the Counties of Meath and Cavan. In 1879, he was appointed as curate-in-charge in the same parish, making his position there more official. Having grown up in the Kerry/West Cork region, he was fully aware of the effects of famine, but he was shocked to find famine wreaking havoc amongst the poor in the Meath-Cavan area, one of Ireland's richest areas. Liking to be in charge, to take control, one of his first projects was to provide support for Poor Relief.

James as Curate

On February 12, 1880, he attended the Local Committee of Relief of Moybologue and Kilmainhamwood. James was appointed as secretary.[30] That day, two resolutions were brought forward:

1. That immediate application be made to the Mansion House Relief Fund for aid to ward off the dire destitution unfortunately existing among many in this district.

   On the motion of the Rev. J.E.H. Murphy, B.A., Pro-Incumbent [Protestant clergyman], seconded by the Rev. P. O'Connell, CC, [Roman Catholic priest]:

2. That letters be sent to the various owners of land in this District, informing them of the Resolutions unanimously passed at this Meeting, and respectfully suggesting that any aid which they may think it well to send, will be

---

30   Trinity College, Dublin. MS 3671 f. 1r, Record book and minute book of the local committee of relief of Moybologue and Kilmainhamwood, Co. Cavan, 1880.

thankfully received and faithfully distributed among the necessitous by this Committee.

As the newly appointed secretary, James wrote to the *Mansion House Relief Fund Committee,* which would have held its meetings in Dublin:

Moybologue, Bailieboro', Co. Cavan. 12th February, 1880.

Gentlemen,

A meeting was this day held in the Edengora National Schoolhouse, attended by the Roman Catholic and Irish Church clergymen, and other representative gentlemen of various religious denominations.

The following resolution, among others, was proposed, seconded, and unanimously passed:—"That immediate application be made to the Mansion House Relief Fund for aid to ward off the dire destitution unfortunately existing among many in this district."

The materials upon which such a statement may be based are lamentably extensive. Within the limits of the parishes to which our district is confined are very many cases of whole families in such distress as borders on starvation. The inhabitants are almost all of the struggling small farmer class, depending on potatoes and turf for food and fuel. The potatoes were last year, in rare instances, worth the digging, and the turf had to be abandoned owing to the heavy rains and consequent flooding. The scanty plots of corn sown were, in the first place, ill-productive, and next, only half saved with great difficulty.

Owing to the excessively low market price of other farm produce, no money was realized to meet the emergency. All these causes conspiring, have reduced the small farmers here to a pitiable condition.

What is apparent to cursory observers is not a tithe of the real distress existing, inasmuch as those very small farmers, in most cases, would suffer almost anything short of starvation before they would brook the shame of a public acknowledgment of their distress. No case of actual death by starvation has as yet, thank God, occurred, to the knowledge of the Committee; but unless immediate relief be procured from some source within a fortnight, we know not what fearful results a delay of even so short a time might bring forth. Many of the small farmers are destitute of food, of fuel, and of clothing. They are at the present moment eating, or have already eaten, their seed potatoes and seed corn, to preserve life. Many of them are perishing for want of ordinary clothes, and, what is far more serious, have no bedclothes to protect them at night from the wintry cold. It was the opinion of our meeting that at least two hundred lives are at the present moment in this perilous condition—reduced to the verge of starvation; their seed potatoes and seed corn consumed, having no fuel, their ordinary clothes, in most cases, reduced to shreds, and devoid almost of any covering at night. With this spectre of distress so excessive brooding over so many in our district, we earnestly and respectfully request such a grant from your Committee as the statement of facts here given seems to your Committee to warrant. Pledging, on our part, that whatever sums may be entrusted to us for the relief of the distress, shall be faithfully distributed by us among those who are most necessitous, in the manner stipulated by the donors,

I am, &c.,
J. E. H. Murphy, B.A., Clk., *Hon. Sec.*

From the *Pamphlet Collection of Sir Robert Stout: Volume 38.*

At the next meeting of the Local Committee of Relief, in the minutes it is recorded as follows:[31]

Rec'd from Mansion House Relief Fund cheque for £20 sterling[32], as well as:

1 stone of Indian meal per person, 80 families = 251 individuals
All the rest to receive ½ stone of meal.
Also rec'd a cheque for £10[33] from *The New York Herald Fund.*

All of this activity was right up James's alley: he was in charge and he was running his own show. James understood how to obtain famine relief and how it should be fairly distributed. And he undertook other projects including the building of a new

---

31   Trinity College, Dublin. MS 3671 f. 1r, Record book and minute book of the local committee of relief of Moybologue and Kilmainhamwood, Co. Cavan, 1880.

32   £20 in 1880 equivalent to £2,380 in 2018.

33   About £1 000, equivalent, 2018

parsonage, the organisation of the local schools, and meanwhile, wrestling with the parochial finances.

At the same time, in 1880, James's father died, and James would have been making trips to Ardgroom and the area, concerned for his failing father, followed by the worry of burial arrangements and costs, and then setting up care for the welfare of his mother.

In 1881, James received his MA from Trinity. He must have travelled a great deal back and forth to Trinity College in Dublin to achieve this level of study. From the northern parts of County Meath in those days, this journey would have taken several hours each way. I'm sure someone in Trinity, perhaps the person who sponsored his master's degree, or perhaps even the provost (Humphrey Lloyd, who died that year) had put in a word, but surely James was at least becoming known to the Protestant Establishment. The bishop of Meath[34] had a position come free near Enfield, farther south in County Meath and much closer to the road east to Dublin. Above all, Enfield had a train station, on the line to Dublin. A perfect position for someone developing further ties with Trinity, who also needed a post as a rector as he had no private money with which to support himself.

James was appointed as Rector of Rathcore in 1881, where he would remain for the rest of his life. Those in the parish where he had done so well were sad to see him leave:

Address to the Reverend J E H Murphy BA,[35] TCD

Late Curate-in-charge of United parishes of Kilmainhamwood and Moybologue. November 1881

Reverend and Dear Sir:

On behalf of the parishioners of the Union of Kilmainhamwood and Moybologne and of your numerous friends in this neighborhood we desire to congratulate you on your appointment to the Rectorship of the parish of Rathcore.
During the three years you have had charge of this parish you have won the highest place in our esteem by your untiring efforts for our spiritual and temporal welfare. We valued most highly the affectionate assiduity with which you laboured amongst us in season and out of season ever speaking the truth in love.

---

34 The Rt. Hon. William Connyngham Plunkett, who later became Archbishop of Dublin. (He was a distant relative of the husband of Eva, the eldest daughter of James Murphy, but all that would be in the future!)

35 **BA:** Perhaps James's MA had not yet been awarded at TCD Commencements, or perhaps the parishioners did not know of James's studies.

To your indefatigable exertions are chiefly due the very satisfactory condition of our Parochial finances and the highly efficient state of our Sunday and Daily Schools as well has the erection of a handsome and commodious Parsonage.

While therefore we rejoice in your well-deserved advancement we are sadly conscious how great is our loss.

You carry with you our best wishes for your success in that work whereunto you have been called and we earnestly pray that wheresoever you labour you may have many soles [*sic*] for your hire.

We trust you will accept the accompanying Time Piece not as a measure of our appreciation of your worth but as a small token of the affectionate regard of those amongst us whom you first ministered.

Signed on behalf of the parishioners:
Churchwardens Thomas Allen and Joshua Williamson Junior
Treasurer Joseph Rowntree
Select Vestrymen Joseph Power, Edward Roundtree, John Roundtree, Alexander Shakleton, Moses Roundtree, William Roundtree, William McWhirter, William Roundtree, William James Roundtree.

Designed and Illuminated by J Hopkins, 39 Great Brunswick Street, Dublin

James moved to the large rectory in Rathcore, and set to work in his new and prosperous parish. He kept his church building in immaculate condition, always doing repairs himself, whether a slate needed replacement on the roof, or a leak had to be repaired, or he had to deal with one of the scourges of woodwork, woodworm or dry rot. His care of his parishioners was over the top. If a member of his parish was absent from a Sunday service, James would stride out after his midday dinner across the fields to the truant's home to discover the real story. Was the absentee truly sick?

At this time, long sermons were the order of the day. One reference to Murphy's sermons:[36]

'Another minister we had was Jim Murphy, a silly, old man, a native Irish speaker from Co. Kerry, I think. He only liked to tell stories from

---

36   "MURPHY, James Edward Hartnett (c.1851-1919)," ainm.ie, Retrieved March 4, 2020, from http:// www.ainm.ie/Bio.aspx?ID=463 (Original in Irish, translated by Helen Faherty of Rusheenduff, Renvyle Peninsula.)

plain or bare incidents, no elaborations. We were tortured with him at the services, he had as much of the Royal Family in them as possible.'

It is difficult to think of James as contented in any way. Perhaps on his train rides up to Dublin he would have had the time to contemplate his life, to reach some degree of happiness. Once he was married, with a wife and a growing family in his rectory, he spent much of his time isolated, alone, and quiet in his study. We can only hope he enjoyed writing and researching. He did not participate in social events or any family activities. He might not have known how to do so. He taught and he disciplined, and, at the same time, caused much fear and pain for those he loved. He was a man trapped, conflicted, and unable to show his emotions. Except, that is, for his anger.

A tragedy.

Rev James Edward Harnett Murphy, Rector of Rathcore, Co. Meath

15.
JAMES THE PROFESSOR

The Gaelic League was founded in 1893 led by Douglas Hyde, who was the son of a Protestant clergyman from County Roscommon, and who was a Celtic Scholar and a cultural nationalist of some renown. He later became the first president of Ireland. The Gaelic League spearheaded a Gaelic revival movement whose aim was to give a sense of Irishness back to the people. Members wanted to fight against the erosion of Irish culture, Irish language, and traditional Irish sports, and supporters argued the reintroduction of Irish back into schools would halt or reverse the decline of the language.

Soon the League was growing more political and forceful. Although Hyde wanted it to remain apolitical, the organisation attracted many nationalists who saw the League as a way to undermine the British presence in Ireland. Murphy joined the Gaelic League very soon after its founding, just to keep himself informed with all things Irish, but certainly not for any political reasons.

Hyde was greatly supported by the many literary Protestants who were busy promoting a revival of Irish literature and along with it, everything Irish. Ironically, English-speaking antiquarians and nationalists from the small educated class, rather than the Irish-speaking minority, were leading the 19th century revival, which in turn was stimulated by the Romantic Movement's interest in Celtic subjects. This group included prominent figures such as W. B. Yeats and Lady Gregory.

This resurgence of interest in Irish language, literature, history, and folklore was inspired by the growing Irish nationalism of the early nineteenth century. By that time, Irish was slowly dying out as a spoken tongue except in isolated rural areas, and English had become the official and literary language of Ireland. The discovery by philologists as to how to read Old Irish (manuscripts written in Irish prior to 900), and the subsequent translations of ancient Gaelic manuscripts, made possible the reading of Ireland's ancient literature. Heroic tales caught the imagination of the educated classes. Anglo-Irish poets experimented with verse that was structured according to

Gaelic patterns and rhythms and which echoed the passions and rich imagery of ancient bardic verse.

The Gaelic Revival was not a widespread, vigorous movement because political nationalism and the need for land reform overshadowed cultural nationalism. The revival did, however, lay the scholarly and nationalistic groundwork for an Irish literary renaissance, the great flowering of Irish literary talent at the end of the 19th and beginning of the 20th centuries.

In 1878 it had been established that Irish should be taught in primary schools, but only outside regular school hours, so that the amount of time devoted to other more important subjects would not be diminished.

There was a great shortage of teachers qualified to teach in Irish in secondary schools, and less than five per cent of students presented for examinations in Irish.

At this time, John Pentland Mahaffy was Professor of Ancient History at Trinity College, and later, in 1914, would become provost. He was a man who had no time for the Celtic Revival, or for the teaching of Irish in schools. 'Of no educational value, a mischievous waste of time' were his declarations. It would be 'a return to the dark ages' should schools devote any time teaching the language. Mahaffy stated Irish literature is 'religious or silly or indecent'. Supporters of the movement for the revival of Irish were aggravated, and Douglas Hyde led the charge against Mahaffy by trying to make him appear ridiculous, and by attacking Mahaffy's almost complete lack of any knowledge of the Irish language. The discussion around the teaching of Irish in schools became a national controversy.

In 1889, and before the founding of the Gaelic League, Murphy was appointed as Deputy Professor of Irish at Trinity College, Dublin. This was eight years after he had completed his MA, and eight years after he had been appointed as Rector of Rathcore. He was Deputy Professor under Professor of Irish, James Goodman, a Kerryman from Dingle, who would have understood everything about Murphy: his origins, his background, and his rise through intelligence and determination. Goodman would have recognised Murphy's authentic Irishness. Goodman must have felt Murphy should get experience as a Deputy Professor, and the Board of Trinity College should be given an opportunity to see Murphy in the deputy role, with an eye on him as a possible future professor. This was at a time before interviews and resumés, and who you knew and how you performed on site were what counted. Today, we might say Murphy was being groomed for the job. The Church of Ireland made him a rural dean in the same year, in 1889 – Rural Dean of Clonard, an area about twenty-five miles from Rathcore.

On March 16, 1895, Murphy was elected as a Member of the Royal Irish Academy. Based in Dublin, the RIA is an all-Ireland independent academic body that promotes study and excellence in the sciences, humanities, and social sciences. It is one of Ireland's premier learned societies and cultural institutions, and members are elected in recognition of their academic achievements.

Professor James Goodman died in 1896, and the Chair of Irish at Trinity College fell vacant. Murphy applied for the job, but so did Douglas Hyde. Hyde was supported in the world-wide academic community outside Trinity College, but those on the inside, some even good friends of Hyde, had major doubts as to Hyde's chief motivation in seeking the Chair. Was his application politically motivated? Many rose to Hyde's defence in this battle, one being Standish O'Grady, writing letters in support from London on March 19, 1896. Standish O'Grady himself was an acclaimed scholar of Irish, and was known to *champion aristocratic values.* He had been born four years before Murphy in Castletown Berehaven, his father being the Church of Ireland Rector there. Rev O'Grady had been one of the ministers who had taught Murphy, contributing to Murphy getting to Bandon Grammar School. Now Murphy was being assaulted on all sides. Who spoke out in his defence?

The Provost of Trinity College and various professors, nervous about Hyde, and happy to continue with the idea of a Church of Ireland clergyman holding the Chair, elected Murphy to the position. Murphy already had a second salary as a rector of a parish, and he would consider it acceptable to take the Chair as a half-time position with half-time salary.

> Although it was not directly mentioned, the knowledge among both the College officers and their critics, that Hyde had been rejected for the Chair of Irish in 1896 in favour of Murphy, a Church of Ireland clergyman, a fluent Irish speaker and a well-educated man, but with no claim to scholarly distinction, heightened feelings in the controversy. It is clear from a letter written by the Provost that it was the Board's suspicion of Hyde's nationalistic politics, supported by Robert Atkinson, Professor of Sanskrit and Comparative Philology, who stated there was doubt on Hyde's linguistic competence that ruled him out as a candidate. Atkinson had told Provost Salmon that Hyde's book on Fairy Tales[37] was written *"in Baboon Irish, a queer mixture of modern colloquialisms with the old literary Irish, of which Hyde has a very imperfect knowledge."* That this queer mixture might have been just the language

---

37   WB Yeats was especially interested in folktales as a part of the exploration of national heritage and for the renewal of Celtic identity. He completed a study with Douglas Hyde and George Russell of Irish legends and tales in 1888, which was published under the title *Fairy and Folk Tales of the Irish Peasantry.* Hyde had translated some poetry, legends and tales from Irish to English for this publication.

used by elderly storytellers of the day, the dialect of Irish learned by Hyde in his home locality of Castlerea in Co. Roscommon, seems not to have mattered.

Adapted from p. 550, 'Trinity College Dublin, 1592-1952'
R. B. McDowell and D. A. Webb
Published: Cambridge University Press, 1982

Douglas Hyde never forgave Murphy for taking the job away from him, and whenever possible he tried his best to denigrate him. He wrote to W. B. Yeats:[38]

Frenchpark [Ireland]
7 May 1896

My dear Yeats

. . .

I was "mad" about Mr. Murphy getting the Chair of Irish in Trinity. It is a proselytizing institution & the money therefore contributed by the "Irish Society", a proselytizing institution. They w^d not have me at any price & I fancy the worse the man [*appointed*] was, the better pleased they were, so that no attention c^d be drawn to Gaelic studies by him. Yet I had the most excellent letters from the great Gaelic scholars etc.

Yours ever
AN CRAOIBHÍN[39]

The controversy had been widely watched in academic circles, and although Murphy won the Chair of Irish, his reputation was not at all enhanced. He must have wondered what he had to do to improve it. It is unfortunate that R. B. McDowell and D. A. Webb, both very highly regarded Trinity College academics, should unsympathetically describe Murphy as having 'no claim to scholarly distinction'. Neither McDowell nor Webb had family responsibilities. They were living and being cared for on campus, holding full-time positions and having no outside pressures intruding on their research time. Murphy was now a part-time university professor, was a full-time parish rector, he lived thirty miles from the city of Dublin, and he had a family of eight children, many of whom he was educating himself. He was also teaching and disciplining five boarders residing in his house, and he kept some cattle on the rectory grounds. All of

---

38   Richard J. Finneran, George Mills Harper, and William M. Murphy, eds., *Letters to W. B. Yeats, Volume I* (New York: Columbia University Press, 1977), 24.

39   Hyde's Gaelic pseudonym is *An Craoibhín Aoibhinn ("Pleasant Little Branch")*.

these activities were to provide for his family. There was little spare time for research, and there was no spare cash for publishing costs.

Murphy's daughter, Eva, recorded that James had taught from the age of fourteen, which meant he learnt good teaching skills while he was a student at Bandon Grammar School.[40] He was an active examiner in Celtic for the Intermediate Education Board for Ireland, and an examiner in Irish for the Royal University of Ireland. He had wide experience of education in Ireland, so when in 1898 a Commission on the System of Intermediate Education in Ireland was set up by Earl Cadogan, Lord Lieutenant-General and General Governor of Ireland, and was held in Her Majesty's Castle of Dublin, it was only natural that Douglas Hyde as president of the Gaelic League and James Murphy as Professor and Examiner of Irish, should be invited to contribute.

Douglas Hyde was eloquent in support of Irish being spoken, but at one point the chairman asked him: [41]

> 'I suppose you are aware that in Trinity College there is an Irish Professor?'

Hyde replied:

> 'I am aware that there is a so-called Professor.'

Shortly after, Hyde continued:[42]

> . . . Irish does not receive proper recognition in Trinity College. I do not know any more striking contrast in the history of human thought than the true literary instinct which, three years ago, urged 50,000 Irishmen in America to contribute a dollar apiece to the foundation of a Celtic chair in the University of Washington, and to choose out a suitable man and to send him to be educated on the Continent by the great Celticists of the Continent, in the hope that their labour might reflect credit on that far-off country of their birth, while all the time one of the richest colleges in their own land allows its so-called Irish professorship to be founded and paid for, not by a society for the cultivation of Celtic literature, but by a society for the conversion of Irish

40   It was common for the best students in schools to enter a monitoring system, whereby they assisted the teachers and helped instruct students in the classroom. Indeed, young James Murphy may have stayed on as a monitor at Bandon Grammar, an extra year or two after finishing his schooling, as a way to earn some extra money.

41   Palles Commission, *Minutes of Evidence 9233*, National Library of Ireland, B2111, 489.

42   Palles Commission, *Minutes of Evidence, 9311*, National Library of Ireland, B2111, 489.

Papists to their own religion. I consider that Trinity College has not treated Irish fairly in that.

There was one area in which Hyde and Murphy did agree, more or less, perhaps because they did not appear before the Commission on the same day.

Hyde was asked:[43]

'Do you think that in order to cultivate the Irish language efficiently, we ought to have "viva voce" examination as well as written examination?'

Hyde replied:

'I should certainly have it as a test, but to conduct the examination as a written examination with a "viva voce" test . . . I would not allow the "viva voce" to count much or at all, in the examination. It should certainly be introduced. The language is a living language.'

Rev James E. H. Murphy made this statement:[44]

'The present system of examination by papers exclusively, tends to superficialness and mere mechanical knowledge, and cannot be remedied unless the examinations be conducted, in part, orally. The papers of questions set, in many subjects, are too short, considering the valuable prizes and exhibitions at stake. An honour examination and an oral examination should be instituted in each subject in each grade.'

Hyde also referred to the failure by Trinity College in the best use of funds, by spending all its money assigned to research in Irish on developing a dictionary. He declared the university should instead be using that money to purchase ancient manuscripts.

Murphy spent a great deal of his spare time working on an Irish-English dictionary which he had inherited partially completed from his predecessors, all of whom had contributed to the dictionary's development. This was an old dictionary which had been meticulously taken apart and remounted, rebound with great care, blank leaves having been inserted in between each page. On these leaves were written various forms of words and their possible translations.

---

43   Palles Commission, *Minutes of Evidence, 9219 - 9220*, National Library of Ireland, B2111, 489.

44   Pallas Commission, Part II, Section B, *Digest of Answers to Queries*, National Library of Ireland, B2111, 163.

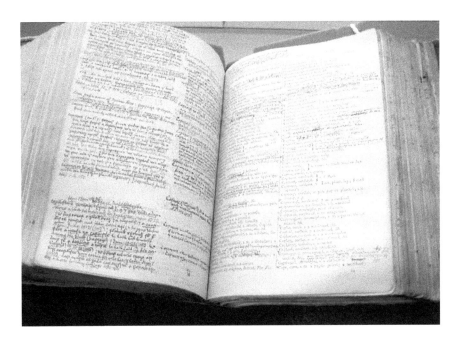

MS 2094, Trinity College, notes on left-hand-side are on letter 'C'
Irish-English Dictionary partly compiled by Murphy, 1910.

It had always been understood that a Professor of Irish at Trinity College would contribute towards developing a translation of the Bible from English to Irish, so that eventually those living in the far reaches of the *Gaeltacht*, the Irish-speaking regions of Ireland, would be able to hear the Bible read to them in their mother-tongue. Murphy had only to think back to his childhood, to when his father as scripture reader would read to the sick and hungry from the Bible, in English or Latin, trying to provide some comfort. The sound of the reader's voice might have been reassuring, but the words had not been understood.

A particular feature of education in the late eighteenth century was the foundation of schools by evangelical Protestant education societies that offered literacy and religious instruction to the Catholic poor. One of these was the *Irish Society for Promoting the Education of the Native Irish through the medium of their own language, (est.1818)*. The objectives of the Irish Society were 'to instruct the native Irish, who still use their vernacular language, how to employ it for obtaining a knowledge of English, and also for their moral amelioration, to distribute the Irish version of the scriptures . . . the Irish Prayer Book, where acceptable, and such other works as may be necessary for school-books.'[45]

---

45   Susan M. Parkes, *A Guide to Sources for the History of Irish Education 1780-1922.* (Dublin: Four Courts Press, 2010), 25.

What research did Murphy manage to get done?

Murphy's research work included:

1. Translation of the four Gospels and the Acts of the New Testament from English into Irish.[46]

2. Translation of part of the New Testament from Greek to Irish, Part I, first published by Hodges Figgis in 1910, and again in 1928. William O'Donnell faithfully extracted it first, in 1602/3, and James Murphy corrected, improved, and modernised the translation before publication.[47]

3. An Irish-English dictionary in three volumes, based on an Irish-English dictionary by Edward O'Reilly (Dublin 1877) with annotations and inter-leavings, all written by Murphy, 1910.[48] Estimated cost to print: 10 guineas.

4. A glossary of Hebrew words with English equivalents.[49]

5. Preparations for the publication of *The Ancient Laws of Ireland, Vols. 2 and 3*, and the Book of Aicill.[50]

On becoming Professor of Irish, Murphy inherited, as was the custom, a large number of papers from his predecessors:

Thomas De Vere Coneys (Professor 1840-1852), *Irish-English Dictionary (1849.)*

Daniel Foley (Professor 1852-1861), *An English-Irish Dictionary (1855).*

Thaddeus O'Mahoney (Professor 1861-1879) ,*Vols. 2 and 3 of Ancient Laws of Ireland (1869-1873).*

It can be seen, Murphy was intent on advancing the work of his predecessors. He may even have given a promise to do so, to his predecessor and benefactor, James Goodman.

In 1904 a newspaper reported:

> The announcement of a Protestant service to be conducted in Irish on St. Patrick's Day, 1904, was reported widely in Dublin. *The Freeman's Journal's* daily column *By The Way* filled in an aspect of the context for this that might have otherwise gone unnoticed. The Irish language

---

46   Recently leather-bound, and held by Rev. Dr. James R. Murphy, great grandson of Rev. J. E. H. Murphy.

47   Part I held by Rev. Dr. James R. Murphy, great grandson of Rev. J. E. H. Murphy.
     Proofs of Murphy's revision c.1907 of Gospels of St. Matthew (MS 3674/1) and St. Mark (MS 3674) held in Trinity College, Dublin.

48   Held as MS 2094-2096a, Trinity College, Dublin.

49   MS 3674/3 Trinity College, Dublin.

50   MS 3677 and MS 3678, Trinity College, Dublin.

could serve the purpose of producing Protestant proselytes: Catholic services were, of course, only ever conducted in Latin.

An unconscious tribute has been paid to the Gaelic League in the matter of having a religious service in Irish by the Rev. Mr. Murphy on the Feast of St. Patrick, at Kevin Street Protestant Church, South Circular Road, Dublin. What the *Irish Times* is good enough to describe as *a service of very exceptional interest* is announced to take place on St. Patrick's Day *to be conducted in the Irish language by the Rev. J.E.H. Murphy, Professor of Irish in Trinity College, Dublin.* But, as a matter of fact, it is quite in the fitness of things that the Professor of Irish in Trinity College should hold an Irish service for those of the Protestant belief, because the lectureship was founded in 1842 for the purpose of instructing the native Irish, through the medium of their own language, in the principles of the *Established Church*. In other words, the Irish professorship, as Dr. Hyde points out, "is only an adjunct of the Divinity School, and paid and practically controlled by a society for the conversion of Irish Papists through the medium of the Irish language.[51]

It seemed as though Hyde was always out to get Murphy and the Department of Irish at Trinity College, whenever possible. In 1992, president of Ireland, Mary Robinson gave an address to mark the quatercentenary celebrations of Trinity College, Dublin, and during her address she spoke of Douglas Hyde, as summarised in an Irish newspaper:[52]

Recalling some of Dr. Hyde's battles with the College authorities, including the rejection of his application for a professorship in 1896, the President charted the influence which Hyde had in reconciling Trinity with the emerging Ireland of his day. From lacerating the College authorities in the 1890s – "that Stygian flood of black igno-rance about everything Irish which, Leithe-like, rolls through the portals of my beloved alma mater" – Hyde finally relented sufficiently to accept an honorary doctorate in literature from the College in 1933.

---

51   Editorial comment, *The Freeman's Journal*, March 12, 1904, 6
52   "President speaks of bonds with Hyde," *The Irish Times*, Tuesday, May 12, 1992.

In 1906, another Royal Commission was held, this time on Trinity College, Dublin, and the University of Dublin. Held in London, one of the commissioners was none other than Douglas Hyde.[53]

On November 8, 1906, representing the Gaelic League, Rev J. E .H. Murphy, MA, Professor of Irish in the University of Dublin, was present.

Murphy was questioned on whether the 'Irish Society' had been financially supportive of the endowment of the professorship of Irish. Murphy replied:

> The money was raised by subscriptions by noblemen, gentlemen, and gentlewomen, some of whom, no doubt, were interested in the work of this "Irish Society"; but by the "Irish Society" not one penny was subscribed to this endowment, as an examination of the Society's Reports for the years 1838–1843 will show.
>
> For myself, I have never received a penny in salary or fee as Professor of Irish or otherwise from this "Irish Society." It has been stated that I have. As an expert in Irish, many years ago I occasionally examined at their request some of their Irish teachers and pupils, just as I have also done some expert Irish work for Roman Catholic clergymen; but in the one case, as in the other, without fee or reward. I trust that now, and for the future, statements which are not founded on these facts will not appear.

Murphy was asked:

> 'I should like to know a little of what you have done in the way of teaching?'

And he replied that he lectured three times a week to each of his three classes. His Irish lectures took the form of hearing translations, examining grammar, dependence of words on one another, the study of unusual idioms, a study of certain Irish texts and poems, as well as preparations for *viva voce* examinations and for translations at sight from Irish to English, and from English to Irish. Explanations of historical personages and events were also given. Murphy said his lectures were open to the public, and were attended by students in Arts and in Divinity. Occasionally, men who had long ago left College, returned to attend his lectures, and recently two young lady students of the College attended. In his first year, only five students attended, but currently he had eleven in his classes, a one hundred per cent increase. Many of the pupils who attended

---

53   Full transcripts are readily available on line, under the appendix to the final report, minutes of evidence and documents.

his classes started with only a knowledge of the Irish alphabet, but his pupils in almost every detail have succeeded in acquiring the language.

But, when it came to Commissioner Douglas Hyde's turn to ask questions, he brought up the information that all Professors of Irish so far had also been Church of Ireland clergymen. The questioning then moved to the close ties between the two schools, the School of Divinity and the School of Irish. Murphy said he was frequently asked by the senior lecturer to examine for decisions regarding the awarding of prizes.

The exchange, when Hyde at last seemed reconciled and more reasonable, continued as follows:

> Hyde: 'If you were not called on to examine for a Divinity prize, who would be called upon?'

> Murphy: 'I do not know at all. Somebody, no doubt, connected with Divinity.'

> Hyde: 'And knowing Irish?'

> Murphy: 'Yes.'

> Hyde: 'Is there any such person except yourself?'

> Murphy: 'As a matter of fact, my son[54] presented himself for the Bedell Prize, and they obtained two examiners to examine him for that prize.'

> Hyde: 'Outsiders for the time being?'

> Murphy: 'One of them; yes.'

> Hyde: 'Do you not think because the Professor of Irish does not devote his whole time to the position of Irish, does not receive full remuneration, and therefore has to be also a clergyman, with other functions to discharge, this gives rise to misconceptions about the two schools? Therefore, would you think it desirable that the Professor of Irish in the College should give all of his time to the subject, provided that he got proper remuneration?'

> Murphy: 'Yes.'

---

54   Edwy or Fred. The Bedell Prize was worth £20 at that time

In 1906, there was only one Catholic Fellow at Trinity College, made possible only on the condition that he would have to wait thirty years or more before he could have any real part in the government of the College. The 1907 Commission's report declared what everyone knew to be true, that Trinity was the College of the Protestant minority.

And so ended the challenges by Hyde, although there was one other area in which they could never agree. Murphy always advocated for the voluntary study of Irish. He felt the language would be stifled, would die as a living language, if made compulsory. In 1909, one year after the 1908 setting up of the National University of Ireland, UCD, a campaign led by Hyde sought to have Irish made compulsory for matriculation. Of UCD he said, 'If this University does not learn to love the Irish Nation, and to make itself beloved of the Irish Nation, it is doomed to sterility.'

When the Irish State made Irish obligatory in schools after 1922,[55] the move did not help to foster a great love of the language amongst students. The requirement for Irish to enter university or to get a job in the Civil Service, set the Irish language as an obstacle to be overcome rather than a part of a rich culture to be embraced. Irish is still compulsory in schools, and currently it is said, 'If it had not been made compulsory, today it would be a dead language. Irish has been taught poorly, with a lack of training for teachers. Also, it has been used as an anti-English platform, ingrained with a sense of repression.'

The educational experience of the majority of people learning the language has been largely a negative one. Irish was the first language of the State according to the Constitution, and it was assumed that people could speak it. Children learning the language were introduced to Irish as a written language before they had any conversational Irish. Secondary students had to read literature and poems in Irish when many could not make simple sentences in the language.

'People should be encouraged to speak Irish, rather than having it forced upon them,' Irish President Michael D. Higgins declared in a speech in Auckland, on Friday, October 27, 2017. 'I am in favour of encouraging people, bringing people to the language rather than forcing it.'

Asked if making Irish compulsory in schools was a help, or a hindrance, the president gave a detailed reply, drawing on an essay by one of his predecessors, Douglas Hyde, who had argued in favour of the replacement of English by Irish:

> English had been imposed on Ireland in a number of ways. At one time you wore a stick around your neck and you put a notch every time you used an Irish word and when you went to school the following day you were punished based on the number of marks.

---

55   In 1928, compulsory in the Intermediate Certificate examinations, and in 1934, compulsory in the Leaving Certificate examinations.

Then again I remember in my time, people referring to the Irish language, they would say about English, 'It's what you needed for the boat' because our people had to learn English to go abroad because of migration.

However, President Higgins said he believed that Hyde's argument had been wrong: 'I think myself that it was a mistake. I don't agree with it.' Welcoming the changing climate for the teaching of Irish, the president said:

> You must encourage and lure them to the language, make the language attractive, the language needn't stand for every antiquated authoritarian idea that was ever dreamed up and imagined in ancient Irish, for example.

Today, the Department of Irish and Celtic Studies at Trinity College, Dublin, is thriving, with a head of department, four assistant professors, one research fellow, one postdoctoral scholar, and one senior executive officer. Research is being conducted in Medieval Irish, Old Irish, Early Irish, Modern Irish and in Scottish Irish. There are about two hundred undergraduates attending lectures, who can take a single degree in Irish, or study Irish as one of two languages, or even combine computer science and Irish. A further option is available, one of taking Irish Studies.

Perhaps all of this would make Murphy smile, for there has been a flowering of interest, some students arriving to the School of Irish and Celtic Studies at Trinity College having taken all their schooling though Irish in Irish Immersion Schools, known as *Irish Medium Schools*.

Trinity College, Dublin   *Photo Credit: Paul Sharp*

16.
EDWARD EMMANUEL LENNON

1857 – 1940

Dr Edward Emmanuel Lennon had decided early on that the rural life was not for him, even if Newcastle House could have provided him with a livelihood. He had very little money but somehow found his way to enrol in the somewhat lowly training school of the Apothecaries' Hall in Dublin. After his father's death in 1889, when Edward was in his early thirties, he used to walk the thirty miles from Dublin to Enfield to see his mother, Mary (Lucas) Lennon at the weekends, returning to Dublin on foot on Sunday evening.

His practice grew rapidly, and he soon acquired a reputation as a spot diagnostician, and became known for his wisdom and kindness. He was asked to join the medical staff of the Meath Hospital in the 1890s, a position he held until his death in 1940. Soon after qualifying, he became House Physician at the Meath Hospital in Dublin, thus beginning a long family connection with that institution. He inspired a generation of nephews and even one niece to become doctors. It could be said that his influence spilled over into the following generations with the qualifying of his Murphy great-nephews: Edwy Murphy's sons Jim and Willie, and also Edward Ross, grandson of Alice (Lennon) Ross. And perhaps there are echoes in the present as his great-grand-nephew Robin Wormell is a doctor who also served his time in the Meath Hospital.

There was a brass plate in the hospital commemorating Dr Lennon's contributions to the medical community, but the building is now closed, hospitals having been amalgamated and rebuilt in the suburbs. Stories are told today as to how Edward carried around his medical instruments in his top hat, rather than in a bag.

Edward Emmanuel lived at 22 Merrion Square in Dublin until he moved to smaller accommodation around the corner at number 38. When he was fifty-one, on December14, 1908 he married Eileen Mary Cole Metge of Navan. They had two children, Maeve and Edward, the latter being always known as *Ted* in the family.

Edward Emmanuel was a handsome man-about-town in his time. Very gregarious and often found at social gatherings, he could be seen surrounded by a group listening to one of his many anecdotes. When he entered the wards, the nurses' hearts were 'all of a flutter'. The following passage is taken from *Dublin's Meath Hospital, 1753 – 1996*, a history of the hospital written by Peter Gatenby, and published in 1996 by Tower Hill:

> Lennon was the son of a well-known Irish landowner in Co. Meath, and one of a very large family. Brought up in the belief that there would be plenty of money for all, he was not educated for any career in particular. But finding *res angusta domi* ("things at home are tight") on his father's death, he set out to seek his fortune in America. He worked his passage out and, in the USA, he learnt various trades including cobbling shoes. He made half a dollar a day as a stone cutter, and worked as a 'wracker' in a drinking saloon. Finally, having earned enough money trundling a wheelbarrow in Armour's canning factory in Chicago to bring him home, he returned to Dublin and decided to become a doctor. He had a brilliant medical course in the Royal College of Surgeons' School and at the Meath, was elected fellow of the Royal College of Physicians in Ireland in 1892, and physician on the hospital staff in 1893. He soon developed a very large practice and was one of the best teachers of clinical medicine ever at the Meath.

> He rarely missed a trick. For instance the story is told, that when King Edward VII came to Dublin after his coronation, Edward Emmanuel followed the vice-regal party to Phoenix Park, where there was a polo match, but first he packed his doctor's bag so that if there should be an accident he would be available and could bring himself to the notice of the royal party. For all that, it is said that he refused a title which would have been bestowed on him as one of the leading physicians of the time. His reason? 'Too many butchers and bakers were being knighted, and he did not think he should be among their number.'

> Edward Emmanuel retired about 1936 to Newcastle House, which he had taken over from his brother

Percy[56] in 1916, retrieving him from debt. There his wife Eileen devotedly cared for him until he died in the autumn of 1940, of coronary thrombosis, at the age of 83. He had known his heart was failing. When his great-nephew Dr Willie Murphy was driving on assignment northwards from Dublin to Londonderry, and passing through Enfield, he called in to see Edward and Eileen in Newcastle House, unaware Edward would die one week later. Willie later wrote:

> He was very far gone but with a clear mind. He presented to me his death certificate, devoid of date and time of death, which he had arranged to be filled in by Eileen. He gave me a stethoscope to examine his heart and lungs, and then said: *I don't want Cyril[57] to have anything to do with this.* I signed.

Dr Edward Lennon was the tallest of the Newcastle Lennon family, a man with long bones. A common belief holds that to be a good physician, a doctor would have to have long fingers. The few photographs taken of him show a man with extremely long fingers! Apart from his contributions to medicine in Ireland, Uncle Edward Lennon was an inspiration to his nephews and nieces, encouraging them in their medical studies and prospects.

In 1895, he delivered the Introductory Address at the One Hundred and Forty-third Session of the Meath Hospital, when he said, in part:

> To my younger listeners I would like to say a word in conclusion:- You are young and buoyant in spirits, and look at most things with the cheerfulness of youth; but do not forget that all around you here is misery and sadness, and that your duty in after-life, as it is your duty now, is to do all in your power, and you will find it in many cases that all is very little, to alleviate some of that dreadful total of suffering and sorrow.

> As you grow older, and your experience enlarges, you will find that your estimate of poor suffering humanity steadily rises.

> There is no place on earth where grander examples of human courage can be seen than in a Hospital. You will see here men and women, without a murmur, or sign of fear, listening to the words in which the saddened medical man conveys to them that they are suffering from some incurable malady, and that their days are certainly numbered.

---

56 *Percy:* Youngest son of Charles and Mary Lennon of Newcastle House, Enfield.

57 *Cyril:* One of the Murphy great-nephews Edward Emanuel had encouraged to take up medicine!

Imagine any one of you being told that you would have to undergo an operation of the greatest hazard, necessarily accompanied by prolonged suffering, and a tedious convalescence if successful, and picture to yourself what your feelings under such circumstances would be – yet you will see men and women here cheerfully accepting the prospect, and with a confidence in medical science that approaches the sublime, walk fearlessly into the operation theatre, and place themselves absolutely and without reserve in the hands of the surgeon.

Never forget that around each patient, be he ever so humble or uninteresting, are grouped the hopes and fears of loving friends and relatives. Never forget that what to you is the interesting sarcoma, too often means bitter want and suffering to the widow and the orphan.

There are few of us who have not lost some beloved friend or relative. When you see the sorrow-stricken friends around the bedside of some poor suffering fellow-creature, think of what you felt yourself when someone very dear to you was taken away. Remember that all the patients you see here are suffering, and that all are poor. Go out any cold winter morning to the out-patient department, and add the pangs of bitter weather to those of sickness and poverty, and he must indeed be hardened and devoid of human sympathy who does not feel his heart sad within him at contemplation of all this misery, not a tithe of which he can assuage. You must remember, also, that there is another side to the picture – that the black cloud of sorrow is illuminated by the sunshine of human kindness.

This hospital, and countless similar institutions, throughout the world, are maintained by the generous contributions of those whose lot is cast in pleasanter places than that of our poor patients, but whose hearts are touched by the sufferings which they try so nobly to alleviate. *One touch of nature makes the whole world kind* and, thank God for it, in the darkest hours of our country, our wealthier fellow-countrymen have never failed to respond to an appeal for help, and no hospital in Ireland has ever yet had to shut its doors through want of funds.

Tree for the Murphys of Rathcore Rectory

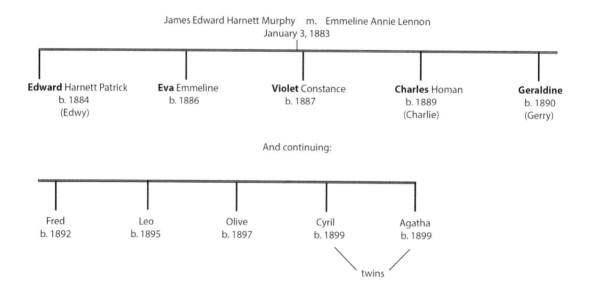

James Edward Harnett Murphy   m.   Emmeline Annie Lennon
January 3, 1883

Edward Harnett Patrick
b. 1884
(Edwy)

Eva Emmeline
b. 1886

Violet Constance
b. 1887

Charles Homan
b. 1889
(Charlie)

Geraldine
b. 1890
(Gerry)

And continuing:

Fred
b. 1892

Leo
b. 1895

Olive
b. 1897

Cyril
b. 1899

Agatha
b. 1899

twins

17.
EDWARD HARNETT
PATRICK MURPHY

March 17, 1884 – December 28, 1936

James Edward Harnett Murphy   m.   Emmeline Annie Lennon
January 3, 1883

|

Edward Harnett Patrick Murphy

Edward was the first child, the eldest son, of Rev Murphy and Emmeline Annie Murphy. Born on St. Patrick's Day, he was named after the saint. His birth took place on Achill Island (according to his son) or at Rathcore Rectory (according to his birth certificate). It seems unlikely James would have taken his heavily pregnant wife on the arduous journey from Meath to Achill, before the Christmas season with stormy weather unpredictable. The baby would have been welcomed by everyone in the family, especially the Newcastle Lennon grandparents. James gave his new son his own father's first name, Edward, and his own mother's maiden name, Harnett.

Edward was always known by his family as *Edwy*, and he spent all his childhood at Rathcore Rectory. As mentioned earlier, Edwy was frightened by his father, crawling in behind the living room sofa at the sound of his roaring voice. Rev Murphy considered his eldest to be a weakling, and decided Edwy would do better if kept at home and taught by himself. Edwy never looked robust, and might have had a weak heart. He never went to school, and was taught with the aid of *ashplants*, a switch or cane made from saplings of the ash tree. And, at times, Rev Murphy cut the clothes off his son if studies were neglected or if the boy misbehaved. One time, Edwy wanted to run away, and he got as far as borrowing a pound from his sister.

When he was little, Edwy had a long strip of white blanket he kept wrapped around his thumb. When the small family went to Achill Island for a few weeks' holiday,

Emmeline Annie thought she would break him of the habit, and had persuaded him to leave it behind at home. He wasn't supposed to have it. But, when sitting in the cart between the train station and their holiday house, he pulled it out from his sailor blouse. He was seven years old.

Another summer, when the family was up in Skerries and Edwy was now a teenager, he became very keen on a girl who lived there. His sister Eva teased him, and he refused to speak to Eva for a full year.

These stories tell of a serious child, fearful of his father and appearing quiet and shy beside his younger, outgoing siblings. However, he was a clever lad, too, and had been taught well by his father. In 1909, when he was twenty-five, he became a licentiate of the Apothecaries Hall, no doubt influenced strongly by his gentle uncle, Dr Edward Lennon, who noticed his nephew's potential. Edwy went on to take the MB degree and the diploma in Public Health at Trinity College, completing both in 1915, after the start of World War I. He did not sign up for military service of any kind, unlike many of his acquaintances, but his health may not have passed muster, anyway. Meanwhile, during his later years of study, he spent some time in Wiltshire as Assistant Schools Medical Officer, from 1911 to 1914. He would have returned to Ireland during the long summer holidays.

Late in 1911, Edwy married Elizabeth Strang, a hospital nurse from Glasgow, whom he had met while in Wiltshire. Elizabeth was known to family members as 'Bessie' and some in the Murphy family were upset she had married their Edwy. However, Bessie showed great kindness to other Murphys when they were in need. Edwy and Bessie had two sons, Jimmie and Willie, both named for their grandfathers, James Murphy and William Strang. Both of Edwy's sons became doctors.

1915 saw Edwy fully qualified and setting up his practice in DunLaoghaire, then known as Kingstown, where he lived for the rest of his life. No doubt a deciding factor for him would have been the bracing sea air which would have benefitted his health.

Edwy with his wife Bessie and two sons, James Edward (L) and William Robert (R) c. 1916

How many times did Edwy stop by the kitchen when Bessie was busy elsewhere in the house? How frequently did Bessie find missing a dozen eggs, a pint of milk or a loaf of bread, all taken from the fridge or the shelf, to be given to a patient on his medical rounds?

Edwy
Murphy, 1929

On Edwy's death in 1936, when he was fifty-two, a number of appreciations of his life and work were published in newspapers.

The following example best describes how he was held in high esteem:

The passing away on Monday last of Dr. E. Harnett Murphy is a matter of real sorrow to his host of patients and friends. I purposely couple the last two words, for, when you secured Dr. Murphy as your doctor, you also secured a true and helpful friend.

He was, I think, more particularly the friend of the poor. He was ever as ready to respond to the call from the poor as he was from the well-off. No better proof of this could be asked for than my own first introduction to this man, who afterwards became my good friend. At 2 o'clock one cold winter's morning, I urgently required a doctor for a person who had suddenly taken ill, and who, by the way, resided at a humble address.

I rang at several doctors' doors but either got no reply or else, on hearing the address of the patient, they said they would call "later in the morning." Dr. Murphy was a stranger to me then, but in desperation I rang at his door. Presently he put his head out of a top window. "What's the address?" he asked, after I had explained my need. "The same old story," I thought, as I gave him the address – but I was wrong. "Right," he shouted, "I'll be with you in ten minutes" – and he was.

This was typical of Dr. Harnett Murphy throughout the many years I have known him. He was ever ready to answer the call of the sick, be they poor or rich. If you could pay him, you did. If you couldn't, well, - he would never ask you.

To his obituary writers I will leave his career. For me it is more pleasant to recall his many acts of kindness, his gentle manner, and his self-sacrificing devotion to duty. Indeed, it may have been the latter that brought about his untimely death.

He has now received the last Call. May he rest in peace.

To Mrs. Harnett Murphy and his two sons we express our sincere sympathy on the loss of a very dear husband and father.

R. H. Christie

At the funeral service, amongst the general public present was a long list of names, including some from Enfield, representatives from the Apothecaries Hall, an ex-TD, Church of Ireland ministers, and doctors and businessmen. The chief mourners listed were his two sons, three of his brothers, Sharman Ross (a Ross cousin), and George H. Lennon and Dr Edward Lennon (his uncles). His mother was still alive, but an invalid, unable to attend. Also not mentioned is Bessie, Edwy's wife, which can be explained by the estrangement which had occurred between them, Edwy having had an affair with another woman.

The Murphys knew well that Edwy had a drinking problem. Two further issues from his rough childhood arose for Edwy – the telling of untruths and a lack of trust in family members. These issues were summarised by his son, Willie, the son who loved him best, when writing to a cousin:

Dad was a rather sober rider, but a very good G.P. He worked hard and lied continuously. Mother had nearly cured him . . . All Emma's children, even Geraldine, whom we loved, could change a truth, and easy. They were all fond of alcohol . . .

On the back is written by one of Edwy's sons:
'Dad Murphy, in 3rd position at this stage!' c. 1910

18.
EVA EMMELINE MURPHY

May 24, 1886 – July 20, 1962

PART I – IRELAND

Eva was the eldest daughter of James and Emmeline Murphy. She was known in the family as the 'fairer beauty'; not that Eva had fair hair, but Eva was not as dark as a younger sister, who would later be called the 'dark beauty'.

Baby Eva was named after her mother, Emmeline, and after her mother's youngest sister, Eva Consuelo Lennon, who would turn twenty, six days after the baby's birth at Rathcore Rectory. This Eva Consuelo was the renowned beauty of the Lennon family.

All the traditional responsibility of the eldest daughter, filling in for Mother in every area, fell on Eva's shoulders: caring for younger siblings and helping the maids with daily house-cleaning chores such as cleaning out fireplaces, blackening the stove, and scrubbing the floors on hands and knees. Like most of her brothers and sisters, Eva adored her mother and hated her father. All her life she would suffer from anxiety caused by childhood years of watching the great and fearful terror of her older brother Edwy, trying to deal with his father's violent outbursts. Repeated patterns of physical abuse are also likely to lead to a person feeling she is only of value when meeting another person's needs.

Eva was taught at home, initially by her father, and later by tutors, alongside her brothers and sisters, and the boys who boarded at the rectory. During the summer months, the family usually set up in Dunroe, the house in Skerries by the seaside. Everyone would move, including servants, tutors, and boarders. One day, when Eva was about eight years old, one of the boarding boys rented a boat, and he rowed along to where Eva and some other children were sitting on rocks. He asked Eva, 'Why don't you step into the boat to see how nice it is in here? Don't you want to be grown up, like all the other girls around?' Eva did indeed, and in she climbed, and they rowed away, off to a nearby island. Eva recorded: 'When I got back, Mother pelted me with questions. Everyone was horrified. I didn't know what all the fuss was about.'

Eventually, when she was seventeen, she obtained a scholarship to Victoria High School in Londonderry, where she boarded for the year before her final examinations. She came first in Ireland the year she wrote the exams.

She returned to Rathcore Rectory. It was customary for the eldest girl in a family to remain at home to help her mother, even during school age. The idea was that the boys needed an education so they could get a good job and so provide for their own future families. If money was an issue, and it certainly was in the rectory, any spare savings had to be used to help the boys through university.

As a rector's wife, Emmeline Annie had many duties to carry out in the parish, visiting and advising parishioners. Emmeline Annie had an innate wisdom and provided a calm presence in times of emergency. Accompanying her mother in the horse and buggy on these visitations, Eva, who was ambidextrous and had difficulty remembering her right hand from her left, would check with her mother as to which was her right hand. As Emmeline Annie drove the horse down the rectory avenue, Eva would place a handkerchief in her right hand, clutching it tightly until the destination was reached. This was how she knew which hand to put out for a handshake greeting. Emmeline Annie would scold her daughter if she got it wrong, saying, *They will think you're a badly brought up girl if you try to shake hands with them, using your left hand.* Eva was careful not to disgrace her mother.

Eva lived at the rectory until she reached twenty-three. She learnt many practical skills: sewing, nursing the sick, and gardening. And she had bred and reared hens for a number of years, selling the eggs and saving every penny. Her Lennon grandparents had bought her a bike, as indeed they did for all the rectory grandchildren, and she succeeded during several productive egg-laying summers in riding an average of three hundred miles a month delivering eggs.

Eva was saving the pocket money made from rearing chickens and selling eggs, but also from shipping her chickens, dressed for the table, for sale to acquaintances in Dublin. On one occasion, Eva thought she would put in a little extra touch, and she added some freshly cut parsley – not readily available in Dublin. The customer in Dublin wrote back: 'Thank you very much for the parsley' but never paid for the chickens. Thereafter, when anyone wanted to tease Eva they could say, 'Thank you very much for the parsley.'

Eva was twenty-three when her father threatened to get rid of her hens, and when Eva declared, *If they go, I go!* Early in the summer of 1909, she gladly left the rectory where she had been born, but leaving her mother behind broke her heart. Eva was not permitted to visit her mother, not even at Christmastime, although during the next few years they did manage to meet a couple of times, in secret.

So, Eva had ridden her bike to Dublin and had stayed for a while with her Uncle Fred Lucas. In the autumn, she was visited there by two sons of her aunt, her mother's eldest sister Mary Alice Ross, all of whom lived in Liscarney House in County Monaghan. These two lads, Charlie and Sharman Ross, a couple of years younger than Eva, arrived with a proposition. Their mother's health was poor, and they needed help to care for her. Their eldest brother was away touring Canada and their younger sister, Gladys, was blind. Would Eva consider moving to their house, running the household, and caring for their mother? An added bonus for Eva would be the possibility of establishing a proper farmyard home for her hens.

Eva had developed practical nursing skills watching her mother at home. All ministers' wives were called upon to aid the sick in the parish, and Eva had gained her knowledge through the experience of watching her mother in action.

Eva decided this was a reasonable offer, and she moved to Liscarney, where she ran the household and nursed her Aunt Alice for over three years. She brought her hens with her and managed to earn some pin-money selling eggs. She looked after Gladys, too, later recording: 'Uncomplaining Gladys was the nearest human being to a saint I ever met. Sadly, she died while I was at Liscarney.'

The house in Monaghan was out in the country, and as such was fairly isolated. Eva became friends with Florrie Walby, who was caring for a blind man in the adjoining estate, at Bessmount Park. Meanwhile,

Florrie

the Ross brothers took to travelling – the eldest, James who had gone out to Canada, was now home again, and full of stories of his experiences on the Prairies and life as a cowboy. The second son, Charlie, had a friend, Cooper, who was a recovering alcoholic and who begged Charlie to accompany him on a trip around the world designed to help Cooper break his drinking habit. Charlie was delighted and was away about two years. James had been the first to return, and his stories of the *Wild West* had so intrigued Sharman that he too set out for a summer's exploration of parts of western Canada.

Eva was in charge at Liscarney, and not long after arriving, Eva and one of the Ross boys fell in love. Although Eva and Sharman were first cousins, their mothers being sisters, this was not uncommon as first cousins saw a lot of each other, visiting back and forth between their houses, and socialising together. Many years later, Eva said: 'Sharman and I were engaged, but there was never a ring. Sharman wanted to return to Canada, and he thought we should emigrate and get married out in Canada. There was talk of selling Liscarney House. Then the engagement was off, and then it was on again. He was unable to make up his mind, obstinate one moment, weak the next. We actually didn't go out very much together, as a couple. It was all very unsettling for me.'[58]

Aunt Alice gradually became more of an invalid and grew difficult to nurse. It seemed 'Nobody mattered to her, except her three sons. Even blind Gladys had been sidetracked for the boys.' When Eva was twenty-seven, and after four years at Liscarney, she decided she needed a break and she left Liscarney in the summer of 1913 for six months, to take a cooking course in Dublin. She had arranged for someone to come in and take care of Aunt Alice while she was away. At this point, Eva and Sharman were still unofficially engaged.

Aunt Alice suffered a stroke late in 1913, and Eva and her mother, Emmeline Annie, Alice's sister, went back to Liscarney and together they cared for Aunt Alice until she died on December 9, 1913.

Most of the brothers of Emmeline Annie had emigrated to the United States, where they settled happily and did very well. In 1911, one of these brothers died, and in his will, Fred Lennon had left £1 000 to his sister, Emmeline Annie, back in Ireland. It had taken a while for Fred's will to be settled and the money to arrive for Emmeline, but she could now afford to offer £100 as a loan to her daughter, Eva. It was now decided Eva should go on out to Canada, and her fiancé, Sharman, would follow on later. Eva's Monaghan neighbour, Florrie Walby, was also keen to emigrate to Canada, and together, Eva and Florrie purchased tickets to travel on *Lake Manitoba*, a 10 000

---

58   See Chapter 9 for photograph of the Ross family.

tonne vessel. Sharman accompanied them to Belfast, as did Florrie's sister, Irene, to see them off, and Sharman purchased a ticket for himself on the tender so he could accompany them out to the boat. At the last minute, Florrie's sister became so upset at seeing Florrie in the tender that Sharman handed her his ticket, and so he was unable

to accompany them. Eva was to contemplate the symbolism of all this for many years to come! It seems they said 'Goodbye!' with a wave of a hand.

Before following Eva's journey to Canada, here is an explanation of what happened to those she left behind in Ireland:

James Ross returned from his Canadian travels and married in Dublin in 1910. He and his wife Nan then emigrated to Canada, settling in Edmonton, Alberta, where James practised as a lawyer. Eva visited him there once, but it was not a happy encounter as James was adamant his mother had suffered a stroke because Eva had abandoned her to go to Dublin. Eva was so upset she never returned to visit the Ross family in Edmonton.

Charlie Ross would be married in 1934 to Olive Murphy, Eva's sister, as described in a later chapter. Charlie and Olive were first cousins.

Sharman Ross never did make it out again to Canada, to marry Eva. Instead, he married Lorna, a girl from Enniskillen, in 1924, ten years after Eva emigrated, and nine years after Eva had married someone else. When Lorna gave birth to a girl in 1927, Sharman was keen to call her Valentine, as he had recently heard Eva had a young daughter named Valentine. Eva's daughter had been born just before Valentine's Day, and she was named for the saint. However, Sharman was keen to name his daughter Valentine because Eva had chosen that name. At a family reunion in the 1980s, when both Valentines were present, Eva's Valentine was asked, 'Why don't you tell Sharman's daughter Valentine about the link you both have?' She replied, 'I wouldn't dare!'

PART II – CANADA

Eva and Florrie set sail from Belfast for Canada on board the *Lake Manitoba,* leaving on May 7, 1914. Landing in Montreal, they were shown around the city by the first mate.

After this happy day they boarded the CPR train for the cross-country trip. Their plan was to cross Canada to Vancouver, stopping off in Calgary for a few days' visit with one of Eva's brothers, Charlie, who had gone there the previous year as an apprentice surveyor and engineer, having completed his engineering degree at Trinity College.

The first night aboard the train, Eva noticed a bug running across the sheet. 'That looks like a bed-bug' she mentioned to her friend; but believing this to be part of the Canadian scene to which she must adjust, she did not complain. By morning the two girls were covered with bites. An embarrassed CPR official was summoned. He eliminated the mattress and whisked the girls to another part of the train where they received royal treatment and no further bites.

James Nevin (J. N.) Wallace

Charlie and Eva

The train pulled into Calgary at 2 a.m., and Charlie was waiting for them on the platform. Charlie loved his sister Eva, later in life describing her as *having great heart*. He organised the girls' trunks, and then took Eva's arm to walk her and Florrie down the platform. 'I have arranged so much for you, to have a happy visit here.' He took the girls to the best hotel in the town, the Braemar Lodge Hotel, and Charlie and Eva sat up until 6 a.m., chatting and discussing family news. Charlie left to get some rest but was back at the hotel by 9 a.m. for breakfast, making plans for the day. They were to hire a car and take a drive out to the Sarcee Native Indian Reserve, and then they were to have dinner that evening with some of Charlie's friends, including Charlie's boss, JN Wallace. 'There's someone I would like you to meet. I've done some work for him out in the bush. He's from Foxrock, County Dublin. His father was a Church of Ireland minister, like ours.' Eva asked, 'Did he beat his family, like ours?'

James Nevin Wallace came to dinner that night, and the next morning before breakfast he returned to the hotel to take Eva for a walk. Eva recalled: 'It was a lovely spring day, the air was so clear, and we walked along 4th Avenue to Louise Bridge, over the Bow River. He was quite deaf, difficult to talk to—he had to lip read what I was saying. On the way back, he proposed to me.'

Eva was dumb-founded. On reflection, she wondered if every man in Canada would become a suitor for her hand? She was also quite sure she had not broken free from ties to Rathcore and Liscarney to go jumping into a marriage of any kind. Some girls did marry to obtain Canadian citizenship and security, but not Eva.

Eva explained gently that she was already engaged, but JN persisted. He was truly smitten.

Charlie accompanied the girls to Vancouver and arranged for them to be comfortably settled. Florrie was eventually to assist in the running of a girls' school while Eva was to seek work as *a Lady's Help*. This was a category where *Old Country girls of good family* could help in the household and be treated not as a servant but as one of the family. This was carried out to the letter in some instances while others delegated *the Help* to the kitchen.

Eva had brought three references from Ireland with her:

#1

The Rectory
Monaghan

30th Sept. 1913

I have known Miss Murphy since I came to Monaghan about three years since. I consider her a most pleasant, obliging, helpful, upright young lady. She has lived with a delicate aunt in my parish and not only acted as companion but did the housekeeping also. I look upon Miss Murphy as a most practical young lady. She is at the same time most respectably connected, her father is Professor Murphy in Trinity College, Dublin. I believe this young lady will be found reliable, trustworthy and anxious to give satisfaction in any position she may undertake. Needless to say her moral character is above reproach, and I can conscientiously, and without reservation of any kind, recommend her in the strongest possible manner. I consider the household into which Miss Murphy may enter a fortunate one indeed.

I am truly sorry to see young people of such sterling qualities leaving my parish. I wish we could keep them here. I can only say that Miss Murphy can never attain to such heights of success and happiness as I could wish her. I hope I may hear of splendid achievements, in her case.

Signed: J. Macmanaway, M.A., T.C.D.,
Rector of Monaghan and Canon of St. Patrick's Cathedral, Dublin.

#2

The Rectory
Ballivor
Co. Meath

April 15ᵗʰ 1914

I have known Miss Eva Murphy from childhood and it is a great pleasure to me to testify to her personal worth and high character. She is a
young lady of considerable ability and attainments in all branches of
household and domestic concerns. I have had frequent opportunities
of observing her capable management of family duties and I trust she
will obtain a post suitable to her abilities.

I am quite sure she will always give of her best to the entire satisfaction of her employer. She is of a bright and cheerful disposition,
naturally active and energetic, and will be found trustworthy in the
highest degree.

Signed:R. J. Merrin
Rector of Killochonnigan, Diocese of Meath.

——

#3

Rosehill
Carysfort Avenue
Blackrock
Co. Dublin

2ⁿᵈ May, 1914

I have known Miss Murphy for some years and can speak highly of her
character and capabilities. She will fulfill any duties entrusted to her in
a thorough and efficient manner.

Signed:G. W. Ledwich
Chief Clerk, Consolidated Taxing Office
Supreme Court of Judicature, Four Courts
Dublin

Charlie helped Eva to get booked into the Queen Alexandra Hostel, a clean, reasonable hostel set up for young ladies. She was awakened the next morning by a knock at her door.

Maid: *Good morning, Miss. There is a man to see you down in the lobby.*

Eva replied: *There must be some mistake. I know no one in Vancouver.*

The maid insisted: *Oh, Miss, he's very persistent. Please come downstairs.*

So Eva went down, to find JN in the hostel lobby waiting for her. He had taken a few days off work and had come out to Vancouver to check on how she was getting along. Was she all right? She was. JN took her to Stanley Park, and then hired a car and they went for a drive.

For the next few months Eva held various positions. She spent the first summer on Thormanby Island in Georgia Strait, between Vancouver and Vancouver Island. The name *Thormanby* was given to the island by Captain George Richards, who had surveyed the area with his ship *Plumper* in 1860. *Thormanby* was the name of the horse who had won the famous horse race, the Epsom Derby in 1860. The island was uninhabited and forested until 1905, when John William (Jack) Vaughan built the first cabin and a wharf on the island.

Here Eva was *the Help,* and she worked hard, but was treated well. She slept under the stars when she could, and later remembered:

> 'There was a gorgeous view looking out to Texada Island. I slept under
> the pine trees and saw chipmunks and snakes. There was a hut where
> I could go if it rained, and there I could sleep on a stretcher under
> the veranda.'

In that summer Eva formed a lifelong love of the British Columbia coast. And she was there when World War I was declared by Britain, on August 4, 1914.

From Thormanby, she went to the Interior of BC, near Kamloops, to a job in a fishing lodge where Sharman Ross and Cooper had visited years before. Sharman had advised Eva to visit there, but it proved to be a disastrous work situation. She was 'treated like dirt'. She stayed only a few days and booked into a local hotel. The first person she met in the lobby was JN. He had been worried about her, perhaps he knew of the lodge, and he had taken a week's holiday to travel up to see her.

By the time he left, Eva had secured a position with a sister of her Thormanby employer. She was happy enough although not well paid. She received five dollars a month plus room and board. Here she stayed until after Christmas.

In January 1915, Eva answered a newspaper advertisement for a governess and in her letter, she stressed her father was a professor in the Old Country. She got the job, at a farm near Innisfail, ninety miles north of Calgary. She loved her new family and became a lifelong friend of the mother, Mrs Milligan.

While she was there, JN phoned almost every evening. The unsympathetic telephone operator would put through the call to the party line and say, 'Calgary calling Miss Murphy AGAIN.' By now, Eva was calling Mr Wallace *Jim.*

Eva and Mrs Milligan were out walking the four miles into Innisfail one evening when a man stopped them on the street to say he believed there had been a call from Calgary for Miss Murphy. When they arrived home, one of the children confirmed the telephone had rung, and he thought Mr Wallace was coming to visit, but he didn't know when.

'I'll just phone Mrs Walker. She always listens in to all the party line calls no matter to whom, and she'll know when Mr Wallace is due,' said Mrs Milligan.

Mrs Walker confirmed the message. Mr Wallace would arrive on the 1:30 train from Calgary on Saturday afternoon.

Eva slipped into town by herself on Saturday and went down to meet the train. There she found a great crowd had gathered at the station. On enquiring what the commotion was about, she was amazed when told the whole of Innisfail wanted to catch a glimpse of that strange Mr Wallace who phoned each evening and who was arriving on the 1:30 train from Calgary.

Such persistence paid off. Eva returned to Calgary in April 1915, to keep house for her brother Charlie, who had returned from Ireland where he had undergone an operation.

Early in June, Eva decided to marry Jim, and her Irish engagement to Sharman was broken off. Years later, one of Eva and JN's daughters recorded:

> Eva finally decided that the next time J.N. proposed, she was going to accept. But the next time they went out, J.N. didn't propose. Being Eva, once she had decided on a course of action she would charge in and do whatever she had planned. So she brought up the subject herself, and years later, when Dad was in an expansive mood, he would

say, "Did I ever tell you children about the time your Mother proposed to me?"

James Nevin Wallace, referred to by his grandchildren as *JN*, was an eccentric Canadian Dominion Land Surveyor at the time when Canada's West was opening up. He led expeditions on Dominion line surveys and meridian surveys, and he surveyed part of the Yukon-British Columbia boundary and part of the Alberta-Saskatchewan border. He represented the Dominion Government on the Alberta-British Columbia Boundary Commission throughout its term, from 1913 to 1924.

Eva Murphy

JN named many mountains, rivers, lakes, creeks, and islands. Family names given for or by JN are Wallace Mountain, Wallace River, Wallace Creek, Eva Lake for his wife, Daphne Island for his eldest daughter, and Dillon and Dillon River for his mother and her family. The most romantic of these is, of course, Eva Lake, situated close to the Wood Buffalo National Park in northern Alberta. Not long after his marriage to Eva, JN was leading a survey team and one night they camped on the shores of an unnamed lake. Coming out of the bush onto the lake's gravelly edge, JN thought the view of the lake with small islands near the shoreline looked exactly like the picture he had loved at his Irish childhood home of *The Lake Isle of Inisfree*, immortalised in a poem written by W. B. Yeats when JN was eighteen years old. JN and his surveying party slept lakeside that night by this gorgeous view, he dreamed of his new wife, and he named the lake, *Eva Lake*.

When JN and Eva became engaged, JN wrote to inform Eva's father of his intentions, and Reverend Murphy wrote back:

Rathcore Rectory July 15th 1915
Enfield,
Co Meath

My dear Mr. Wallace,

I have received your letter of June 4th. Although, through my son Charlie, not alone your name but your personality, and your kindness to him, were well known to me, it was quite a surprise to me to hear that you and Eva had decided to join your futures in marriage.

I rejoice to find that she has found for a future husband, one who has already, through Charlie, been thus reputedly known to us as a thoroughly good man, who hails from the old Country, and from the old University of Dublin, and (as I have heard from the same commending source) who has ancestral connection with the clerical order of the Church of Ireland. These are the chief grounds of satisfaction to me. I heard also that your success in your profession whereby you have secured for yourself a respectable competence and standing, is a further proof that Charlie's and Eva's trust is not misplaced.

Both Eva and yourself have her mother's and my blessing in your proposed marriage, which we pray God may be a blessing to you both.

Eva has written to her mother to say that after your marriage you both, pace submarines,[59] hope to take a trip to Ireland. It would be even a more happy arrangement to come to Ireland to be married.

Yours very sincerely,

Jas. E.H. Murphy

---

59   *Pace submarines:* "if submarines go quiet". Written in 1915, the First World War was in full swing.

Emmeline Annie also wrote to JN:

July 1st, 1915

Dear Mr. Wallace,

Having heard so much from Charlie of all your kindness to him and also how pleasant you have made a foreign land for Eva, I must say I welcome you most heartily as a future son. I only wish that you and Eva could come over to the old country to be married. But you will be very welcome whenever you can come. It is nice for me to feel that Eva had someone to take care of her, and I know she knows how to make a home happy. I missed her more than anyone could imagine. Hoping to meet you in the near future and with my love and best wishes to both of you.

Yours very sincerely,

E.A. Murphy

They were married on August 18, 1915 in the Calgary Pro-Cathedral of the Redeemer. *The Calgary Herald* described the marriage of Miss Eva Emmeline Murphy and Mr James Nevin Wallace, BA, BAI, DLS, Superintendent of the Dominion Topographical Survey office in Calgary:

> The bride, who was given away by her brother, Mr. Charles H. Murphy, B.A., B.A.I., was becomingly gowned in a fawn coloured silk poplin suit, and a black picture hat. …After the ceremony, a luncheon was served at the Palliser, after which Mr. and Mrs. Wallace left for an extended trip to the coast. On their return they will reside in Calgary.

Charlie was best man, coming south from Edmonton where he was now stationed. After the ceremony, they went off to the Palliser Hotel for lunch, where Charlie had created and ordered a special menu *à la Rathcore*, with all of Eva's favourite dishes from her childhood. Eva was twenty-nine and three days later, Jim turned forty-five.

> We set out for our planned honeymoon in Hawaii, travelling around, first by train to Prince Rupert, then down to Vancouver, where we stayed with Florrie Walby, my old friend. Boarding a ferry, we went over to Victoria, staying at the Empress Hotel, which looked exactly as it does today, standing at the head of the bay and covered with reddening Virginia Creeper. There were forest fires everywhere, and

we couldn't see the scenery for the smoke. Going back to Vancouver, we took the train to Seattle and Portland, and then a steamer to San Francisco. There we met up with Uncle Percy Lennon, my mother's youngest brother, who knew the city and showed us around. In a few days, we set sail for Hawaii.

Around this time, Eva met Marie Symes, in Calgary. They were to be lifelong friends. Marie recorded:

Once I had settled after my own emigration journey from London to Calgary, I went to a tea at Bishop Pinkham's home. There I met nice Eva Murphy. She was brought over and was introduced to me. "You two should be friends because you're both from Ireland." Eva had arrived out only a short time before, and she was staying with her brother, Charlie Murphy. Very soon afterwards we knocked up a great friendship, we two, Eva and me. It would last a lifetime. And in no time she told me she was going to be married to Jim Wallace

Marie Symes   *JN and Eva outside Pro-Cathedral*

Marie continued:

Once Eva was married, she kept in touch with me, and soon she was going to have a baby, and she asked me would I go to her. But, in the meantime, I had met my Justus, and I was wanting to get married. So, I said I'd go to her until the baby came and then I'd have to get married. Eva was out at Bowness; it was empty in those days, she didn't know people, and she was very lonely. So I went and stayed with her until the baby came, and then, as it happened, she made a very slow recovery after Daphne's birth in June, 1916. Eva wasn't getting over it very quickly, and I was inclined to have to stay.

I was Daphne's Godmother. I didn't like to leave Eva and Daphne, and I was putting off my wedding, postponing everything so as not to abandon them. Finally, my Justus wouldn't wait any longer. My man had waited patiently for more than a year. I had to leave Eva.

Wallace House at Bowness

Eva and Jim lived for ten years at Bowness, just outside Calgary and during this time their five children were born.

In 1924, with her four children presently born, Eva went home to see her mother in Skerries.

A year later, the Depression now in full swing, there was no government cash for a surveyor, and Jim was given an office job in Ottawa. In 1925 the whole family moved to Canada's capital city for seven years, where Jim was given the position of a director in the Geodetic Survey.

Jim took an early retirement and the family with the five children now returned to their house which they had left empty in Bowness. Eva continued to hope this would be a temporary stopover on the way to a family move to her beloved West Coast, but it was never to be. Jim loved Alberta's distant vistas and wide-open spaces and was reluctant to leave them.

Eva (50) in 1936 photo

Eva had one trip back to see her mother in 1937, before her mother died. JN, Eva, and their five children had had a family photograph taken in Calgary and copies were sent out at Christmas 1936, to all of Eva's Irish relatives. Eva's brothers were so shocked at the appearance of their sister Eva, that they got together, pooled their resources and sent Eva the cash to purchase a trip home. Eva had suffered over the years from thyroid gland troubles, she may have been anaemic, and one summer she had endured a bout of typhoid. While Eva was in Ireland, JN was keeping things going at home, and he wrote letters, which Eva kept and left us in her personal treasures, to be passed down:

Bowness, 20 April, 1937 I hope you are gaining more and more weight, and that you have locked up the worry compartments and lost the keys … Tell your Mother she would have to do a lot of thinking before she thought more of her daughter than I do …

Bowness, 26 April, 1937 Well, now, my own darling, don't stay away too long. I have pictured meeting you on the C.P.R. platform about a thousand times. Won't that be a great meeting, and, darling, I love to think you will be as glad to see me as I will be to see you. I love your affectionate remarks in your letters. Ever, darling Eva, Your loving Jim.

Eva had always wanted to see the West of Ireland, and who better to take her on a road trip than her brother Charlie's wife, and son, Harry? They took black and white photos of famous views, and of donkeys and carts, and visited close to where their father had grown up on the Beara Peninsula, but not too close! However, the best photo taken of that trip is one of Eva herself standing looking out across the Atlantic Ocean, hair windswept, and no doubt thinking of her family across the ocean, not of any nearby.

When Eva returned to Calgary to a tumultuous welcome, she found Jim exhausted and spent, worrying himself into a decline over his children and having already had some minor heart attacks. Eva grew afraid to leave him alone in the house for those years, arranging for someone to be with him if she had to go out.

Jim died early in 1941. Eva stayed on in the house until 1944 when she sold it. She went to stay with her son, Hugh, in Ottawa, where she waited for the release of a troop ship so she could obtain a passage to Ireland. In June 1946 she sailed to Ireland, stayed one year with her daughter Daphne, and returned to Toronto for ten months to keep house for her sons Brian and Hugh who were attending university in Toronto, before finally travelling out to her spiritual home on Vancouver Island. She stayed with her old friend Marie, now remarried, and eventually Eva bought a field and a cottage from her friend. Eva planned to build a home, but her health failed. She convalesced with her daughter Dorothy in Calgary after major surgery before flying to Ireland where she died in 1962.

Twenty years later her daughter Valentine wrote:

My mother had a warm welcoming personality. Our friends gravitated to her house which was always full of people. To this day they remember the welcome she gave everyone. My sister maintained that Mother was always more relaxed when she had overnight guests, and a house full of people than when the house was empty. Luckily, my father was partially deaf and although he witnessed the activity, the noise could never irritate him.

She had an abiding love for her garden which bloomed all summer long despite the lack of water and the long, hot Alberta summers.

It was a great pity she was the only Murphy, other than Eva's youngest sister Olive, not to receive a University education. Eva was an avid reader, followed world politics with intense interest and would have been a whiz at Mathematics. She loved to work out geometric problems as a hobby, and volunteered help to our friends who were having difficulty in Mathematics at school.

Eva was a real Lennon. She had such humour and love of life which I think is present in all the Lennons. She also had the nobleness of character so evident in her mother, Emmeline.

Years later, a friend of the family wrote:

"Oh, I'll never forget that Bowness house of yours. There were people coming in the front door, and going out the back door, and there were people on the stairs, and your Mother always seemed so serene."

Another friend wrote:

There were people hanging out windows shouting at friends downstairs, or calling out "Come on over!" From the moment I heard that, I became a member of the family. Usually I was there for meals, and your Mother accepted me as one of the kids. I always had the best time at your house. It was dull in comparison at home.

In December 2015, in London, the following was recorded by Eva's grandchild, Richard Wormell:

I was working one summer while at University, 1962. I hitchhiked around England. I ended up sleeping under the Pavilion at Evesham Cricket Ground. Suddenly, there was a police dog there, and a torch flashed in my face. I said, "I'm a penniless Irish student. Would you give me a dry cell for the night?" The Bobby said, "I don't give a damn, mate. You can bloody well stay where you are for the night."

I ended up running a chicken farm where I was paid 4 shillings per hour. I was staying in a house where I slept by day, but I was working in the chicken house at night.

One evening I was sitting in the central area of the chicken house, and on either side of me were thousands of chickens. The wind was blowing, the curtains were moving and four or five times when I looked up I saw Eva coming down between the chicken rows. There was a definite feeling of seeing Eva several times, walking down the passageway. That was the night she died. I am her eldest grandchild.

1937, a windswept Eva looks out over the Atlantic Ocean
'… The best photo taken of that trip is one of Eva herself standing in West Cork, looking out across the Atlantic Ocean, hair windswept, and no doubt thinking of her Canadian Wallace family across the ocean, not of any Murphy family nearby.'

19.
VIOLET CONSTANCE

October 19, 1887 – January 11, 1892

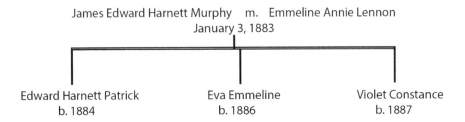

James Edward Harnett Murphy   m.   Emmeline Annie Lennon
January 3, 1883

Edward Harnett Patrick
b. 1884

Eva Emmeline
b. 1886

Violet Constance
b. 1887

The day Violet was born was a wonderful one for Emmeline Annie. Her new baby was the most beautiful she had ever seen. With a shock of black, wavy hair, creamy white skin, and eyes of a vivid blue, Violet looked unlike any Lennon before her, and her mother thought she came straight from the wilds of West Cork. Emmeline Annie decided this baby was a flower, and named her accordingly.

But Violet was delicate, and soon a nurse was hired to care for her, to watch over her. The rectory was a busy household, in a few months Emmeline Annie was pregnant again and Nurse Hattie cared for the baby – and talked of nothing else.

By this time, two of the Fitzgerald girls had settled into the rectory – Blackie and Chota, carrying TB, coughing all the time and unable to play much, their breathing and energy levels being very poor.

In 1887, when Violet was a baby, the children at the rectory were:

Chota 16
Blackie 12
Edwy 3
Eva 1
Violet a few months

Any memories Eva had of these years, while Violet was alive, would have been amongst her earliest memories, when she was brushed aside by everyone and everything. Later in life, in her seventies, she said she had been intensely jealous of her baby sister Violet.

Predictably, Violet soon was infected with TB. Perhaps one of the Fitzgerald girls leaned over the charming babe and coughed. No one would have noticed. In spite of Emmeline Annie's renowned nursing skills, Violet's condition grew worse. By Christmas 1891, Violet was struggling and had developed a touch of meningitis. She died soon afterwards.

Eva said, 'The day Violet died, something in Grannie Mary Lucas Lennon died also.' Perhaps Mary recognised how Violet had become infected.

Emmeline Annie's granddaughter, Daphne, remembered Emmeline Annie still grieving in her eighties for her little girl with the lovely, curly black hair.

20.
CHARLES HOMAN MURPHY

February 2, 1889 – October 25, 1966

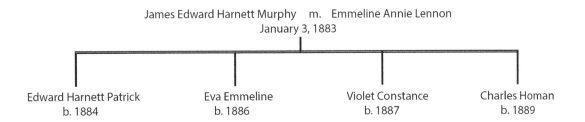

James Edward Harnett Murphy   m.   Emmeline Annie Lennon
January 3, 1883

| Edward Harnett Patrick | Eva Emmeline | Violet Constance | Charles Homan |
| b. 1884 | b. 1886 | b. 1887 | b. 1889 |

Charles Homan Murphy was named after his grandfather, Emmeline Annie's Newcastle father, Charles Homan Lennon, who died the year Charlie was born.

In the summer of 1891, Reverend James Murphy had offered to take care of the Church of Ireland parish on Achill Island, staying in the rectory while the rector took a holiday. This time, both he and Emmeline Annie thought it would be a healthy way for their four children to spend a few weeks by the seaside. They were thinking especially of Violet, whose TB was causing concern. Rev Murphy had already been out on Achill for a few weeks, when in July, Emmeline Annie, along with Nurse Hattie and the four Murphy youngsters, set out by train for Westport, in County Mayo. They could catch the train from Dublin at the Enfield train station, and travelling on the Midland Great Western Railway, they would have passed through Mullingar and on to the West.

On reaching Westport, they were met by a pony and trap sent from Achill to meet them. The drive to the Achill Rectory was forty miles, and the trap was open style. Rain poured down on them the whole way. They were soaked through. There was a rug on the seat of the trap to wrap around their knees for warmth, but instead, Emmeline Annie threw it over the children, who remembered water dripping off the rug's edges and trickling down their backs for hours. Let's hope Nurse Hattie somehow managed to keep the sickly Violet dry. They reached the rectory late that night.

Next morning, the children saw the sea for the first time, and there would have been sunny days spent on the beach, digging in the sand, splashing in the sea, and picnicking at mealtimes. The rectory was a ten-minute walk from the beach.

Violet was delicate, and took all of Nurse Hattie's time. Charlie was a baby, cared for full-time by Emmeline Annie. Eva was jealous and years later declared she had felt absolutely miserable on Achill Island.

When it came time to go home, a carriage with long side seats was offered by a parishioner for the return trip to Westport to catch the Dublin train. Two horses pulled them along, one horse being blind. A lovely late-summer day, Emmeline Annie sat with Charlie on her knee, and when Charlie needed to 'spend a penny', she held him out so he could do so over the side, as the carriage continued to move along.

When Charlie was eleven or so, about 1900, he was very ill, another victim of TB. But Charlie was a big-boned, robust, vigorous child and could fight off the disease. He could not go to school, where children with TB were not welcome, so he stayed home alongside his older brother, Edwy, and was taught mostly by his father. Three governesses came at various times, but none stayed for long. The TB did linger, however, settling in glands in Charlie's neck. Subsequently, during the First World War, he wore a band on his arm which said 'medically unfit', wearing it even in Ireland. Later on, after working abroad, he returned home briefly, 'to have his neck glands fixed'.

As a boy of fourteen, Charlie rode his first motorcycle around Enfield, Co. Meath, though he was not yet old enough to hold a licence under the new law, the Road Traffic Act. Living in the countryside and the son of the local clergyman, no one would challenge the lad.

Charlie was as bright and quick as his siblings, and he entered Trinity College, Dublin University, in 1907, graduating with a degree in engineering, a BAI, in 1911, when he was twenty-two. He immediately became active as an architect in Dublin.

Charlie's cousin, James Ross, eleven years his senior, had been out to Canada on a trip, and had returned to Ireland in the same year Charlie graduated, in 1911. James regaled his Irish family with tales from Canada. Then, James married in January 1912, and the newlyweds returned almost immediately to Edmonton, north of Calgary, where James had a job as a solicitor (called a lawyer in Canada). Through all of this, James had got on very well with Charlie – indeed, who didn't? Now, James wrote glowing accounts back to Charlie, who decided to set out on a trip to Canada on his own, hoping to serve out his engineering apprenticeship there. The following tells the tale:

Names and descriptions of British passengers embarked on the Ship **Oceanic**, *White Star Line, at the port of Queenstown. Departing April* 17th *1913, bound for New York:*

Chas H Murphy, 1 adult, 2nd class, Gentleman, Age 24, no wife, country of destination: Canada

He had no idea what he had started. At first, Charlie got a job in the city of Calgary, levelling roads. Then he went up to Edmonton, knowing his Cousin James Ross was up there, and this time, Charlie obtained surveyor work. The head office for Dominion Surveying was in Calgary, and Charlie decided to seek out office work there. Perhaps his neck glands were causing him some pain, and a consultant doctor was in Calgary.

At this time, Eva travelled out to Calgary, knowing that her dear brother Charlie would take care of her. When she arrived, Charlie had been in Canada for a year. He was working as an engineer for surveyors of the Federal Government and his boss was JN Wallace, who was in charge of the Calgary office, the western office of the Dominion Surveyors of Canada. No doubt, JN liked the look and sound of Charlie, fresh from Dublin, JN's birthplace, and a recent graduate of JN's alma mater, TCD. These connections counted for a lot in those days, when phone calls were too expensive, made only after a crisis such as a death in the family, and when letters between Canada's West and Dublin took weeks, if not months, to arrive. Besides, Charlie had the Lennon charm in spades, and could talk *the hind leg off a donkey*. He would have made great company, passing the time on a surveying expedition or over a cup of tea in the office, full as he was of stories, anecdotes, jokes, and literary quotes.

The following year, in January, Charlie dashed back to Dublin for three weeks, to have a neck operation, which may have involved removal of some lymph nodes. He returned as fast as he could, to find his sister Eva was now almost engaged to his boss. On his return to Calgary, he and Eva decided they should start a house together in April, in a suburb of Calgary called Parkdale. Charlie was now fully fit again, and he spent weeks and then months at a time

This Articles sheet, Form B, shows the agreement reached between Charlie and J.N. in Calgary on February 10, 1915. The sheet is signed by both J.N. and Charlie

out in the field working for JN. Eva took care of the house until she got married, August 18, 1915. Charlie came in from the bush specially to give Eva away at the altar. They all went to the Palliser Hotel for a lunch reception, which consisted of a special menu *à la Rathcore,* Charlie having made up and specially ordered the dishes.

In 1917, World War I was still going on, and Charlie received his affidavit from Dominion Land Surveyor, E. W. Berry, which stated:

> 'Chas H. Murphy always conducted himself with all due diligence, honesty and sobriety with me in the field on surveys.'

But Charlie always was, first and foremost, an Irishman. His heart was back with the Old Country. Having completed his apprenticeship, he left Canada and returned to Dublin in 1917, where he worked on munitions. Shortly afterwards, he was transferred to Ipswich in England, not far from London, for further munitions work. Everyone would have been relieved to have him home, safe, at the end of the Great War.

Charlie's father died in 1919, and Charlie was a great support to his mother, Emmeline Annie, who was now glad to have possession of Dunroe, on the seafront at Skerries. All her possessions had to be moved from Rathcore, the new rector needing to take up residence there as soon as possible. Dunroe became the family home. Charlie lived there for the next few years. His business card is reproduced below:

> **CHARLES H. MURPHY**
> B.A., B.A.I.
>
> *Architect, Engineer & Surveyor*

He was picking up any jobs he could get, but it would have been difficult with the economy in chaos after the War. A favourite story goes that in 1923 he was on the train

from Dublin to Skerries one day. Everyone on that train would have been chatting to each other, and Charlie, especially, would have known them all. Someone in the carriage compartment quoted from an ad in the *Irish Times:* 'I see they're looking for a Secretary for the new Automobile Association they have started.' Charlie jumped off the train at the next station and took the first returning train back to Dublin. He got the job. Thus began a career to which he was superbly fitted and where he remained for forty years until his retirement. He knew Ireland in a way few are privileged to know it. The

Automobile Association stars for excellence were in jeopardy every time he walked into a hotel. One could see the maids scurrying to fix up the rooms the minute his shadow fell on the lintels. But he commanded respect and love and was known in every town in the 'Free State'.

During his career with the AA he was the constant champion of the motorist's rights, and helped to pioneer the association's signposting scheme in the twenties. He also encouraged the government to facilitate the temporary importation of cars. In 1938, a newspaper clipping of an article written about Charlie states:

> There are few more eloquent advocates of "safety first" than Charles Homan Murphy, Irish Secretary of the Automobile Association – whose description incidentally seems to cause a great deal of confusion; for he is often mentioned as "Secretary of the Irish A.A." or some other non-existent organization. At Rotary gatherings and meetings of traffic and tourist bodies he is regarded as the great authority on motoring questions, which is as it should be. Since his present appointment in 1923, he has worked hard to develop the A.A. in Ireland.
>
> He has a remarkable knowledge of places and people, and can be a most amusing companion when he really gets going.

By 1927 he was architect to the Church of Ireland Diocese of Meath, and also to the united Dioceses of Dublin, Glendalough, and Kildare, a position he held until at least 1951. He was a very keen lay-member of the Church of Ireland. He was responsible for all the Church of Ireland buildings in those dioceses, and if he was going down to inspect a rectory or a church, he would take a family member with him for company. He knew all the clergy, and had a lot of lore. He was a great character, and people would remember having met him. In fact, it seemed Charlie knew half of Ireland. He was a great talker, and at dinner he could be absolutely hilarious, telling story after story after story. A great raconteur.

Charlie was involved with the architectural plans for two structures known to many: (a) St. Andrews Church and parochial hall, in Dublin, in 1928, and (b) the new rectory in Athlone, in 1941.

In 1924, Charlie fell in love with a girl who had been born near Limerick, but who was working as a secretary in Dublin, and now living in Skerries. It is thought they noticed each other on the trains between Skerries and Dublin. Walking to the train station each morning was a trial for the girls going to work, as the boys used to tease them with a shout: 'Here comes the train. Hurry! You're going to miss it!' The girls would be wearing tight skirts and high heels, and would have had to cross over the railway, up steep steps, and down again on either side of the footbridge. Charlie was always an expert at this kind of *divilment* and would have stood out and been commented on. Ada Massy Royse, known at this time as Amy Royse, certainly noticed Charlie. They were married in Holmpatrick Church in Skerries on September 6, 1924. One of the signatories of the register was a younger sister of Charlie's, Olive Murphy. And Olive decided the mix of names *Ada-Massy-Royse* to give *Amy* was objectionable, so Olive decided to call her *Amos*. For some reason, that name prevailed, and, after that, Amy was always called *Amos* in the Murphy family.

Amos and Charlie lived first at Dun Laoghaire, until 1929, at #1 Royal Terrace. But, house prices were depressed at this time, and shrewd Charlie longed for a big house with an estate. He had his eye on a place near Malahide. Ada Smith, an aunt of Amos from Limerick, offered to help them buy a house and a car, if in return she could live with them. When she died, Charlie and Amos received her share. So Charlie went out and bought *Auburn* for £2 000 (and many years later he sold it for £22 000, and now it might be worth £2 million!). Fields surrounded Auburn on all sides, farming became Charlie's hobby, and there was a magnificent walled garden in two parts, with a charming gate between the vegetable section and the flower garden. He brought Amos out to view his purchase, in 1933, and she was horrified at the isolated remoteness of it. She shuddered at its size. However, she grew to love the place, and they lived in the 'Big House' until 1958, when they built a bungalow in a field in the corner of the property, and sold off the rest.

Charlie and Amos had two sons, the elder named after his father and great-grandfather, Charles Homan Lennon, and always known in the family as *Harry*. He became an engineer. The second, named after his great-grandfather *Edward*, carried on his father's tradition, becoming the managing director of the Scottish and Northern Irish branch of the Automobile Association. For this work, Edward was awarded an OBE[60] by the Queen.

---

60 ***OBE:*** The Most Excellent Order of the British Empire is a British order of chivalry, rewarding contributions in several categories, and with Edward it was for public service outside the civil service. It was established on June 4, 1917, by King George V.

Charlie and Amos

Both Charlie and Amos were avid golfers, and at various times each was captain, even vice-president of the Malahide Golf Club, a well-known links course. Their names are displayed on the walls of the clubhouse.

One niece wrote:

> Charlie and Amos affected so many of our lives that I feel inadequate to write about them; especially Charlie. I remember how he helped my sister Daphne and her husband Donald Wormell strike a deal for their new house, of the good cheer we all imbibed at Christmas time, how he arranged with the rest of the Murphys for my mother, Eva Wallace, to fly home to Ireland after her illness, the countless times he arranged sailing tickets, bookings, advice and comfort to all of us.
>
> His son, Harry often refused invitations from his father for lunch at the University Club, the reason being that the distance from the AA office to the University Club was about a third of a mile. Charlie's 'buddying' as his son called it, meant that it took an hour and a half to arrive at the Club.
>
> For myself, I remember being tapped on the shoulder at Holyhead, when, at three-thirty in the morning, waiting to board the ferryboat to cross the Irish Sea and scarcely able to stand from weariness, I queued with nothing to declare, at the Customs Post. "Are you Mr. Murphy's niece? Then follow me." Miraculously, I was whisked up the gang-plank and safely aboard before I knew it.
>
> Or the time I walked with a friend into the ferry terminal at Malmo in the south of Sweden, having hitch-hiked for days down the peninsula

from Stockholm. We were tired and footsore, worrying about money exchange, totally isolated, as we hadn't seen anyone or anything in over a month to remind us of home. As we entered the building a lady came forward, hand outstretched and in broken English said, "You must be Mr. Murphy's niece." Surely Dr. Livingstone could have felt no more surprise. It was all the more remarkable since Charlie, to my knowledge, had never set foot in Sweden."

Eva's grandson said:

Auburn was a huge house. It was just wonderful to go out there, partly because, having no family car, to travel to Auburn was a long journey, all by bus. From the South, we went into the city, across the city and then out to Malahide. We loved those trips.

Before Mum and Dad were married, and when they were dating, they went out to stay with Charlie and Amos for a few days. They offered to go and pick some gooseberries in the garden. Charlie announced, "Daphne and Don are going out to pick gooseberries, and they don't want any human gooseberries to go along too."

Charlie was very generous. Whenever Dad went out to visit, Charlie would give him all sorts of vegetables, food, fruit, lots and lots of things, just for nothing. And he was always very caring. I think people in those days were more generous and more giving, and kinder, than we are these days.

It seems our generation, today, is the most greedy, selfish generation. Charlie's generation had very little, they had no money. But there was a certain *joie-de-vivre* in Ireland, they enjoyed themselves. It was infectious, it spread around. We loved to go to Auburn as children. They were very hospitable, always.

Charlie died in England on October 25, 1966, when he was seventy-seven. He was buried in the Sutton graveyard, in Dublin. Amos lived on for another nine years, dying on November 12, 1975. She was buried with her Charlie in Dublin.

Charlie and Amos were sorely missed by relatives; their presence in our lives had been huge and they are well remembered in stories told of them, ever since.

Charlie Murphy standing by the front steps of Rathcore Rectory
An iconic family photograph of one Murphy who successfully managed to overcome his childhood.
Every Christmas, Charlie sent out family updates of Newcastle Lennon and Rathcore Murphy news.
(Co. Kerry was never mentioned.) These typed out pages were mailed with Christmas Greetings to India,
Australia, Canada, the Middle East, the United States, South Africa, and around the British Isles, wherever
Lennon and Murphy relatives had settled.
A treasure trove for a family historian.

149

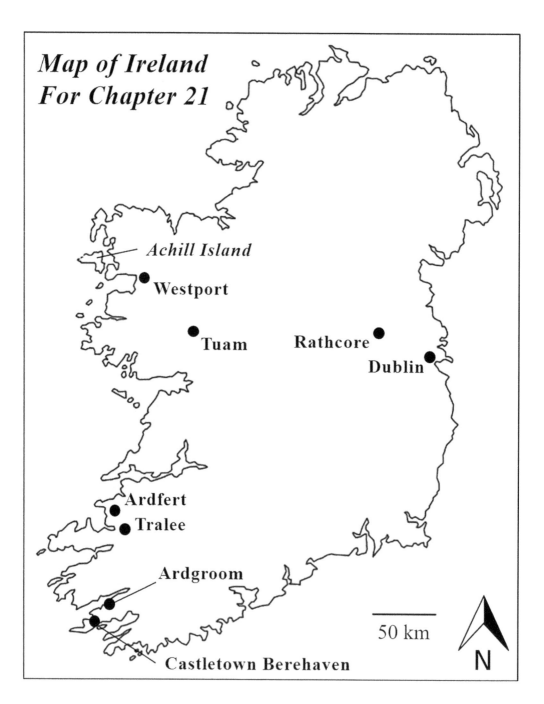

Map 5

21.
ACHILL ISLAND

A: HISTORY OF ACHILL ISLAND

Achill Island is the largest island in Ireland, being 148 km² or 24km x 19km, in area.

Today, it is accessible from the mainland by bridge. Its magnificent sandy beaches, sea cliffs, and warm hospitality bring many visitors. The resident population is about 1 700.

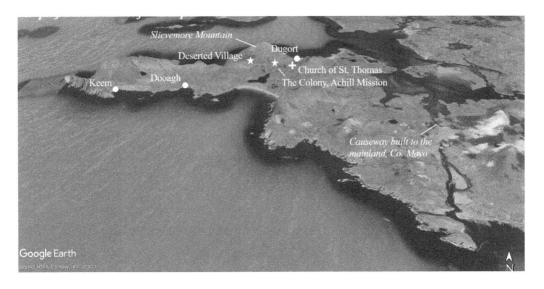

Map 6

One of Achill's most famous historical sites is that of the Achill Mission or 'the Colony' at Dugort. In 1831, the Protestant Reverend Edward Nangle founded a proselytising Mission at Dugort. The Mission included schools, cottages, an orphanage, a small hospital, and a hotel. A village was built of about eighty stone cottages, each dwelling consisting of one room only, which was used as kitchen, living room, bedroom, and shelter for animals too. The Colony was very successful for a time and regularly produced a newspaper called the *Achill Missionary Herald*.

After Nangle moved off the island, the Achill Mission slowly began to decline and was finally closed in the 1880s. Edward Nangle died in 1883.

Beyond Dugort today, at the base of Slievemore Mountain lie the ruins of the village, known as the 'Deserted Village'. Lazy beds and stone-walled fields can still be seen all around the village site.

The Mission, near Dugort
The Mission village in its heyday

In July 1847, Achill's total population was estimated at 7 000, of which about 5 000 were receiving famine relief from the Mission. The Mission also planted twenty-one tonnes of blight-free foreign potatoes, and the Colony became the food distribution centre for the island. In November 1848, the barque *William Kennedy*, delivered 220 tonnes of Indian meal to Achill from Philadelphia, enough to feed 2 000 people. The cost of £2 200 was paid out of mission funds collected in England. In 1848, about 3 000 people were working for the Mission, clearing land and building roads and walls. Nangle and his Mission are credited with saving Achill during the Famine, for without them, thousands might have starved. Hopes were expressed that Achill might soon become a Protestant island. This was the zenith of the Mission's fortunes. Author Theresa McDonald wrote in *Achill Island*, 2006 (*p. 163*):

> [In 1849] Divine service was now being celebrated in Dugort, and three other centres, and plans were being advanced to open another station for preaching the gospel in Duagh (Dooagh) … Eight Protestant clergymen were employed in Achill, five churches had been constructed, another was in progress, and there were five stations where divine service was celebrated.

For many years people had thrived in the village but the Famine did eventually ravage the population, as it had in much of the West of Ireland. Many Islanders emigrated. Others moved beside the sea, to the nearby settlement of Dooagh where fish and shellfish were easily accessible. Soon, the village was completely abandoned, and today it is known as the *Deserted Village*.

No one has lived in the village houses since the time of the Famine, but the families that moved to Dooagh, and their descendants, continued to use the site as a *booley village*. During the summer season, younger members of families, teenage boys and girls, would take the cattle to summer graze on the hillside and they would stay in the house ruins of the *Deserted Village*. This custom of *booleying*, not unique to Achill, continued until the 1940s.

However, the Achill Mission settlement had become the focal point for one of the most bitter religious conflicts in nineteenth-century Ireland. Religious coercion by the Achill Mission during the Famine, when Catholics were encouraged to deny their faith, to become Protestants, in return for food and for education for their children, has been rumoured. The conflict was greatest between Protestant Rev Edward Nangle and the Roman Catholic Archbishop John MacHale, a fierce opponent of the proselytising movement. MacHale had been appointed Archbishop of Tuam in 1834 and now the battle was on for the souls of Achill Island! Archbishop MacHale denounced the Mission's activities, making highly-charged visits to Achill, setting up schools adjacent to those of the Mission, and urging island clergy to act against Mission activities.

B: THE MURPHY FAMILY ON ACHILL ISLAND

With less than 5% of the population of the Republic of Ireland being Protestant, it is only natural that the community of the Church of Ireland has always been tightly knit. Everyone seems to know everyone else. Inter-marrying has been endemic. Those who know how everyone is related, how the jigsaw fits together, tell the best stories at social gatherings.

One of the parishioners in Rathcore parish when Reverend James Murphy was the rector there was a Mrs Fitzgerald, connected to the Fitzgeralds from Kerry. She herself was widow of a County Carlow Church of Ireland minister, Rev Joseph Fitzgerald, who at thirty-three had died, possibly of TB. He had left his wife with two young boys to raise. One of these was Richard Fitzgerald, who had married sixteen-year-old Henrietta Lennon, an older sister of Emmeline Annie. Mrs Fitzgerald had 'private money', and Richard had no trouble purchasing a commission, to serve with the British Army in India. But Richard had contracted TB as a child, likely from his father, and he, too, died young, serving out in India [See Appendix II].

Now a widow, Henrietta had left two of her four children with their grandmother, Mrs Fitzgerald, to raise as best she could. This grandmother's household was stuffy and rigid, and not long after arriving, these two girls were sent to re-unite with their sisters at Newcastle House. They, too, went on to live at Rathcore Rectory. The Murphys were now linked to this Fitzgerald family. Perhaps the care of the girls brought in a little bit of cash to help pay the food bills. Never discussed, of course, but managed discreetly, quietly on the side.

However, for Rev James Murphy there was another link with the Fitzgerald family, and this dated back to James's childhood in Ardgroom. During the Famine, the rector in Ardgroom had an assistant, Michael Fitzgerald, who had started out there as a scripture reader. Michael was in Ardgroom, proselytising and converting for the Protestant cause. He was not ordained a deacon until thirty years old, in 1875, and in 1877 he was priested. He himself had come from a Roman Catholic family that had *jumped*, growing up not far away in Ardfert, north of Tralee, in Kerry. He must have known Eamon Murphy in Ardgroom, also a scripture reader and also a jumper, and perhaps he taught Eamon's son, James, as a boy.

Rev Michael Fitzgerald was based in Castletown Berehaven from 1875 until 1882. His next appointment was as Rector of St. Thomas's Church in Dugourt, Achill Island, just as the Achill Mission was closing down. This promotion would have suited Rev Michael, himself a native Irish speaker and a proselytiser. He stayed as rector from 1882 to 1897.

When it came to the summertime, and when Rev Michael needed to take a summer holiday, he remembered Eamon's son, now ordained. He asked Rev James Murphy to fill in. Rev James was the perfect choice: a native Irish speaker, also with Roman Catholic roots and interested in 'doing mission work', as he would have described it. Rev James spent maybe three weeks on Achill Island for several summers. He would stay in the rectory, and preach next door in the Church of St. Thomas, beside Dugort.

One of these years, 1891, when Rev James's youngest daughter Violet was growing weaker from TB, her parents thought the bracing sea air would do her good. So Emmeline Annie took her children and Violet's nurse on an excursion to the Achill Island seaside, to join the father and to stay at the rectory. This holiday was described by Eva, eldest daughter of Rev James and Emmeline Annie, as follows:

> We caught the train to Westport, Co. Mayo. We were met at the station by an Achill man with a horse and cart, and he took us the forty miles to the Rectory. We didn't arrive until very late at night, and it poured with rain the whole way. We covered ourselves as best we could with a rug, but there was water dripping down our backs. We were soaked through.

At the Rectory we had Nurse Hattie to care for Violet, who was three and was delicate. Edwy was six, Charlie was a toddler and I was in the middle of them all, at five years old. I remember the whole trip in great detail because I felt absolutely miserable the whole time. I was jealous of Violet, and got fed up with my brothers. Why couldn't Violet have been better as a sister?

Finally it was time to go home. For this return trip to Westport, the parishioners arranged for us to ride in *a longside car*, a larger, fancier cart, with the benches being sideways. And we were provided with two horses, one of which was blind. The weather was gorgeous that day, making the trip go even faster. Mother sat with Charlie on her knee, and when Charlie needed *to spend a penny*, she held him out as the car went along. I laughed so much on that ride, and I was happy at last. We were going home! When we got back to Rathcore, there was old Mrs. Fitz at the house to meet us, anxious for news of her relative's congregation in Achill.

Mrs. Fitz was the parishioner who came to Church every Sunday, driven by her son, and Father would spend a long time after each service talking to her, mostly about "Who's Who" and about Royalty. We would all leave them behind at the Church, talking away, and then, at home, we had to wait for him to return to the Rectory before we could have our Sunday Dinner.

One Sunday, the Old Lady was sick and she didn't come to Church. She sent a message to the church for Father to come and see her, immediately. So he set out for her house. Her son met Father with a shotgun, and wouldn't let Father go up the road to the house. Mrs. Fitz died two days later. She was buried as a Roman Catholic. Father went to the funeral service, and following that, he held another funeral service for her in his Protestant Rathcore Church.

Years later, three generations later, some of the great-grandchildren of Mary Fitzgerald erected a tombstone in her name on the site of the Newcastle Lennon and Rathcore Murphy plot in the graveyard of St. Ultan's Church of the parish of Rathcore, Co. Meath.

Tree for
Chapter 22. Geraldine Murphy

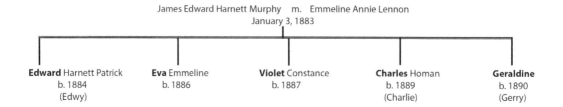

James Edward Harnett Murphy   m.   Emmeline Annie Lennon
January 3, 1883

Edward Harnett Patrick
b. 1884
(Edwy)

Eva Emmeline
b. 1886

Violet Constance
b. 1887

Charles Homan
b. 1889
(Charlie)

Geraldine
b. 1890
(Gerry)

22.
GERALDINE MURPHY

December 28, 1890 – September 11, 1939

Geraldine Murphy, third daughter and fifth child of James Edward Harnett Murphy and Emmeline Annie Lennon, showed early academic promise by teaching herself to read while hiding under the dining-room table at the age of four. She went on to become one of the earliest women graduates in medicine at Trinity College, Dublin.

Known in the family as *Gerry*, she was a bright and cheery child. Many told her she was 'the dark beauty' in the family, and Eva was 'the fair beauty'. Her father told everyone she looked just like one of her cousins living down in West Cork. They would never meet.

By this time, on a salary as a Church of Ireland Rector, Murphy was earning £220 per annum. It would be three more years before his appointment as a professor in Trinity College, Dublin, when his income would rise somewhat. He decided that a few students, all boys, should come to live at Rathcore, so they could join the children in the schoolroom for lessons. For these boys' parents it would be cheaper than boarding school, and it might do their sons good to be 'under the cane of a Reverend'. Some of these boys were pleasant, while others were very slow, with all kinds of special needs. The boys slept three in one bedroom, two in another.

Some of these boarders met tragic fates. One boy died from TB. The father of another was a lawyer and a stockbroker, but the boy was 'a bad type', who later went out to farm in Alberta. He attended a Farmers' Convention, and that night the place where he was staying on 9th Avenue, in Calgary, burnt up in fire, and he was frozen in his bed from the fire hose water! Back in his Rathcore days, 'that same character used to go to all kinds of straits to get whiskey into the house.' Then he sexually molested Geraldine when she was about seven years old. This was not the first time a Murphy girl had been assaulted by one of these boarding lads taking advantage.

Gerry went on to attend the boarding school 'Londonderry (Victoria) High School'. where all the Murphy girls boarded over the years, and did very well. Gerry was the only one of the girls to attend university – she studied medicine, part of only the second medical class to permit women students. She often spoke of the experience, of being one of a very small minority in the Medical School and of how the few women huddled together at lectures and in the anatomy room, where Geraldine fainted the first time she tried to dissect a corpse. She lived with the rest of the Trinity women students in Trinity Hall, the women's residence about two miles from the university. Here, a small and select band formed themselves into a club modelled on a family with designated roles for each member (father, mother, sisters, brothers, cousins, and so on). One of them was to marry the Dean of St Patrick's Cathedral, another a future Vice-Provost of Trinity College. Geraldine qualified in September, 1915. In the final year, the students did: 1) medicine; 2) surgery; and 3) obstetrics. She won the Gold Medal in Surgery in her final exam, the Medal for Surgery being the most prized medal, for surgery was the most difficult subject studied. Being top of the class was exceptional for a woman. She was fond of telling the story about how, several times before exams, she danced all night and then went into the examination still wearing her ball gown and without any sleep.

Upon graduation, and with World War I in full swing, she immediately joined up to serve as an officer in the Royal Army Medical Corps, based in Aldershot, England. Perhaps the establishment was not sure how to deal with a qualified woman doctor interested in helping in the war effort, and in January, 1916, her first appointment was as House Physician to the Chester Royal Infirmary. Her work there must have reassured her superiors, for in December 1916, Gerry was contracted to work as a *civilian surgeon* attached to the RAMC. Her salary was 24 shillings per day, a gratuity of £60 to be awarded at the end of the contract. On December 9, 1916, Gerry embarked for Malta, as part of the Women's Medical Unit, RAMC, and was assigned to the military hospital there, the same hospital where Vera Brittain, who wrote *Testament of Youth*, was serving as a VAD.[61]

---

61   **VAD:** The Voluntary Aid Detachment referred to a voluntary unit providing field nursing services, mainly in hospitals. The system was founded in 1909 with the help of the Red Cross and the Order of St. John. There were 74 000 VAD members in 1914, of which two-thirds were women and girls. *Testament of Youth* was made into a BBC television drama in 1979 and a motion picture in 2014.

Women doctors were classified as civilian surgeons attached to the RAMC. Women serving as fulltime doctors in the Army and doing precisely the same work as their male colleagues, had neither rank nor status, receiving the same pay as temporary, commissioned male officers of the RAMC. Uniforms were not introduced until after April, 1918.

The casualties from operations in Gallipoli (April 25, 1915 – January 9, 1916) and Salonica (October, 1915 – September 30, 1918) were initially treated in Malta and Egypt; but in 1917, submarine attacks on hospital ships made it unsafe to evacuate from Salonica. Five hospitals were then mobilized from Malta for service in Salonica, but Gerry was kept in Malta.

Between August 1916, and July 1917, eighty-two lady doctors served in war hospitals in Malta. They worked alongside their male RAMC colleagues and carried out all but administrative duties.[62]

On February 22, 1918, Gerry was moved to a similar hospital in Egypt, serving there until May 9, 1919, when demobilisation was occurring. She was officially demobilised on May 27, 1919, receiving the Victory Medal, for services as 'Lady Doc. Hosp'.

Anaesthetics were in full use in World War I, chiefly chloroform and ether. However, supplies were not always available. But, there were always difficulties with secondary, often fatal infections setting in, one of the greatest challenges for all doctors working with wounded soldiers at that time. The first antibiotic, penicillin, was discovered in 1928, by Alexander Fleming.

While in Egypt, Gerry discovered she had some psychic powers that took the form of dreaming who was to be the winner of the horse race scheduled for the next day. Partly for this reason, but more especially because she was such an outgoing person, Geraldine was very popular amongst the staff, but she reserved her affections for a young Irish naval commander, Richard Chevenix Fleury, who declared he was serving on a torpedo boat destroyer, and was known henceforth to Geraldine and in the family as *TBD*. One of Gerry's nephews would later report: 'Chenevix was Gerry's gallant man: he was a TBD! In fact, he had nothing to do with a destroyer at all. He was actually involved with the Intelligence of the Royal Navy, and the TBD story was his cover.'

TBD was born in Kilworth, a village a couple of miles north of Fermoy in north Co. Cork, on April 10, 1887. His father was a Church of Ireland minister from Kinsale, near Cork in Southern Ireland; his mother came from Co. Fermanagh in Northern Ireland. Before he was eighteen years old, TBD had entered the service as an Assistant Clerk on board the *Implacable*. In the next four years he had to write exams and there

---

62   See "British Army Medical Services and the Malta Garrison, 1799 – 1979" *maltaramc.com*.

were reports on his conduct and his ability. He was described as a 'promising young officer' and was 'recommended for employment as a Secretary Clerk', which may have been code for intelligence work. He was also passing exams for *Paymaster 1st Class*. Apart from a couple of months' sick leave, having been diagnosed with anaemia when he was twenty-two, his career was flying high: 'zealous, capable, hardworking, promises very well', were all reports on his record. In March and April, 1911, he was on board the *Bulwark* as Secretary's Clerk to Vice-Admiral Prince Louis of Battenburg. Then he was posted to Africa for an additional assignment with King Edward VII, followed by a posting as Secretary's Clerk to Admiral Hamilton. Following on, he was on the staff of various Royals and of Admirals, and his reports state: 'Has good judgement, is excellent at performing the difficult job of demobilizing officers, capable, loyal, reliable, zealous, considerable tact, common sense.' An Admiral wrote: 'During the War, his duties have been very varied and arduous – and he has performed them throughout with great ability and in every respect to my satisfaction.'

In 1919, he was formally assigned as *special service,* and was sent from London to Bombay on 'Government work', and this is when TBD may have met Geraldine Murphy, en route in Egypt. TBD was thirty-two, and Geraldine was twenty-eight. They became engaged, and then parted ways again – TBD continuing as instructed, beyond Bombay to a posting in Japan.

Returning to Gerry's story, we find on October 17, 1919 on her record: 'Miss G. Murphy, departing for St. John, N.B., Canada, from Liverpool on board *Empress of France.*' Gerry continued to travel across Canada by train, and she had planned a couple of days' stopover in Calgary to see her dear sister Eva and to meet her brother-in-law JN and their four-year-old daughter, and also to take time to write a report back to their mother, Emmeline Annie, as to the health of Eva, who was expecting her second child any moment. Most unfortunately, Gerry's train was delayed several days. Heading by train for Vancouver, where she was booked onboard a ship to take her over to her TBD in Japan, Gerry couldn't take the risk of missing her boat, which would have made her sailing ticket invalid. A very pregnant Eva, at home in Bowness with a four-year-old, could not get to the Calgary Train Station. Eva's distress must have been great, but JN offered to leave his office and go sit for a few moments with Gerry on the train. When the train finally pulled in there was a bad scene on the train: JN anxious to give advice and Gerry very agitated at missing her sister; Gerry talking at high speed, concerned about her ticket being wasted in Vancouver, and JN, deaf, unable to keep up with her words. When JN finally got home that evening, he was in a state of high irritability!

Gerry did catch her boat in Vancouver, and she and TBD were married in Yokohama on February 4, 1920.

Richard Chenevix Fleury and Geraldine Murphy, in Japan, at the time of their marriage.

They were both expecting to leave on a return trip to England, passage having been bought and their names drawn up on the passenger list. However, at the very last minute, TBD had to remain behind, intelligence work demanding he stay, and his name on the passenger list is crossed out. Gerry made the return trip alone, again travelling across Canada by train, and boarding the ship *Canada* in Montreal, sailing for Liverpool. She arrived on June 21, 1920. There is no record of her having met up with Eva on this trip either, but perhaps Gerry managed a phone call from the Calgary Station.

TBD was back at Headquarters in London by July 1920, so Gerry did not have too long to wait for them to be reunited. TBD was now appointed as an Admiralty Assistant Liaison Officer, and he was spending time also in the Government Code and Cypher School. He is also listed as a *Paymaster Lt. Commander.*

Perhaps TBD was growing weary of the fast pace of life in the Navy. Perhaps he wanted a more leisurely style of living, and needed to spend more time at home. There is no doubt they were both exhausted from their war experiences. Geraldine persuaded her husband to retire on pension. They lived for some leisurely years in Sunbury-on-Thames, until a surfeit of leisure convinced them that it would be advisable to commute

TBD's pension for a lump sum and to buy a haulage business, based on the Thames in Oxfordshire. There they had an attractive house on the river called 'The Warren', where many of the Murphy family received warm hospitality. They soon designed and built their own house in Long Crendon, nearby, but sadly the Depression caught up with them, the haulage business dwindled to nothing, and they found themselves practically penniless.

Their niece who knew them both well, Daphne (Wallace) Wormell, eldest child of Gerry's sister Eva, wrote in 1982:

> They told me afterwards that they were actually hungry at this time; they borrowed where they could and started job-hunting. TBD applied for any kind of work, including sweeping the streets, and did eventually find an opening in the London Army and Navy Stores, where he was responsible for outfitting ships' companies who were being posted abroad.
>
> Meanwhile, Geraldine had decided to return to medicine. She went to Dublin for a three months' refresher course at the Meath Hospital under the auspices of her brother, Dr. Cyril Murphy. She was then appointed as dispensary doctor in a rundown area of Stoke Newington in London. The house assigned to the doctor had formerly belonged to the Rothschild family, and for an urban dwelling, it still had a remarkably large and agreeable garden, which much pleased two such ardent gardeners as they were. The Depression was still at its height when I visited them there, and the experience of walking round the streets with Geraldine and observing the outward scene while she visited her patients was an eye-opener even to me who had seen the effects of unemployment in Canada in the Depression of the thirties.
>
> Geraldine was a very warm and humorous person, and was loved and respected by her poor patients. She also got much amusement from their remarks and attitudes. I recall her account of the little man formally dressed, who swept off his bowler hat, a derby, as she entered the room, bowed low to her, and said, "Madam, would you attend to my bowels?"
>
> But war-clouds were already gathering, and in 1939, just before the outbreak of hostilities, the Admiralty approached TBD and asked him to take up the intelligence work he had been engaged in during

the First World War in *Room 11*. He was put in charge of codes and cyphers based at Mansfield College, Oxford. Geraldine's health, never robust since an illness in 1924, had deteriorated further, and they thought it wise for her to leave the uncertain conditions of war-time England. She went to Dublin, where she stayed with her brother Cyril and his bride Maureen. She was now suffering from headaches. One evening, Cyril and Maureen went to the theatre, and on their return home, they discovered Gerry in a coma. At the early age of forty-six she had suffered a brain haemorrhage from which she did not recover. I was to have spent the next few days with her in 15 Lower Fitzwilliam Street, when Maureen and Cyril had planned to go on a brief holiday.

TBD came over for the funeral which took place to Rathcore cemetery. The epistle appointed for the Sunday nearest, had the words: "I thank my God upon every remembrance of you," and these words TBD later had inscribed on her tombstone, little realizing that within eighteen months he himself was to have a heart attack and would shortly join her. Appropriately, their joint grave bears the legend: *Reunited*.

They were a very affectionate and hospitable couple; it was a great sadness to them that they had no family. But they maintained their love of children (and of dogs), and Geraldine was known among her nieces and nephews as a very caring aunt. Every year a parcel would arrive for the children of Eva and JN in Canada containing Christmas presents for all seven of us; when they had little or no money, these took the form of carefully handmade garments of one kind or another.

Geraldine was gifted in many areas. From her mother she inherited a great interest in domesticity and in music. Her sister, Olive, said she could make a piano speak. She was an inveterate talker with a quick ear for an anecdote or an amusing phrase. She also had boundless energy. I remember her, even when she was quite ill, sitting up in bed, hooking a rug.

Above all she had an endearing warmth of personality and interest in people. TBD once told me that the surprise of his life was that he fell in love with, and married, a woman doctor. He wrote in my autograph album when I was eight years old the words from Charles Kingsley: "Be good sweet maid and let who will be clever" (see below), so one can imagine what his reaction would have been to Women's Lib. It is a measure of what we would today call "Gerry's charisma" that TBD fell in love with one of the earliest supporters and practitioners of the suffragette movement.

A Farewell

Charles Kingsley (1819–1875)

My fairest child, I have no song to give you;
No lark could pipe to skies so dull and grey:
Yet, ere we part, one lesson I can leave you
For every day.

Be good, sweet maid, and let who will be clever;
Do noble things, not dream them, all day long:
And so make life, death, and that vast for-ever
One grand, sweet song.

Geraldine Murphy
This spectacular photograph only recently came to light. Running across it were many cracks and creases. Somebody had crushed it deep down in her handbag. 'Any chance of a fix-up?' was the query which flashed from London, UK, over the Atlantic and across the States to Canby, Oregon, to the computer of Wallace Cousin, Brenda Gundersen. A wizard with Photoshop, Brenda managed the restoration job, done to perfection, and in record time. In the return email Brenda wrote: 'Gerry looks to be a sturdy sort of frontier woman – was she?' Considering Gerry's life, that just about sums her up!

DUBLIN FAMILY OF DOCTORS

PROFESSOR'S FIVE CHILDREN
M. O. DAUGHTER
"Daily Express" Special Correspondent.[63]
THAME (Oxfordshire), Tuesday.

A young, attractive woman doctor sat in an armchair before a fire in her study here today and roared with laughter when I suggested that she had made history.

Then she became serious and – a faint smile hovering on her lips – said: "Well, I can't help being one of a family of doctors, can I?"

She was Dr. Geraldine Fleury, the only university-educated daughter of the late Professor Murphy, of Trinity College, Dublin, four of whose sons are now doctors in various parts of the British Isles or the Empire.

Which is where "Dr. Geraldine" has made history.

England's Nearest

There is no other family in England – or probably in the world – where four sons and a *daughter* have all become doctors. The nearest England can go is a family where the four sons are doctors.

"I'm probably going to spoil your story," said Dr. Geraldine, her eyes twinkling maliciously, to me. "You see, I am not practising now. I had to give it up four years ago for reasons of health, so you can't say we are all diagnosing human ailments at the moment.

"Two of my brothers, however, have practices in Dublin, another is attached as Medical Officer to the Royal Air Force in India, and the fourth is a doctor in Prestatyn, North Wales."

"And yourself?" I asked, rather timidly.

"Well, doctoring is the most wonderful profession in the world," smiled back Dr. Geraldine. "It's so wonderful – and my own health is so much better that you can say that I shall probably be taking up a new practice in the very near future."

War Experiences

"A woman can make just as good a doctor as a man, and at times a better one. Woman doctors, you know," she added, "have come to stay."

---

63   Author's Note: Every effort has been made, unsuccessfully, to date and credit this newspaper clipping, found amongst family papers. Many cousins over many years have laboured in vain. It is not possible to write about Gerry Murphy's life and not include this wonderful interview. I would be delighted if the source could be identified and full credit given where due.

I asked Dr. Geraldine about her war experiences. She was for three years a Medical Officer attached to the Royal Army Medical Corps in Malta and Egypt.

"There's not much to say about that," she replied rather gravely. "The war was a horror, from the doctor's point of view, made only bearable by the amazing bravery of the men."

"You had to operate, then?" I hazarded, and she smiled tenderly.

"Of course – but –" she shook her head suddenly, and said quickly: "Let's talk of other things – of Dublin – dear, darling Dublin – or, of a cock grouse calling on the Wicklow hills."

23.
FREDERICK JOHN MURPHY

CB, CBE, MB, BCh, DPH, CStJ
(FRED or RUMTUM or RUMMER or PAT or SPUD)
September 25, 1892 – May 22, 1969

Frederick John Murphy, the third son and seventh child of James Murphy and Emmeline Lennon, was born September 25, 1892. He was outgoing, making a splash everywhere he went and with everything he did. Although he inherited the names of his great-uncle, Uncle Fred Lucas, the Church of Ireland minister, it is no wonder he was known by so many first names, for he was always the centre of attention, the life and soul of any gathering. People loved to be in his company, sharing jokes, laughing a lot, and thoroughly enjoying themselves. The nicknames they gave him were a sign of affection. The origin of *Rummer* or *Rumtum* is not known, but in the Murphy family he was always *Rummer* or *Uncle Rummer*, having grown out of the childhood nickname of *Rumtum*.

As a young boy, no doubt Rumtum was mischievous and unruly, and likely he received the worst end of the beatings doled out by his father. The most remarkable thing about him was that although his father was so hard on him, and in spite of his great successes, 'all for England', one might think he would become the one Murphy with the least Irish connections. In fact, he was the one who retained a noticeably Irish brogue until the end of his life.

One summer's Sunday afternoon, after Sunday dinner was finished, all the Rathcore children and their parents piled into the pony and trap and set off down the rectory's avenue on their way to visit the family of a neighbouring clergyman. They got to the gate, and when Rumtum did something naughty, his father announced: 'Rumtum being disobedient, we shall now return.' All very sad, especially for the parents who could have done with a break. Perhaps Rumtum could not bear sitting squished in the trap, being bumped around for an hour or so. Not long afterwards, the children were given a huge treat, perhaps organised by Uncle Edward Lennon or Rev Fred Lucas, up in Dublin. They were taken to the theatre, possibly a children's play of some kind. When they returned home, Rumtum declared 'he was going to go on the stage', and none of the children were ever taken to any theatre again.

Rummer was the first of the boys to be sent to the Abbey School in Tipperary, a school for post-primary students. Here he was well prepared for his next step – attendance at an Erasmus Smith School[64] in Drogheda. He did well, and went on to Trinity College, Dublin.

He graduated from TCD in medicine in 1916. His personal background found in RAF records, states in part:[65]

> 'This doctor was academically excellent, possessing a Bachelor of Arts, Bachelor of Medicine, Bachelor of Surgery, Bachelor of Obstetrics and Doctor of Public Health qualifications. He also spoke fluent French and Russian.'

Fred joined the RAMC[66] in Dundalk on August 25 as a Lieutenant. As part of the recruiting procedure he was asked, 'Are you able to ride?' He replied, 'I have hunted since childhood.' There were no hunting horses in the Murphy stables, but I am quite sure this simple response was the truth – what Rummer had been hunting was not fox or hare, and he had not been riding hunting horses! He was a quick learner.

His reference from A. Francis Dixon, School of Physic, TCD, dated July 19, 1916, notes: 'F. J. Murphy is clever, quick and steady. His conduct has always been excellent.' He received another reference from Dr Edward Lennon, and who was to know this was Rummer's uncle? It reads:

> Dr. Lennon presents his compliments to the Director General, Army Medical Service, relative to Dr. Frederick J. Murphy.

---

64 **Erasmus Smith:** (1611–1691) He was an English merchant and a landowner with possessions in England and Ireland. Having acquired significant wealth through trade and land transactions, he became a philanthropist in the sphere of education by creating an eponymous trust whereby some of his Irish property was used for the purpose of financing the education of children and providing scholarships for the most promising of those to continue their studies at Trinity College, Dublin.

65 Fred's RAF Record kindly provided by **Stuart Hadaway**, researcher and author.

66 **RAMC:** The Royal Army Medical Corps is a specialist corps in the British Army which provides medical services to all British Army personnel and their families in war and in peace. The RAMC is responsible for maintaining the health of servicemen and women, and is represented wherever British soldiers are deployed, providing medical support to operations, exercises and adventurous training expeditions all over the world. The RAMC was formed in 1898.

Dr. Murphy is a very capable surgeon. He was my clinical clerk at the Meath Hospital in Co. Dublin, and in the Co. Dublin Infirmary, and also a Resident Pupil. He has been a Resident Surgeon in England, where I believe he gave satisfaction in the discharge of his duties. He is thoroughly sober, clever and practical in his work and will fulfill any duties he may be called upon to discharge with efficiency and skill.

Dr. Murphy is a somewhat 'rough diamond' but nevertheless is genuine. His conduct and character merit all commendation.

22 Merrion Square.11 July, 1916

Rummer first went to Stockton-on-Tees as a Locum, and mid-August found him in Ripon. Now a Captain, Rummer was posted to Salonika, in Greece as a doctor. Early in 1918, he was suffering from synovitis in his right knee.[67] The medical report states: 'Initially injured at football about 1914, and aggravated while playing football again in Salonika. Trouble since at frequent intervals, unable to walk rough ground any distance. Aggravated further by marching, or riding a horse. Loose cartilage, operation not recommended.' On February 23, 1918, he 'embarked', arriving home on March 16, 1918. He immediately reported to Irish headquarters, which were based in Dublin Castle, where he was declared as 'unfit for service'. He applied for a six-month leave of absence, but received only three weeks, from April 27, 1918, to May 17, 1918. The day after his leave expired, on May 18, Rummer was *posted to Irish*, and on June 17, 1918, the Medical Board in Athlone has him listed as *Reserve Duty* on June 17, 1918.

With the approaching end of hostilities of World War I, and suffering with his knee, it would have been easy for Rummer to retire to a more leisurely way of life in the Irish countryside. But that wasn't his style at all, he loved adventure, and by the summer of 1918 he had applied for transfer to the Royal Flying Corps. On June 17, 1918, he was 'lent to the RFC', meaning he was seconded to the Royal Flying Corps, where he acted as Medical Officer to operational flying squadrons. The RFC had come into being on the March 13, 1912, and towards the end of World War I the RFC and the RNAS (the Royal Navy Air Service) had been joined together as the RAF.

In 1918, after formation of the Royal Air Force, he elected to transfer to that service, and so became one of the founding members of the RAF medical branch. On July 13, 1920, he officially relinquished his Army Commission, and received a commission in the Royal Air Force. Between the wars he served in Iraq, Egypt, and India as well as at a number of stations in the UK, and was, in fact, serving in Egypt and

---

67   Knee joints are surrounded by a synovial membrane which encapsulates the joint and lubricates it by secreting synovial fluid. This lining can become inflamed, causing pain and stiffness in the joint.

the Western Desert as Deputy Medical Officer, specialising in hygiene, when World War II began. He returned to Britain in 1942, and the following year was appointed Principal Medical Officer to the Second Tactical Air Force.

Air Vice-Marshall Frederick John Murphy c. 1936.
Wearing a black arm band due to the death of George V

He served during the Normandy landings and, following on, in Germany. He was responsible for the evacuation of the wounded during the invasion period, which included the evacuation of all the beaches on D-Day. His keenness and dedicated service during the war was recognised by the fact that he was mentioned in despatches three times.

One of Rummer's nieces noted:

> He was the first doctor into Belsen, Belsen being the first Concentration Camp the British went into. It was pretty bad, and apart from caring for survivors, his great concern was for the mental soundness of his soldiers. Rummer told me that he led his soldiers in, and his men went crazy. They were releasing all these skeletons.

> He said, "What we need to do is to set up a hospital." So Rummer went down to the Red Cross Hospital, which was closed, and where they didn't speak a word of English. He went over and he patted the sheets on the bed, to indicate he needed beds. And the Matron was terrified. "The Enemy had come!" She took off her clothes and jumped into the bed, thinking that was what the Commander wanted! Rummer told me he turned to his Junior Officer, and he said, "Now's your chance!"

The above account is so typical of Rummer – he would tell a story, the listener might wonder was it all true, and frequently the undertone would have a slight off-colour whiff to it. But he was always so interesting to listen to, one laughed till one's cheeks were sore when Rummer was present.

On November 9, 1947, the *Sunday Dispatch* stated:

> When the 2nd Tactical Air Force crossed to Normandy, in 1944, it included one very remarkable County Meath man, known throughout the RAF as "Spud" Murphy.

> He wore that broad ring of Air Commodore, and as principal Medical Officer of 2nd TAF, he arranged the evacuation of casualties (including army) by air. Right up to the last battles in Germany this system saved countless lives.

> This sturdy character now has another ring, and is principal Medical Officer of Technical Training Command.

> He has a passion for being out of doors, and spends nearly all his spare time fishing, game shooting or gardening.

After the war he became Principal Medical Officer of Bomber Command, and during 1947 – 48 held a similar position in Technical Training Command. For his last tour of duty in the Royal Air Force, he returned as Principal Medical Officer to the Mediterranean and Middle East Commands, where his early service had been spent, and he remained there until he retired from the Royal Air Force in 1951.

From the Irish Times, 1949, page 5:
An Irishman's Diary

From Egypt:

I have had quite a lot of news from Egypt this week. To begin with, I had a visit from my old friend and sparring partner, Air Vice-Marshall F.J. Murphy, who is boss of the RAF's medical services in the Middle East. Fred Murphy, who is a son of a former Professor of Irish in Trinity, has been nearly thirty-five years in the air service. He joined it immediately after he had been qualified in TCD, and served through two World Wars – not a bad record for a young fellow! At the moment he is stationed in Ismailia, but he has a medical staff of something like two hundred Air Force doctors to look after, and spends about a fortnight out of every month in the air, flying between Egypt and the Persian Gulf, hither and yon over the desert to the remotest Air Force stations.

After Fish:

He has been over here trying to kill unfortunate trout in the West—how is it that every distinguished medical man seems to take a delight in the massacre of these innocent little creatures—and he has been remarkably successful. His only complaint is that he did not contrive to kill a salmon.

Air Vice-Marshall Murphy, who will be retiring fairly soon—how I envy him his pension and his bright prospects afterwards—is a brother of Mr. Charlie Murphy of the Automobile Association, and Dr. Cyril Murphy of the Meath Hospital. I quite forgot to ask him if he still spoke Irish. His father, if I remember aright, was a native speaker: but I should imagine that life in the Middle East does not make very heavy claims on an Air Vice-Marshall's knowledge of our ancient tongue!

He was appointed CBE in 1946 and CB in 1949. He was appointed Honorary Surgeon to King George VI in 1947, and he held this appointment until his retirement from the Royal Air Force in 1951. After retiring, he served as a Medical Officer with the Ministry of Health until 1959.

Air Vice-Marshall Murphy was a fine all-round sportsman. He played hockey regularly for the RAF and captained the team for four successive years from 1925–28. From 1946–9 he acted as chairman of the RAF Hockey Association. He also represented the RAF at tennis, and for many years was a member of the golfing association.

At every step of Rummer's career, there are stories recorded. A favourite one in his family goes like this:

> Did you hear the story about Rummer at the hockey match? He played as captain for the RAF four years running. He was invited to play for England, and he refused because he was an Irishman. He was never invited to play for Ireland, because he was in the British Services.
>
> The British Interservices' teams were playing and the King arrived to watch the action. King George V came along the row of players, shaking their hands, and said to Rummer, "I believe you're an Irishman, Murphy!" Rummer replied, "Begorrah, I am, Sir!"
>
> And the next year, King George came along again, and said to Rummer, "Begorrah, how are you, Murphy?" We have no record of Rummer's reply, so perhaps, for once, he was speechless!

Rummer married twice, but had no children. His first wife was Margaret Vera Oliver, whom he married in 1924, a few years after joining the RAF.

Vera (née Oliver) Murphy

She it was who noticed that life was awkward for their niece, Daphne, Eva's eldest daughter, who was living with Rummer's youngest brother Cyril and running his household at the time of Cyril's marriage. Daphne had no money, but Vera saw the problem, and in 1939 provided money for Daphne to move to the Women's Residence of Trinity College, to Trinity Hall. Daphne remained most grateful, all her life.

Rummer's nephew recorded:

> Some members of the Murphy family felt Vera was a bit of a snob, without cause to be so. Did you know we had a relation called Sir Francis Knowles? He was a Master at Marlborough School. Sir Francis was a nice man. He was a Baronet. I met him once. His mother was Lady Knowles. And Vera was introduced to them without any titles being mentioned, and afterwards she heard that she had been talking to Sir Francis and Lady Knowles, and she was most upset. She hadn't realised their stature.

Vera died in her forties. On April 25, 1950, Air Vice-Marshal Murphy married Félice Grant McIntyre Mulholland, widow of Group Captain D.O. Mulholland, CBE, AFC. Félice was popular with some of Rummer's family, but others were not so fond of her: Here are some comments recorded:

> Félice and Rummer came to visit, and we had the best fun with them, for a whole weekend. They were just terrific.

> Rummer was Félice's third husband, each having died in turn. She was never divorced. Her second husband had been a great buddy of Rummer's from the RAF, so this was, in their older age, really a very happy and satisfactory arrangement. They were married for almost 20 years.

> Félice could be difficult, very difficult. If things went a bit wrong, she could behave strangely, and be sharp with her tongue.

> We came across the father of a friend of ours, at a dinner party. He had been a very famous fighter pilot in the Battle of Britain, and he, too, had become an Air Vice-Marshall in the RAF. I asked him, "Did you know my Uncle Fred Murphy?" He said, "Oh, yes, indeed! And, how terribly pleased we were when Félice Mulholland married your Uncle Fred." They had all known each other very well. Both Fred and

Félice were two lonely people, and so they had got together, when both wanted company.

Fred and Félice at their wedding in Cairo, 1950.

On May 22, 1969, Rummer died, slipping away peacefully. One of his many obituaries is below:

AIR VICE-MARSHALL
F. J. MURPHY

The death has taken place in London of Air Vice-Marshall Frederick John Murphy, C.B.E., C. St. J., of The Lodge, California Lane, Bushy Heath, Hertfordshire, who was Honorary Surgeon to King George VI from 1947 to1951.

Air Vice-Marshall Murphy, who was the only surviving son of Professor J.E.H. and Mrs. Murphy, Rathcore Rectory, Co. Meath, was educated at the Abbey and at Trinity College, Dublin, where he qualified as a doctor in 1916.

He joined the Royal Air Force in 1918 and served throughout the Second World War in Egypt, the Western Desert, Normandy and Germany. He was Wing Commander at the outbreak of hostilities and was Principal Medical Officer of the 2ⁿᵈ Tactical Air Force from 1943 to 1945 when he was transferred to Bomber Command for a further two years.

In 1947 he was promoted to the rank of Air Vice-Marshall with the Technical Training Command. From 1948 until his retirement in 1951 he was Principal Medical Officer of the Royal Air Force Mediterranean and Middle East Command. From 1951 onward he was Medical Officer with the British Ministry of Health.

Air Vice-Marshall Murphy who was 77, was married twice, first to the late Margaret Vera Oliver, daughter of Mr. and Mrs. R. C. Oliver, Morpeth, and secondly to Félice Grant Mulholland, widow of Group Captain D. O. Mulholland, C.B.E., A.F.C.

Rummer's second wife, Félice, died on November 13, 1976. She is remembered as a warm, elegant, well-dressed lady who took time to talk to young relatives of her husband.

Eva's grandchild, Robin recorded three memories as follows:

Close to the Meath Hospital in Dublin, there was a shop called Colcloughs – just a tiny sweet and tobacconist shop. When the Murphy students were working and studying at the Meath, they used visit this shop, buying mainly cigarettes and chocolates. And every time Uncle Rummer came back to Dublin on holiday, he would always call in to see old Mrs. Colclough. I heard about this, so when I was a student doctor at the Meath, in about 1975, I went in to the shop, which was still standing. And I asked, "Is Mrs. Colclough here?" And they said, "Oh, no! She died last year." A pity – I missed her by about a year.

We visited Rummer and Félice in Stanmore, when I was nine years old, in 1958. The Underground had just been completed, and Stanmore was at the end of the line. There were the three of us kids. About five minutes after we had arrived, Rummer said, "There are rabbits on the stairs for each of you!" Halfway up the stairs we discovered three half-crowns (2/6d), each imprinted as they were with a rabbit. We were all delighted, never having owned so much money before!

Rummer was said to have come out of the Rotunda Maternity Hospital as a student, saying "Thank God I'm a man!"

Rummer's nephew, Geordie, noted:

> One time when I was in a taxi on my way to meet Uncle Rummer, I mentioned to the driver who I was going to meet. He asked, "Your uncle wasn't an MO?" The driver had been on some medical drugs, and had grown addicted to these. He had then run into Uncle Rummer in the early 1920s as a young MO in the RAF, and he remembered him. Then the driver said, "He wouldn't remember me. I was a naughty boy in those days."

> After Rummer had been with the RAF in Iraq, he said it was only when he saw flocks of animals in Iraq that he understood the Biblical expression of "sorting out the sheep from the goats." It is extremely difficult to tell them apart, when they're all running in the same flock. In Iraq, the sheep all have long ears, like the goats. And goats and sheep are able to interbreed, when their offspring are called "shoats." There seemed no way to sort them all out.

Rummer's niece was fond of telling a story about her Uncle Rummer, about when he would be trying to pass through the Customs at Dublin. He had to explain all the goods he would be carrying into Ireland. Rummer would have all kinds of gifts for all sorts of people, and especially for his mother, Emmeline Annie, living up in Skerries at the time. The restrictions were many and the Customs officials were intense in their searches. Rummer would say: 'Well, me name is Pat Murphy, and I'm just bringing some old things back to me poor old mother.' On hearing his accent, and of his love for his mother, he always got through, no bother.

Rummer was a legend during his lifetime, and he will long remain so in his family's hearts for generations to come.

24.
HENRY JAMES LEOPOLD MURPHY

LEO
August, 2, 1895 – April 7, 1960

This is the first son to carry his father's first name. Rev Murphy included *Leopold* also. By this time, Rev Murphy had developed a fascination for all things Royal, and the eighth child and youngest son of Queen Victoria had been Prince Leopold, now deceased. King Leopold II was the well-known King of the Belgians. This was a fashionable name. Rev Murphy was overlooking that king's atrocities, his exploitations, and the high death toll of his subjects in Africa … or we can persuade ourselves Rev Murphy was not well informed.

It is likely Emmeline Annie admired the strength of the name Leopold – *Leo* is a lion. She knew the young lad would need a stout heart to get him through his childhood.

Far from being a 'king of the jungle', Leo was a sensitive, small-boned child, who suffered around his father. His sister Eva said: 'Leo was temperamental and nervous. He walked in his sleep. When Rev Murphy was at home and not working in his study, Leo would get scared and would cower behind the furniture. His father frightened the life out of him.' His mother, on the other hand, gave him a lot of affection, and he was happy being around her in the kitchen, in the garden, or wherever she was busy at the time. When Rev Murphy was out, Leo could join in the fun created by his two boisterous brothers, Charlie and Rummer, and he would tag along as best he could.

Leo followed Rummer to the Abbey School, in Tipperary. The Murphy family's finances had improved somewhat, and although Rummer later returned to the rectory for schooling alongside Charlie, everyone thought Leo would fare better if away from his father. His niece noted 'Leo loved company' and he must have learnt about enjoying being with others from his older brothers.

Drogheda Grammar School was founded under Royal Charter in 1669 by Erasmus Smith and is one of the oldest secondary schools in Ireland. An all-boys school, Leo next boarded there for his schooling until he entered Trinity College, Dublin, in the School of Medicine in 1913. He was 18 years old.

Life in the university was full of talk of the looming Great War, which formally began on July 28, 1914, after Leo had written his first exams. He was interested in contributing to the war effort, and starting his second year of studies, in October 1914, he signed up for the DUOTC, the Dublin University Officer Training Corps. He attended meetings and instruction, but mostly the unit marched around and around the grounds of Trinity College – around Front Square, Botany Bay, and New Square. It was called 'drilling'.

In 1914, Ireland was, of course, part of the United Kingdom of Great Britain and Ireland, and most Irish people, regardless of political affiliation, and both Catholic and Protestant, supported the war in much the same way as their British counterparts. Over 200 000 Irishmen fought in the war, and 49 400 died.

According to military historian John Terraine in his book, *White Heat—the new warfare 1914–18*:

The war of 1914–18 was an artillery war: artillery was the battle-winner, artillery was what caused the greatest loss of life, the most dreadful wounds, and the deepest fear.' The first day when shells were fired during the Battle of the Somme, windows rattled in London and the sound of the guns could heard on the south coast of England. It is discussed today how 30% of British shells fired proved to be duds.

November 30, 1915, Leo was granted a commission in the Regular Army for the period of the war. Leo signed up for the Royal Garrison Artillery, the RGA, based in Weymouth. His papers were signed by his father.

The RGA was equipped with much larger weapons than the RFA, the Royal Field Artillery. Howitzers of 6" and 9" bore were common as were 60-pounder heavy field guns. These weapons became the first to be hauled by motor tractors rather than horse power. Some of the guns were so large that they could only be deployed on railway tracks, which had to be especially laid down if the guns were to be moved. Therefore, the guns were not moved frequently, but the longer they stayed in one position the more likely the guns, and those who worked with them, would themselves become targets.

The London Gazette, 21ˢᵗ December, 1915:

War Office
21ˢᵗ December, 1915.

SPECIAL RESERVE OF OFFICERS

The undermentioned to be Second Lieutenants (on probation)
Dated 17ᵗʰ December, 1915:-

Royal Garrison Artillery
(among other names)
Henry James Leopold Murphy

On **August 23, 1916**, Leo was wounded. The wound was classified as *slight* and he remained on duty. He was wounded again on the Somme Front on September 16, 1916, and this time his name appeared in casualty lists. But he remained close to the Front, and was then moved around to several Heavy Artillery Groups, as needed. Men were either killed or wounded at an alarming rate, and fit, surviving men were moved frequently to provide maximum effect. For example, on **January 5, 1917**, he went to the 6ᵗʰ Heavy Artillery Group, and by **January 7, 1917**, he was with the 66ᵗʰ Siege Battery, RGA. Leo had been promoted to Lieutenant, and he was showing promise as an officer capable of taking charge.

By **April 30, 1917**, he was full-time with the 51ˢᵗ Siege Battery, in France, part of the XV Corps, 3ʳᵈ Army. Officially, he was the second-in-command, and his record states he was Acting Captain. Then he was Acting Major, and the youngest Major serving in the Army, and this promotion meant he could command the Battery for a month or so, while the original Commander took a month's respite. Once this Commander rejoined the Battery, Leo reverted to rank of Acting Captain, all of which provided an opportunity: an insurance for the Unit against the Commander himself being wounded, or taking ill.

The 51ˢᵗ Siege Battery was moved around, first to support 3ʳᵈ Corps 4ᵗʰ Army, then to 10ᵗʰ Corps, next to II Anzac, followed by V Corps 3ʳᵈ Army. Most of their positions are shown on the following map, drawn from notes made in a war diary of the 51ˢᵗ for that period and still preserved in the UK National Archives. It is tempting to believe this record was written by the second-in-command, Captain Leo Murphy, as it began shortly after he joined the Battery, and the handwriting changed after he had left.

'Oh, Murphy, you're a medical student, your writing must be OK—they're getting after me for a better record. You take it on.'

'Yes, sir!'

Map 7

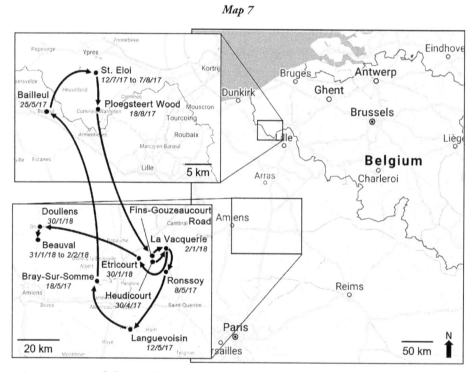

Movements of the 51ˢᵗ Siege Battery , May 1917 - February 1918

Positions shown by black dots.

When the men were not involved in battle, they were having target practice, known as 'requisition shoots', occasionally with assistance from an aeroplane. If an order had been received to change their position, they were putting a huge amount of energy into moving the gun, ammunition, and gear off-position to a railway and, following the train journey, detraining them out to a different site. Sometimes they had to lay down the railway tracks themselves. The enemy was skilled at finding a gun's position, recorded in the war diary of the 51st as *Enemy 77 mm gun shelled the battery throughout the day.* The men were beleaguered by shelling and flying shrapnel.

Sometimes equipment failed, as in 'having trouble with the gun pits due to bad weather.' Unremittingly stressful, eventually they were pulled back. They spent one night at a rest camp where 'we detrained the guns, and our personnel proceeded by motor lorries to Beauval and were billeted here for a rest period of two days.'

The Siege Batteries of the Royal Garrison Artillery were equipped with heavy howitzers, sending large calibre high explosive shells in high trajectory, plunging fire. The usual armaments were 6-inch, 8-inch and 9.2-inch howitzers, although some had huge railway-mounted or road-mounted 12-inch howitzers. As British artillery tactics developed, the Siege Batteries were most often employed in destroying or neutralising the enemy artillery, as well as raining down destructive fire on strongpoints, dumps, stores, roads, and railways behind enemy lines.

51st Siege Battery assisted in the **Battle of Cambrai**, a British offensive from **November 20–December 8, 1917**, on the Western Front, that marked the first large-scale, effective use of tanks in warfare. The battle demonstrated the evolution of technology and tactics on the Western Front which would eventually end the stalemate of trench warfare.

Although best known as the first effective deployment of tanks, these hostilities were also notable for the calibre of predicted shooting by British artillery.

An unidentified British soldier standing with a 9.2 inch howitzer on the Somme. The camouflaged box in front of the gun is known as a dirt box, which was filled with soil and attached to the gun to act as a counterweight to the force of the blast and to keep the gun in position. Hanging on the side of this box is a horseshoe. Note in the background (left) an observation tower and rows of shells standing in front of this structure. [Reproduced here with kind permission of the Australian War Memorial]

Carried out by the 3rd Army in order to relieve pressure on the French Front, the Cambrai offensive consisted of an assault against the Germans' Hindenburg Line along a 10-mile (16 km) front some 8 miles (13 km) west of Cambrai in northern France. The chosen terrain, rolling chalk down-land, was especially suitable for tank movement. Nineteen British divisions were assembled for the offensive, supported by tanks (476 in all, of which about 324 were fighting tanks; the rest were supply and service vehicles) and, unbelievably, five horsed cavalry divisions. For the initial attack, eight British divisions were launched against three German divisions.

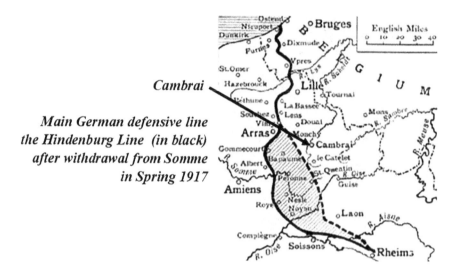

Cambrai

***Main German defensive line
the Hindenburg Line (in black)
after withdrawal from Somme
in Spring 1917***

*[Taken from 'Die Württemberger im Weltkrieg', by Otto von Moser.
Published by Chr. Belsar AG, Stuttgart, 1927, p. 89]*

The Germans had abandoned their old positions along the Somme Front in a carefully staged series of withdrawals beginning **February 23, 1917**, and completed by **April 5, 1917**. Much of the withdrawal was conducted under cover of night and included numerous attempts at deception, including skeleton crews who remained behind until the last moment to keep up a screen of fire from machine guns, rifles, and mortars. The line so formed was named The Hindenburg Line, after its developer, Field Marshal Paul von Hindenburg.

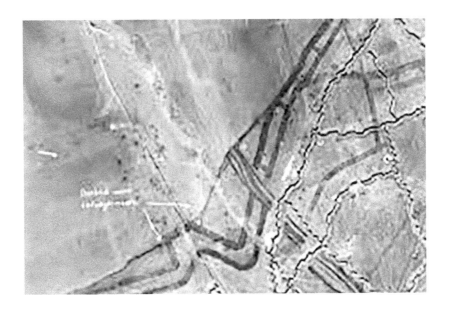

An aerial view of the Hindenburg Line. (Serrated lines are trenches)
(https://www.britannica.com/event/Battle-of-Cambrai-1917)

Spent shell casings from the Battle of the Somme.[68]

---

68   *This image from:* https://www.pinterest.com/pin/4644405845333109/
And from: https://peashooter85.tumblr.com/post/148750501468/
And from: 'Spent artillery shell casings, Battle of the Somme. World war. Somme'

Field Marshal Douglas Haig was in command of the British Expeditionary Force on the Western Front from late 1915 until the end of the war. While the Battle of Passchendaele was being fought **July 31–November 10, 1917**, Haig approved a plan to take on the Germans by sweeping round the back of Cambrai and encircling the town. The attack would use a combination of old and new: cavalry, air power, artillery, and tanks that would be supported by infantry. Cambrai was an important town as it contained a strategic railhead. In front of it lay the very strong Hindenburg Line – a defensive position in which the Germans put a great deal of trust. Haig's plan included an attack on the Hindenburg Line and the use of three cavalry divisions that would encircle Cambrai, thus cutting it off. While Haig's plan won the approval of some, others were less than inspired that it included tanks, as these new weapons had yet to prove their worth in battle in the eyes of some.

The attack started at 06:20 on **November 20, 1917**. The Germans were surprised by an intense artillery attack directly on the Hindenburg Line. 350 British tanks advanced across the ground supported by infantry – both were assisted by an artillery rolling barrage that gave them cover from a German counter-attack. The bulk of the initial attack went well. One Division covered more than five miles from their starting point. Compared to the gains made at battles like the Somme and Verdun, such a distance was astonishing.

However, not everything had gone to plan. A Division of Cavalry had a problem crossing a canal when a tank went over a main bridge and its weight broke the back of the bridge – the same bridge that the cavalry were supposed to use to advance to Cambrai. Elsewhere, British units became bogged down in their attack.

By November 30th, the Germans were ready to counter-attack and defend Cambrai. Many British Army units had become isolated and their command structure was breaking down in places. The German counter-attack was so effective that on **December 3rd**, Haig gave the order for the British units still near to Cambrai to withdraw with the least possible delay, to a more retired and shorter line. The failure to build on the initial success of the attack was blamed on middle-ranking commanders – some of whom were sacked. The initial phase of the battle did show that mobility was possible in the war but that to sustain it, a decent command structure was needed so that impetus gained in one area of the attack was aided by gains elsewhere in the advance.

While losses did not equate to the Somme or Verdun, the British lost over 44 000 men during the battle while the Germans lost about 45 000 men. That was 89 000 men lost in 18 days.

The Battle of Cambrai, fought in November/December 1917, proved to be a significant event in World War One. Cambrai was the first battle in which tanks were used en masse. In fact, Cambrai saw a mixture of tanks, heavy artillery and air power being utilised. Mobility, lacking for the previous three years in the war, suddenly found a place on the battlefield – though it had not lasted for the duration of the battle. Of course, these troops regrouped, fought further battles and went on to win the war.[69]

Leo was at the end of his tether. He had survived so far, he had not suffered major injury, but in every other way he was a wreck. He was granted Special Leave to England from **May 31, 1918–July 7, 1918**. He embarked for England at Boulogne on **June 1, 1918**. Likely he made his way to Ireland, and the comfort of being with his brothers, and friends. He would have been embraced and fêted by all. At first his leave was extended to **July 10**, and then officially to **July 20**. But on **July 11, 1918**, he was placed on *Special Reserve*, and wanting to continue his studies at TCD, he had to officially relinquish his acting rank of Captain, and cease using his title as a Battery Commander. His record states:

> 'On July 20, Leo was on leave in England to enable him to resume his Medical Studies, effective July 15, 1918.'

Leo returned to Trinity College, Dublin University, to complete his Medical Studies with a bachelor's in Medicine, Surgery and Obstetric Science, graduating in **1923**. His address during this period was:

> Captain H. J. L. Murphy
> Late Captain Royal Garrison Artillery (Special Reserve)
> 39, Trinity College
> Dublin

Leo was writing letters, trying to set up his pension, and other remunerations. He was told:

> You will receive full pension

> There is no regulation for any allowance to continue your Medical Studies

> As you relinquished acting rank of Captain on ceasing to be Second-in-Command of a Battalion, but as a demobilized officer you remain on the strength of the Royal Garrison Artillery, Special Reserve, and you are permitted to wear your uniform when attending ceremonials and entertainments of a military nature.

---

69   C. N. Trueman, "The Battle of Cambrai," History Learning Site, December 18, 2019, https://www. historylearningsite.co.uk/

And that was the end of word from headquarters. He received medals for his participation in the War, but from here on, he was on his own. How fortunate he had his studies to keep him focused on something other than the nightmares and flashbacks he was experiencing. He only had to walk out of Trinity, through Front Gate, and out onto the streets of Dublin, to see the broken bodies and physical sufferings of returned soldiers on all sides, to be reminded of the battlefields in which he had fought. Over 200 000 Irishmen fought in the war, and thousands came home. Many of those who returned had been wounded, and now found themselves destitute, broken down, and homeless on the streets of Dublin.

There can be no doubt Leo was suffering from PTSD, post-traumatic stress disorder. Unheard of back then, today we know PTSD is a mental health condition triggered by a terrifying event, or events – either experienced or witnessed. Symptoms may include flashbacks, nightmares and severe anxiety, as well as uncontrollable thoughts about the experiences. Sometimes symptoms may not appear until years afterwards. These symptoms cause significant problems in social or work situations and in relationships. They can also interfere with ability to go about normal daily tasks. Further symptoms may develop when stressed in general, such as prior to the relentless number of medical exams for which Leo had to prepare. When he came across reminders of what he had been through, such as hearing a car backfire, he would have relived combat experiences, been easily startled or frightened, finding himself immediately on guard for danger. Further symptoms for Leo would have been: insomnia, trouble concentrating, irritability, angry outbursts or aggressive behaviour, overwhelming guilt or shame, negative thoughts about himself or other people or about the world in general, hopelessness about the future, memory problems, including not remembering important aspects of traumatic events, difficulty maintaining close relationships, feeling detached from family and friends, lack of interest in activities he once enjoyed, difficulty experiencing positive emotions, feeling emotionally numb, with recurrent, unwanted, distressing memories of the traumatic event.

Not that anyone would be swamped by all of these symptoms all of the time. Leo tried to cope with his condition, but there was little sympathy, no willing listener, anywhere:

'Come on, Leo, get over yourself.'

'Pull yourself together, man.'

'You're alive, aren't you?'

'Look at what happened to your friend. Two legs missing! Who are you to complain?'

While Leo had been away, Ireland had undergone its own changes, with the 1916 Independence Uprising, the execution of sixteen of its leaders and the 3 000 prisoners taken. Like many veterans returning to nationalist areas, he would have met grudging acceptance, hostility, or even physical violence. For all of the returnees, the high public honour and celebration with which they had departed contrasted sharply with the changed circumstances of their return. The disillusionment which, across the world, many returning soldiers felt with the outcome of the war, that the prodigious costs had not been matched by commensurate benefits, was felt especially sharply in nationalist Ireland. One returning officer wrote:

'I'm a coward if I return, a hero if I fall.'

Another recorded:

'These men, the executed 1916 leaders, will go down in history as heroes and martyrs; and I will go down - if I go down at all - as a bloody British officer.'

What a remarkable achievement for Leo to finish his studies successfully. A nephew explained:

"Leo was shell-shocked in the Great War. When he re-entered Trinity, he was the only Rathcore Murphy around who had any money—he had his army pension. But he became a drinker to ease his torments. The two may have been linked: easy money, cheap booze. My mother used to say Leo had gone mad, but he had good reason."

On graduating, and encouraged by his eldest brother Edwy, Leo set up a practice in Kingstown, today known as DunLaoghaire. The good sea air, a train available for easy transport and a less costly lifestyle would have all been enticements. And Leo made another decision. On **September 16, 1924**, he married Vera Goligher, daughter of William Goligher, Professor of Ancient History and Classical Archaeology, and later Vice-Provost, of Trinity College. Both bride and groom were twenty-nine.

Vera (née Goligher) Murphy

But Leo's drinking quickly caused trouble in his marriage. He was a medical doctor with a drinking problem, and his wife Vera would often have to hold off patients in the waiting-room until he became sober. They moved to Prestatyn in Wales for a few years, Leo continuing to practice.

However, the following appeared in *The London Gazette, 5 June, 1934:*

> Notice is hereby given that the Partnership heretofore subsisting between us, the undersigned, Henry James Leopold Murphy and Daniel Kinsella, carrying on business as Medical Practitioners, at Prestatyn, under the style or firm of MURPHY AND KINSELLA, has been dissolved by mutual consent as from the fourteenth day of February, 1934.
>
> – Dated this thirty-first day of May, **1934**.

Clive Murphy

Before returning to Dublin, Leo and Vera had a child, a son called Clive Hunter, born in **1935** when they were both forty.

In **1936,** Leo's brother Edwy died, and Leo took over what had been Edwy's Surgery, on the main street in DunLaoghaire. Leo, still suffering from PTSD, continued to have difficulties in his work and his relationships. He made an effort to detox by admitting himself to *St. John of*

God Hospital, a religious-based care facility. He then tried working as a ship's doctor for a while.

Leo's son, Clive, an author and now 82, says:

> I saw my father rarely. Being an alcoholic, he appeared to behave oddly, and I didn't like the smell of his breath or the Jeyes Fluid he added to his bathwater. He rather scared me.
>
> All my memories of him are negative or embarrassing. During the period we were in DunLaoghaire before his medical practice had to be abandoned and before we went to live with Grannie Goligher in her bungalow in Sutton Cross at the foot of Howth Hill, I recall his reproving me impatiently in DunLaoghaire's George's Street with "Don't drag your feet, son!" And to entertain guests, to their consternation and my discomfort, he would fling me into the air in a kind of somersault and catch me coming down when I'd almost reached the floor.
>
> He had an epidiascope on which he would obsessively watch war photos. Once, when a film party had been arranged for me, he was too drunk to operate the film projector, and when Mummy took me to a concert in Dalkey and we caught the last train home, he created a scene in front of our house. Mummy hadn't told him we were going out.
>
> After we moved to Grannie's I remember Mummy and the housekeeper searching for him in the rockery one morning after one of his late night binges at the Marine Hotel. I would hear him and Mummy bickering in their bedroom. She told me long afterward that he often tried to throttle her in a drunken rage.
>
> He was against my being sent to Boarding School, Castle Park in Dalkey, where I was very happy. "The fees are pretty stiff," he said. It was Grannie Goligher who paid them.
>
> It wasn't long before he left Ireland to become a Ship's Doctor, regarded in those days as something rather "infra dig." He came to my bedside to say goodbye, and left saying, "He doesn't love me! He doesn't love me!" "Of course he does," my mother reassured him. She was wrong.
>
> I don't think it is generally known that they had a son, who did not live even a year, before me. Much later, when I was a student at Trinity,

I was set with a clergyman at a table in the canteen of the Spiritualist Association of Great Britain, when he pointed: "Look! Your brother's sitting over there. You need never worry. He'll always take care of you." And he, or some other power always has watched over me, through thick and thin.

But my father wasn't of assistance, though I'd receive from him occasional letters about flying fish and the like, and trivial presents such as a shark's tooth, or a sponge. But he sent my mother nothing, ever. She had been Secretary to the Provost of Trinity College. When we moved to a lovely part of Dublin called Merrion Avenue, she worked her socks off taking in student lodgers to make ends meet.

Given my father's medical knowledge and my mother's tiny frame, my brother was born in the normal way. But, I was born, unexpectedly and by Caesarian Section.

I asked my father only once for help. I wrote, when I was apprenticed to a Dublin Solicitor, to his British address in London, for enough money to buy an umbrella and a mackintosh. No reply was forthcoming, and I never heard from him again.

I do not recommend the lack of a stable father to anyone.

My mother loved Leo to the end, and was terribly hurt by his deserting us.

Leo's nephew recorded:

> The Murphys blamed his wife, Vera, for the marriage breakup. She wanted to have Leo certified "mad." She rang up his younger brother, who was a doctor himself, and who was also married to a doctor. Vera wanted to ask them both to certify Leo. You had to have two doctors sign the form. It was the wife who answered the phone, and she said "I will have nothing to do with any such thing" and put the phone down, thinking what a crazy thing for Vera to have gone to her brother and sister-in-law to have her husband certified.

Leo returned to Ireland for a while, but eventually he left again, this time permanently. The Murphys said, 'He took up with another woman.' He wrote letters to his sister Olive, trying to get news of his son, Clive.

Vera was a great support to some of the younger Murphys, especially Leo's nieces. These girls found Vera sympathetic, understanding, and compassionate. She supplied them with good, sound advice on their boyfriends, on the running of households, on the hiring of maids, and on the managing of depression. Regarding the latter, she would say soothing phrases like 'Don't dwell on the past', and 'Always look towards the future, up ahead.' These two phrases are still quoted by the following generation, and credit for their origin is given to Vera.

She attended St. Bartholomew's Church, a loyal member of the congregation, where she had many friends. Sometimes, after church service on a Sunday, she would be invited for dinner by a niece. The table would be full, the food plentiful. Vera was small, a bundle of fun. She had a distinct, slightly husky voice, which she combined with her quick wit to regale the assembled family. The children hung on her words, and even today some of her comments are remembered with laughter and affection. She was very perceptive, not easily fooled, but living alone as she did for so many years, she in turn thoroughly enjoyed the company.

It is tragic Leo could not enjoy his wife and son, as others have done. It is sad both Leo and his wife felt rejected by the Murphy family.

Thread Mark

O angel of history, must we forget
those hard-earned vestiges in our clay,
sweat of heritage, arrears we owe?

The dues paid, the debt assumed,
our thread mark of owing between
those who were and those who follow.

[...]

In these fragmented times we wonder
will those who fit the prints we leave
remember feet that walked before them.

Micheal O'Siadhail,
Collected Poems (Bloodaxe Books, 2013)
Reproduced with kind permission of Bloodaxe Books
www.bloodaxebooks.com

25.
OLIVE LILIAN MURPHY

March 26, 1897 – August 28, 1970

Olive was the third daughter of Rev Murphy and Emmeline Annie. When she arrived there were four boys and two other girls in the family. She grew into a tall, slim girl, with a great sense of humour.

Olive went to school in Londonderry, finishing there in 1915. There was talk of her going on to study at Trinity College, but she preferred to remain in the rectory. The Great War was now in full swing, everyone's life felt unsettled, even down in the Irish countryside, but Olive thrived in the country society of Meath. She never expressed regret at her choice.

There was a further reason for her choice. Much later, her son recorded:

> You see, my Mother had a boyfriend, maybe even a fiancé, who was killed in the First World War. I know very little about him. I don't know his name. There's a locket in my top drawer at home, with a picture of a young lad in uniform, and that was him. One time I asked, "Who is this?" and my Mother said, "Oh, that's my boyfriend from the First World War." How serious their relationship was, I don't know.

Olive was twenty-one when the Great War ended, and was twenty-two when her father died, in 1919. She was living in Rathcore Rectory when Emmeline Annie was nursing her husband before he died. Olive soon discovered nursing was not especially to her liking. Emmeline Annie moved the home to Skerries, and at first, Olive enjoyed living by the sea and visiting the households of old friends dotted around the countryside. But eventually this began to wear thin, and Olive could see the writing on the wall. 'She did not fancy getting stuck looking after her mother, nursing her mother, being confined to the fulltime care of an ailing parent. That is the reason she went to America, to stay with relatives of her mother's siblings, in Sioux City and elsewhere.'

Before Olive took off for the United States, her sister Eva arrived back in Ireland, her first visit since emigrating to Canada in 1914. She brought her four children, the youngest being a baby. Years later, Eva's eldest would write the following:

> When Aunt Olive, Eva and all the other Rathcore Murphys were growing up, down in Meath, there were a lot of stories which had a summing up in some kind of expression. Today, I often try to work them out with one of my cousins, and between us we can manage most of them. One particular day the children were making speeches, taking turns to climb a pillar, one of the gateposts of the Rectory. A workman came to go through the gate, but they persuaded him to "obtain permission to do so"—he would have to climb a pillar and give a speech. Up he went, he on one side of the gate, and Olive on the other. Poor man! All he could think of to say was *"Miss Olive is on the pier and she is sounding her voice exthorny!"* That extraordinary phrase became one of the Murphy sayings. Years later, on the morning Eva and her children's ship from Canada was due to arrive at the docks in Liverpool, the Ship's Purser found Eva and said, "There's a cable for you, Ma'am, but I can't understand it. It seems to be in code." Eva read the cable which said *"Miss Olive is on the pier and she is sounding her voice exthorny!"* Eva knew at once that Olive had gone over to Liverpool from Dublin to meet them off the boat, and would be waiting for them on the pier.

Arriving at Dunroe in Skerries, Eva wanted to spend time with her mother, and Olive stayed around to help out with the children. Olive also wanted to hear all Eva had to say about emigration, about life in North America, and even about travelling long distances by ship or train. Eva would have greatly encouraged her baby sister, hoping Olive would make a long side-visit north from the United States to where Eva lived in Calgary. Olive never made that trip to Canada.

In Iowa, *Olive was always intending to come home.* But she stayed longer and longer, altogether five years, and wired home for more money to be sent out to her. Money was found and wired to the US, but it all made Emmeline Annie concerned her daughter would not be returning home at all. Really, Olive was having a gay old time in the US. She was tall, slim, and athletic, very much of a figure popular and admired in the 1920s. She could play a mean game of golf, and she could dance away the nights with the best of them. Americans admired her accent, her loud laugh and vivacious manner, and her US relatives were still commenting about her visit in the 1990s.

Olive Lilian Murphy

Eventually, Emmeline Annie wrote saying she thought Olive had been away long enough, an astute observation! Olive would likely have stayed on in the US where she had a 'beau' but at the last minute this relationship seems to have fallen through. She booked her passage to Liverpool and a taxi had been arranged to transport her to the train which would take her to the ship's dock. The cab arrived and sat outside the house for a long while. Inside, Olive was hoping a love-stricken beau would appear with a proposal. It never happened! The driver must have been paid off by Olive's host, and without a passenger he pulled out to depart. Literally at the last possible moment,

Olive suddenly appeared, dressed inappropriately and unprepared for travel, with her bags all thrown together. She ran yelling down the street to attract the driver's attention. She climbed inside and her bags were thrown in after her. Thus, Olive left her relatives in the States in the most dramatic fashion, and she travelled back to live in her homeland, Ireland.

Returning to Skerries, it was now the 1930s, and Olive soon began to feel life might be passing her by. She continued to visit relatives and friends, whether they were in Dublin, or DunLaoghaire or Enfield or Londonderry or England. She lived out of her suitcase, she was good company and relatives were happy to have her and to hear all her latest family news. But this lifestyle was unsustainable, for she had no income, and she survived on the generosity of her doctor siblings, and on Charlie and Amos to keep an eye on her welfare.

One of the big houses where she spent time was in County Monaghan, at Liscarney House. This had been the home of the eldest sister of Emmeline Annie, Alice, who had married James Ross. Eva, Olive's eldest sister had nursed Aunt Alice, who died in 1913. There were three sons, James, Charles, and Sharman: James and Sharman were solicitors, and Charlie was a doctor with a thriving practice in Navan, Co. Meath. Charlie had been with the RAMC[70] during the Battle of the Somme, the largest battle of the First World War on the Western Front, when more than three million men fought in the battle and approximately one million men were wounded or killed, making it one of the bloodiest battles in human history.

Son James had emigrated to Canada ten years previously, and son Sharman had married in 1924. Sharman and his family were now established in Liscarney House. Also visiting Liscarney House when Olive arrived there was Charlie Ross, now in his late forties but still a bachelor. Olive was in her late thirties. First cousins, Olive and Charlie fell in love. They were married in St. Stephen's Church in Dublin on August 29, 1934. Olive's 'home address' was given as 15, Lower Fitzwilliam Street in Dublin, the residence of her mother's brother, Dr Edward Lennon. The signatories to the marriage were *Henry H. G. Dorman* and *Cyril J. Murphy*: Olive's younger brother, Cyril, and Henry Dorman, a relative of Cyril's future wife.

---

70   *RAMC:* The **Royal Army Medical Corps** is a specialist corps in the British Army which provides medical services to all Army personnel and their families, in war and in peace.

Bride Olive arrives at St. Stephen's Church, Upper Mount Street, Dublin, on 29th August, 1934. Olive is being assisted by her youngest brother, Cyril Murphy, and in the back, by her aunt, Eva Consuelo Lennon

Outside the church, Charlie and Olive Ross

Olive and Charlie took up residence in Brownstown House, near Navan:

The house was set on a large estate with a wonderful farmyard enclosed beside, and with a fully operational farm. Olive had a major shock when she discovered her new husband was suffering from a large X-ray burn on his back, which he had received when operating an X-ray machine. The burn turned cancerous and Charlie died less than a year after their marriage, on March 24, 1935, aged 52, in Brownstown House. He was buried in the graveyard of the First Presbyterian Church in the town of Monaghan, in the Ross family plot.

The Ross family were bitter, contesting the settlement of Charlie's estate at every turn. They were certain Olive had married Charlie only to get her hands on his Ross family inheritance. Surely she had known his health was failing and how he was suffering from the burn? How could Olive not have known?

And so the Ross family and the Murphys were now at war. Charlie Ross had not been liked amongst Olive's siblings and certainly Olive was despised by the Ross family. Olive was supported by her brother Charlie Murphy and his wife Amos at every turn. They arranged all meetings, and even drove Olive to Dublin the day before an appointment, driving her back home afterwards, and always accompanying her to every session with solicitors. They were determined she should not be bullied and shoved around by anyone. But they were concerned about Olive living alone out in the country and now running the farm at Brownstown. They wrote to Eva in Calgary, asking if Eva's eldest daughter would consider travelling over to Ireland again, this time when she was 19 years old, to live with Olive, to keep her company for the summer up ahead. Daughter Daphne was thrilled – what an adventure! – and Eva was happy to let her go. Daphne wrote home to Calgary almost daily, regaling her parents and siblings with family news and stories, and with descriptions of the lush Irish countryside all around her. Many of those letters were written as she sat in Charlie Murphy's car outside a Dublin solicitor's office, waiting for Olive and her brother Charlie to finish the legal wrangling inside.

Eventually a decision was reached, that Olive should keep Brownstown House, as well as all the property and buildings that went with it. That all made up about half of what Charlie Ross had possessed. The other half went to the two Ross brothers, James out in Canada, and Sharman at Liscarney House. At the end of that summer, Daphne returned to Calgary and Olive managed well on her own. The farm prospered and she had some good friends around the county. Olive was a young, good-looking woman, a substantial property owner, was good at sports, and was lively company. She was an asset at any dinner party, at tennis parties and lawn croquet parties, at Golf Clubs, at shooting parties, at Hunt Balls, and at every kind of cocktail party. The Lawn Meet[71] was frequently held at Brownstown House. Olive was admired for her farming skills and farm management. The only trouble holding her back, true all around the British Isles, was the shortage of men of her own age. She was now approaching forty, and so many young men had been lost in the Great War.

In December 1937, Emmeline Annie died. Olive had been close to her mother, visiting frequently, the only daughter able to do so. There are many more photographs of the two of them together than of Emmeline Annie with anyone else.

Somewhere along the way, Olive met John Hope Hallowes, who was from Navan. They were married in the parish church in Kentstown, Olive's Brownstown House parish, on March 10, 1938. The four signatories on the wedding certificate were a Mr Dillon, a Mr Kennedy, Charlie Murphy, and the fourth, Daphne Wallace, Eva's eldest daughter. Daphne had so much enjoyed Ireland and her summer with Olive, she had returned to Trinity College in Dublin to study, sponsored by her Uncle Cyril Murphy, Eva and Olive's youngest brother.

---

71   ***Lawn Meet:*** The owner of the house gave drinks, known as *the stirrup cup,* to all before the Hunt moved off, and probably hosted a large dinner party that night for some of the participants.

John Hope Hallowes came from a long line of seriously successful military and naval officers. This can be seen in the sketchy family tree below:

Thomas and Lady Catherine Hallowes
|
Colonel John Hallowes
|
Admiral John Hallowes
|
Major General George Hallowes
|
Colonel John Hope Hallowes
(1873 – 1959)

John Hope Hallowes was born into a large family, on January 29, 1873. His mother's maiden name had been Hope. John had a most illustrious career in India, with the 15th Bengal Lancers, later amalgamated to the 20th, in India, fighting and leading men in the Raj. Officially, he was a Lieutenant-Colonel when he retired, but everyone referred to him as *The Colonel*. On retirement he needed a wife, and Olive fitted his bill perfectly. He was sixty-five, and she was forty-one.

At the time of the wedding, John was living in Navan, but once married, the couple resided at Brownstown House. Their only child, George Richard Hallowes, was born on March 21, 1939, and was always known in the family as *Geordie*.

Geordie

As a child, he grew up in Brownstown House until old enough to go over to England to Shrewsbury School, where he boarded and excelled in everything, especially in academics, rowing, and singing, all of which he pursued throughout his life. He studied at Trinity College, became a civil engineer and then based in London, he travelled to Pakistan, Iraq, and South Africa, building dams and major waterworks.

In 1910, Emmeline Annie had given Olive a thirteenth birthday present of an autograph album, and inside she had written:

> Keep a watch on your words my darling,
> For words are wonderful things,

They are sweet as bees' fresh honey,
But like bees they have terrible stings.

They can bless like the warm glad sunshine,
And lighten a lonely life,

They can cut in the strife of anger,
Like an open two edged knife.
If a bitter vengeful spirit

Prompt the words, let them be unsaid,
They may flash through a brain like lightening,
Or fall on a heart like lead.
Keep them back if they're cold and cruel,
Under bar and lock and seal,
The wounds they make my darling,
Are always hard to heal.

E. A. Murphy

Why her mother chose these words to write in the album is not known, but Olive had been known to have said things in a thoughtless way, and perhaps she needed this advice? Years later, Olive transcribed this entry, headed by the words *To Geordie*, and signed *O.L.H.*, and she gave it to her own son, who kept it as a treasure.

Meanwhile, Olive, John, and Geordie lived at Brownstown House. Olive devoted herself to bringing up her child. He had his own pony at a young age, and she was a very active parent in the Meath Pony Club. Olive would take Geordie out following the local hunts, and they also went for jaunts in the horse and trap along nearby roads. Eventually, a governess was hired to care for Geordie, and he remembered her teaching him how to ride a bicycle. She then took him bike-riding much farther afield than around the small neighbouring roads.

Olive began to grow alarmed about John as a farmer, and she worried more and more that John would bankrupt them. He had very strange and peculiar ideas about how to manage a farm. Olive had farmed most successfully, but now John insisted the way to operate was *to farm rough*. What he meant by this was all of the fields should be farmed together, at the one time, and then, in the following year, all the fields should be left fallow. Where he got these ideas Olive knew not, and unfortunately, John insisted his ideas should dominate.

Geordie recorded:

> I remember in 1946, Mother and I loaded our bicycles onto a train
> on the local branch line of the railway. We travelled all the way to the
> end of that line, to Oldcastle in County Meath. We were to take a
> look at a larger house there, and we were met at the station by one of
> the Kilroy family who was an Estate Agent.[72] First we went to lunch
> with the Kilroys. Afterwards we rode our bicycles to view the house,
> which was called *The Lough Crewe Rectory*. This house had never actu-
> ally belonged to the Church of Ireland, and there was another building
> called the *Oldcastle Rectory* which did belong, and where the Rector
> now lived. The owners of *Lough Crewe Rectory* wanted to sell the house,
> and my parents were interested in a purchase.

The Diocesan Architect in Meath for the Church of Ireland at this time was, of course, none other than Charlie Murphy, Olive's brother, and no doubt he had had a hand in all these arrangements! Furthermore, John Quarry Day, the great friend of Rev Murphy, back in times when they were both interested in courting the Lennon girls of Newcastle House, had been the Rector of Oldcastle. At that time, there was no *Oldcastle Rectory*, the parish was known as *Lough Crewe Parish*, and Reverend Day had resided in this very house, *Lough Crewe Rectory*, that Olive was inspecting.

Protestant Ireland was so small a community and so well interconnected, people would say 'everyone knows everyone else'. In fact, this connectivity continues today, enough to drive some from the shores of Ireland, but it is a great source of conversation whenever any sized gathering occurs. Very close to gossiping, but not quite, for good and bad are jumbled together in a sympathetic, supportive way, in an attempt to share and confirm status and experiences, and to remind each other of the stories and of the times of the past.

The big house in Oldcastle was purchased, and Brownstown House was sold. The first thing John set out to do was to change the name of the house. He said, 'It is unsuitable for us to be living in a house that is called "The Rectory"'. John cast around for a suitable name. The land on which the house stood was called *Fork Hill*, not appropriate, but across the road at the end of the avenue, was an area known as *Knockbrack*, approved by all. The house was re-named *Knockbrack Grange*, a good name for the house of a Colonel!

---

72 "Of their visit to Oldcastle, they were met by Richard Kilroy's uncle, Ernest Kilroy, who worked for Joseph Lowery of *Kells Auctioneers*": *Maureen Goodbody*, 2017.

Knockbrack Grange

Olive and John lived a quiet life, and Geordie was away at school most of the time. Olive still enjoyed the county social scene, a little less hectically than when she had been single. John's health was on the wane and his manner became more and more gruff, and Geordie was somewhat afraid of him. But John did manage to join in with some local events, if they met his approval.

Col. John Hallowes and his wife, Olive, entering a country church for a local wedding

John Hallowes died in May 1959, when he was eighty-six, Olive was sixty-two, and Geordie was twenty. Thus began the most difficult period of Olive's life. She felt very much alone. Sometimes she managed to travel to Iraq, or wherever Geordie was working on engineering projects, but even while there she would be alone, he being tied up with travelling to and from the work sites, and having to spend hours creating

Carnalway Glebe House

and studying drawings and diagrams. Meanwhile she decided to sell Knockbrack Grange, and she moved closer to Naas, in County Kildare, beside some long-time friends, and where she might have some company. She bought another former rectory, this time *Carnalway Glebe House*, not exactly a small place!

A great-nephew recorded:

> We used to drive down to Carnalway Rectory, perhaps once every two or three years. About an hour's drive from Dublin, Aunt Olive would have invited us for lunch, sometimes for a midday Sunday dinner. There would be a servant girl serving us, and usually we were provided with a very large meal. What an outing for us!
>
> Situated in the middle of the countryside, the house was huge and very empty, but it was very pleasant to go down and spend the day there. I used to play with the toys and games Geordie had had as a child. If my brother came, he joined in. We had lots of fun.
>
> Olive was obviously very fond of us, but she was really pre-World War One, and there was a huge gap between us. She was very, very different to us. As Kenneth Clarke said: *They were so charming, so elegant, living with dignity, but most of them were as ignorant about the world as swans.*

In 1965, Olive wrote a letter to a daughter of Eva's, living in Canada. She wrote in part:

> I have started farming again. Had 5 cattle, now they are down to 3, and 20 sheep. It keeps me occupied and it may be profitable!! (Keep hoping) I suppose you heard Geordie has a good job in IRAQ—150 miles north of Bagdad, in a place called KIRKUT. He has been good about writing but he is very far away—I am still where you saw me— (same house). Poor Uncle Charlie is terribly ill—I always counted on him for advice since I was very young. It is so sad to see him now—you

can guess how I feel. The bottom has fallen out of my world between Charlie's illness and Geordie being so far away. Geordie is full of ideas of getting me out there for a holiday. It may come off in the Spring.

Olive had a dachshund called Billy, and in 1969, she approached a niece in Dublin and asked if she would take care of the dog. Olive was planning to travel with Geordie again, this time to South Africa, and she needed a long-term arrangement for her dog. She and Geordie had rented out her house. Olive's health was not good, and Geordie wanted to keep an eye on his mother. While in Lesotho, Olive took a turn for the worse. She died there on August 28, 1970, aged 73. She is buried there.

The news of the sudden passing of Olivia Hallowes caused us all wide-

spread sorrow. There was barely time to put in a brief notice in our last issue. She will be remembered for her gracious charm and her love at all times for her church, a regular attender and one time member of the choir in St. Patrick's, Carnalway.

26. AGATHA

March 26, 1899 – October 15, 1899

In the autumn of 1898, Rev Murphy and Emmeline Annie had planned to go up to Dublin to buy things for the baby, before the expected birth the following spring. They were in the trap setting out for the train station at Enfield, and Rev Murphy was already in a state. Then, for some reason, the reins got caught, and the horse got turned around. Murphy was now in a towering temper. He whipped the horse, which ran into the avenue gate. Murphy fell out on his head, Emmeline stayed in, but the event may have affected the baby.

Agatha, Cyril's twin sister, was born with spina bifida. This birth defect is an incomplete closing of the backbone and membranes around the spinal cord. It is believed to be caused by a combination of genetic and environmental factors. A folic acid deficiency during pregnancy plays a significant role. There is no known cure for nerve damage caused by spina bifida. Being born with this condition in 1899 was a death sentence, a devastating tragedy for everyone.

The translation of the Latin name spina bifida is *split spine*. By the time of birth, the spine may have developed crookedly.

The condition causes leg weakness and paralysis. There may be orthopaedic abnormalities such as a club foot or hip dislocation. The major difficulty, right from birth, is the great risk of infection settling in the exposed spinal protrusion. Emmeline Annie was skilled in nursing and would have kept everything as clean as possible, but current knowledge was a long way from understanding the causes of infection. She was likely breast feeding both twins, and she had a household to run. But, she was not without support.

A nurse soon came to care for Agatha during the day. Eva was now almost thirteen, and Gerry was nine. These girls would have been well able to hold and rock the twins if they became fussy in the evenings.

One evening, Emmeline was seen to go into the dining room with Reverend Murphy, and once there, he treated her very freely with the horsewhip. He declared, 'The *divil* had infected her, had affected the baby girl and needed to be beaten out of her.' Eva's distress was overwhelming. Emmeline had left Rev Murphy a couple of times; she went up to Dublin to visit a solicitor, and started lawsuits for assault against him. He had a great fear of being sued by his wife, but there was little patience in society, at that time, for such legal actions against what went on behind closed doors in a private house.

Years later, Rummer was staying at Cyril's, and they were discussing their father. Cyril said, 'Fine Man!' 'And an awful bugger!' replied Rummer. This comment wasn't well received by Cyril. The older children of Rev Murphy felt that Cyril wasn't aware of the complete background, being younger than they were. When Cyril was born, Charlie was ten and Rummer was six, both old enough to remember Cyril's birth, and the events surrounding that time.

Baby Agatha died at six months. She had lived just over two hundred days. She is buried in the graveyard of Rathcore Church, beside the grave of her sister, Violet.

27.
CYRIL JAMES USSHER MURPHY

(Also known as 'Mad Murphy' or 'Spud')
March 26, 1899 – January 5, 1957

Cyril was one of a set of twins, the last two children born to Emmeline Murphy and the Reverend James. The other twin, Agatha, died after six months. The twins were born on the exact same birthday as their two-year-old sister Olive, which would have caused a stir at the time. Three birthdays on the same date – cause for large birthday parties up ahead!

Cyril was the fifth son in the family. Along with his brother Leo, now five years old, Cyril was also given the name James; but where the names *Cyril* or *Ussher* came from is uncertain. He was born into a noisy, boisterous household, with many children running up and down stairs, racing around the house, clattering along the flagstones in the kitchen, shouting and 'carrying on', and apparently eating huge meals. His siblings were full of vitality and energy, but there were also teenagers boarding and studying under the Reverend's tutelage, enough to occupy two of the bedrooms at night and to fill the room designated as 'the school room' much of the day. Emmeline Annie would expect all these lads and girls to be outside in their free time, leaving the younger ones some peace for naps and rest and even attention from their mother. 'Out you go' they would be told; sometimes doors were locked and the children played in barns or farm buildings if the weather was bad. That tradition continued down through the generations. Fresh air cleared heads and strong bonds were forged between children brought up this way, children left to entertain themselves with spontaneous theatricals, physical competitions, even musical performances. For several years they called themselves *The Balcony Club*, dressing up in any cast-off clothing they could find.

Cyril contracted meningitis as a child. It is not known how he became infected, but possibly one of the boarding students brought the illness into the house. Meningitis is an infection of the meninges, the protective membranes enclosing the brain and spinal cord. Very difficult to diagnose early on, the symptoms of meningitis are closely allied to those of a bad case of the 'flu – fever, headache, vomiting. Without easy access to a hospital, it would have taken experience and nursing skills to discern Cyril's condition as not being a regular or garden variety of the 'flu. However, Emmeline Annie with her experience, was onto his case right away, and Cyril recovered, with the only remnant being a slight defect in the pupils of his eyes. He was fortunate to have avoided loss of hearing, blood poisoning, or even psychological effects. Cyril came through this threat with flying colours, although in later years his medical colleagues would consider him 'off the wall', some even believing 'the meningitis had affected his brain'. He was affectionately referred to as *Mad Murphy*.

Other family members would refer to Cyril as 'the genius of the family'. He was exceptionally bright, and would have learnt his lessons from his father at high speed. No wonder he was sent to the Abbey School in Tipperary, an Erasmus Smith School, and then continued on to Drogheda Grammar School. He would have been a first-class student and a prominent boy in each school, respected by everyone. These schools provided him with an enriched environment coupled with a steady routine and discipline in which to develop. When Cyril entered the Abbey, Leo was already there, and at least two of the older siblings were still studying at Trinity College. The school fees required were an additional expense for the Reverend James and Emmeline Annie, but they managed somehow, mostly by 'doing without".

When Cyril was nineteen, his father was stacking hay, high on top of a barnful of the sweet-smelling crop. Reverend James was now sixty-eight, not so spry anymore. He slipped, a momentary lapse, and down he tumbled. He broke his collar bone, and was confined to bed. Depending on the summer weather, hay would have been cut in June/July, and stacked a month later after drying in the field. It is likely he fell in August 1918. Reverend James was now dependent on his wife Emmeline Annie, and his youngest child, Cyril, who was about to enter the School of Medicine in Trinity College. Eight months later Reverend James died, having contracted pneumonia from lying flat on his back all those months waiting for his broken bone to heal.

After his father's death, Cyril grew very close to his mother, supporting her in the move from Rathcore Rectory to the house in Skerries. Charlie was back from his North American adventure, and he now lived in Skerries with Emmeline Annie. Cyril was happy to head up to Skerries by train from Dublin University to enjoy his mother's good cooking. His fees and rooms continued to be covered by the College, but he received no pocket money, and cash for food was short! He would return to College after a weekend in Skerries with an extra bag full of goodies from Emmeline Annie.

After qualifying at Trinity, Cyril secured the Medical Travelling Prize, which enabled him to work at the Mayo Clinic in Rochester, Minnesota, USA. Here he learnt about innovative medical and surgical practice from the doctors, and he discovered the importance of offering superior educational programmes to ensure the success of the next generation of medical professionals.

In Dublin, there were a number of small hospitals of about one hundred beds, where medical students trained, initially. Most students then moved on to the Meath Hospital, a teaching hospital, which was full of Trinity students, with some students from the Royal College of Surgeons mixed in. Here, there were many very good teachers in medicine.

Cyril Murphy returned to Dublin from the States, and was assigned to the Meath Hospital, where he remained for the rest of his life. He was a loyal servant of the hospital, and Honorary Secretary of the Medical Board for ten years. In 1922 he was elected Assistant Physician, and from 1928 to his death he was elected to senior staff. He was appointed as Anaesthetist 1925–1928 and held the position of Medical Radiologist (specialising in deep X-ray therapy to the pituitary gland) from 1933–1943. He was described as possessing 'irrepressible cheerfulness' and his extrovert personality was an important ingredient in his clinical teaching, where he was apt to give 'a picturesque exposition of clinical signs'.

In 1952, a room on the medical landing was given over to Dr Cyril Murphy for his allergy work. He used it to isolate patients from potential allergens, such as feathers, mats, and horsehair, and he was able to identify sensitising agents which would precipitate allergic attacks like asthma. He was a pioneer in this field.

In a list of transactions of *The Royal Academy of Medicine in Ireland*, the following document was submitted by Dr. Cyril Murphy:

A CASE OF ASTHMA IN WHICH THE PATIENT WAS SENSITIVE TO DOG HAIR:

The patient's dog was given away and she remained free from asthma. Recently, however, she had come in contact with dogs, and the asthma had returned. Dr. Murphy was now treating her with injections of dog hair antigens, and the result was very satisfactory. He thought that wherever the offending protein could be avoided, it was possible to bring about a cure of the disease.

This work and its effect on his relatives, was described in 1983 by a cousin:

Cyril was basically quite a nice chap. But he had this medical allergy thing, at which he was working very hard. And he didn't put it over quite right. He went to great lengths to protect his mother, who was ailing and was living with him at the time. But the rules and regulations around social visits, even family ones, and the required removal of hats and feathers and the like made visiting impossible. He was governed by TIME, and had ten phones. What a man! The last time we tried to visit Aunt Emmeline, I think he had gone funny in the head, or something, because Cyril was ghastly.

In the 1990s, one of Cyril's nieces recorded:

> I was managing the household for Uncle Cyril, and Grannie Emmeline Annie was living with him too. She became quite ill, and Uncle Cyril discovered she was seriously allergic to feathers. She did eventually die of asthma. Other people have said Grannie had a bad heart, which no doubt she had. But I remember my uncle saying to one of his brothers, also a doctor, "Mother died out of her lungs."

In 1952, Dr Cyril Murphy had founded a medal for the best nurse of the year, awarded both for clinical and for theoretical ability. He was well-liked by everyone in the hospital, as he made hospital days more interesting and more lively. He is celebrated in two cartoons created by G. Brewster to decorate the menus of *The Annual Reunion Dinner of the Meath Hospital,* held at the Gresham Hotel, Dublin:

1933>

<1935

Several poems were written about Cyril, calling him 'Spud', by a colleague, Dr Oliver St. John Gogarty. *Patients*, a play on the word, is one:

Patients

The Spud has got a gadget bright
For each man's motor car:
'It points to left, it points to right,
It shuts – and, There you are!'

The Spud has got a new moustache –
No product of his brain –
To left and right it points to mash
The girls; but, ah! In vain!

Gogarty was fond of writing lewd poetry, as well as amusing ditties, but he spared 'Spud' as a subject of any of the more unsavoury verses. I suspect he was somewhat afraid of Dr Cyril Murphy.

In the 1950s, Cyril was 'Doctor to the Gaiety Theatre'. For one hundred and forty-six years, the Gaiety Theatre has given the people of Dublin opera, musicals, drama, revues, comedy, concerts, dance, festivals, and pantomime. Through times of war and times of affluence, The Grand Old Lady of South King Street, close to the top of Grafton Street, has remained a vital and ever-changing expression of Irish culture and Irish society. Since the glamorous night of its opening on November 27, 1871, with the Lord Lieutenant of Ireland as guest of honour and a double bill of Goldsmith's *She Stoops to Conquer* followed by the tuneful burlesque *La Belle Sauvage*, the Gaiety Theatre has remained true to the vision of its founders in presenting the highest quality musical and dramatic entertainment.

Becoming the official doctor to travelling companies of theatrical people who came in from England was a major source of pleasure for Cyril. He would delight in socialising during the intermission as much as he enjoyed the performances. To thank him for his efforts, Cyril was given two tickets for the dress circle every Monday night, and he would invite one thrilled family member each time to accompany him. Over the years, Cyril remained a weekly attendee.

In 1939, when Cyril was forty years old, he fell in love with the new, freshly graduated young anaesthetist who arrived at the Meath Hospital. Maureen Dorman was a quiet, innocent, and somewhat naïve young woman. She would later describe herself as a *Child of Two Continents*, and her memoirs were published after her death under that title.

Cyril and Maureen c. 1940

Maureen was born in 1914 in Lahore, capital of the Punjab in India, to Irish parents. She was their third child. Her father was a civil engineer. Maureen spent much of her childhood in India but received most of her education in Ireland. She told a nephew:

> My childhood was terribly unemotional, as I was almost always separated from my parents. Really, I had a loveless childhood. I was terribly fond of my sister. When she was suddenly killed while caring for a horse, it was a terrible blow to me. The horse must have kicked or suddenly reared its head, and she was found out in a field with her neck broken. It was a severe blow. We could have spent our old age together.

In 1932 Maureen entered the Medical School in Trinity College, Dublin, and qualified in 1938. She then practised as an Anaesthetist in the Meath Hospital, and as a Paediatrician in the Adelaide Hospital, both in Dublin. Inevitably she would meet

Dr Cyril Murphy along the way, and she may even have been taught by him during her student years. They were married in 1939. They would have no children. Both Cyril and Maureen were upright, conscientious persons of deep convictions and were prominent members of their church, St. Ann's in Dawson Street, residing in the parish at 44 Fitzwilliam Square. A plaque to Cyril was erected at the end of a pew in the church, perhaps placed there by his wife. The plaque reads:

IN LOVING MEMORY OF
CYRIL JAMES USSHER MURPHY
M.D., F.R.C.P.I.
WHO FOR 30 YEARS WORSHIPPED HERE
HE SERVED ST. ANN'S AS CHURCHWARDEN
VESTRYMAN, SYNODSMAN
AND PAROCHIAL NOMINATOR.
BORN 26TH MARCH 1899
DIED 6TH JANUARY 1957

_____

"The strife is o'er,
the battle done"

A great-nephew of Cyril's, who had also studied medicine and trained at the Meath, recalls with a friend their own time as students at the Meath, much later, in the 1970s:

> When I studied at the Meath hospital, quite a lot of people still talked about Cyril Murphy. One doctor said "Cyril was a bit of a genius, but quite mad." My father disagreed. He said, "I would put it the other way around. I would say he was a bit mad, but quite a genius." Cyril could diagnose hypothyroidism by pressing the skin of a patient's wrist, and if it was swollen he would say, "That is hypothyroid." He knew by the feel.
>
> He used to have clinics every Tuesday morning, and they were very dramatic; he would always put on an act and the patients loved it. Patients would say, "Today is Pantomime Day as Dr. Murphy is giving his clinic." The student doctors enjoyed it too. It used to be like a theatre in the Ward, Cyril giving a full performance: how patients walked after strokes, or maybe in the last stages of syphilis, tertiary syphilis, when *tabes dorsalis* would occur resulting in a patient walking in a high-stepping, jerky, non-fluid manner, slapping down feet on the ground—everyone loved it. "If he hadn't done medicine he would have been on stage." Cyril was ahead of his time.
>
> His staff nurse would set the stage. If a patient had a rise in blood pressure, Cyril would claim this was due to an offending protein, and he would reach under the bed and pull out a protein, represented by a rubber tyre, or a bundle of chicken feathers. No progress in health would be possible, would not occur if the protein was not removed! If he needed to show the sounds of wheezing lungs, he would blow across the top of a series of different sized glasses to reach the required effect.
>
> Cyril Murphy was considered very brilliant and inspirational. He did a most unusual thing with his pupils, "giving them the eye" you might say, using the fact his pupils dilated in an abnormal way. He had a signature that was a squiggle which he had developed to look rather like a spirochete, the bacteria that causes syphilis. After a clinic he had to sign students' attendance sheets, and he would say, "Stand in line now for the spirochete."

Taken about 1940, this was Maureen's favourite photo of her husband, found in her flat after she had died.

But, Cyril had some strange ideas about the family too. He didn't approve of the fiancé of his niece. 'Must be Jewish', he declared. Then he met the distinguished-looking father of the fiancé, declaring him to be a most impressive person! Now Cyril pronounced that the offending young man 'must have been illegitimate'. Fortunately, the fiancé stayed the course! But Cyril had been deadly serious, writing to the niece's mother to block the marriage. The niece and fiancé did marry, but they never took their children to visit their Uncle Cyril, and he never stopped by their home.

The two sons of Edwy, Jimmy and Willie Murphy, were Cyril's nephews. Both took medicine at Trinity. Before their exams, Cyril would give them each a £1 note on one condition: if they failed the exam they had to give it back; if they passed the exam, they could keep the money. £1 was a fat sum for a student in the 1930s.

Cyril Murphy died on January 6, 1957, at the age of 57. Though he had been suffering for some time with a dreadful carcinoma of the thyroid, which had developed as a result of his work with radiotherapy, he continued with his medical practice without complaint, until shortly before his death.

To quote *Dublin's Meath Hospital 1753–1996,* a history of the hospital written by Peter Gatenby, and published by Town House, Dublin in 1996, page 156:

He had been married to Maureen Dorman, who had been one of the original specialist anaesthetists to the hospital. In 1959 she gave £1,000 to the Medical Board to set up a lending library for the interns and students, in memory of Cyril Murphy. This was the foundation of the present combined medical and nursing library. In 1961 Maureen, a quiet, dedicated person, resigned from the hospital and went to India as a medical missionary.

Maureen's nephew recorded:

After Cyril's death, Maureen now in her early forties carried on, and although she invited the same sort of people to her dinner parties, she found she was not being invited back. And she told me later that there were women who were afraid she was going to entice away their husbands. What a desperately lonely life for a widow. She also found that as an anaesthetist she wasn't getting the work because the young up-and-coming surgeons naturally invited their contemporaries, their friends who had graduated with them, to do their anaesthetics. So all this was part of the scene behind her decision to go to India, in the winter of 1962, five years after Cyril's death. She was staying with Uncle Fred Murphy, south of London, and one Sunday when I was in London, for the first time I was invited down to Uncle Fred's home for the Sunday Dinner just before she went on her way to India.

This was her first trip to stay and work in India. But she had been out there on a holiday since Cyril's death. In Hazaribagh, Bihar, the 'St. Columba's Hospital Report for the year 1960' states in part:

The year 1960 has been a good year for St. Columba's Hospital in many ways...

Then came the blessed new toy, the special anaesthetic machine brought out and donated by kind and generous Dr. Maureen Murphy, one of the leading anaesthetists in Dublin. She came out to us for her holiday, at her own expense, and taught us how to use the machine, which is simple enough: just the type that suits us. We are ever so grateful to her for the gift, her infinite patience in the teaching of us how to use the machine, her encouragement and help with various medical problems and her charming company which has endeared her to all of us. She was with us from 11/7/60 till 14/9/60 always ready to help in every way. I wish she could have stayed with us longer. How we ever did abdominal operations with open ether anaesthesia, I cannot now imagine.

In 1962, Maureen returned to India under the Christian Missionary Society to work for five years as Professor of Anaesthesia in the Christian Medical College in Ludhiana in Punjab. She then transferred to St. Columba's Hospital, Hazaribagh in Bihar, and in 1970 Maureen was appointed Medical Superintendent there, a post she held until 1981. Retiring in 1982, she spent long periods in both India and Pakistan doing locums in Christian hospitals and re-visiting scenes of her youth.

An obituary for Maureen, written by her great friend Elizabeth Ferrar in 1991, describes Maureen's work in Hazaribagh:

> . . . It is as a doctor that we find Maureen at her best. She was totally committed to her work in the medical world and with a single-mindedness that could be alarming. She served and slaved for the hospital, its staff and patients. Her integrity and skill were of the highest order. St. Columba's Hospital—the medical 'wing' of the Dublin University Mission to Chota Nagpur—had been established in the 1890s. The buildings Maureen inherited were built in 1912 and were in sore need of a major overhaul. It is to her credit that the hospital was modernized and 90% rebuilt. The work this entailed was immense: the funding necessary, the supervision and responsibility of construction and, at the same time, the continued running of a hospital, all fell on her shoulders . . .

Everywhere she went, she was happy to give a talk illustrated with slides on her hospitals' difficulties in raising funds for urgently needed equipment and trained personnel. Travelling back to Ireland for a break in 1982, Maureen stopped on Vancouver Island, Canada, where she spoke in a parish hall. She explained how St. Columba's had been originally built for women and for children, but was then expanded to include male patients. Wards for TB patients and for leprosy victims were added, as well as wards for cholera, typhoid, and gastroenteritis. There were also wards for abandoned children, for children without parents and for children whose parents were too poor to feed them. Many children suffering from extreme malnutrition were brought in, the hospital bringing them back to health and arranging adoptions. Funding for all of this came from Maureen's speaking tours made during her holiday periods, from Dublin's University Mission Society, and from a group of churches in West Germany who answered her world-wide appeal for assistance in the 1970s. Eva's grandchildren recall afternoons spent attending the annual sales held in Molesworth Hall in central Dublin. These sales were sponsored by many societies and church groups interested in helping Maureen's missionary work by coming together to raise a great deal of money. There were enormous numbers of attendees at a time when few supporters had cars and most travelled long, tedious distances on public transport, and had accommodations arranged. No one had much money in post-World War II Ireland. Eva's grandchildren remember the loud noise of so many people thus gathered together, all enjoying themselves and all feeling good about giving support. The joy of each child holding a three-penny coin tight in a hand and cruising around the stalls seeking the perfect treasure, still remains. Suddenly silence would fall, and someone, once even Maureen herself, gave a brief update of the hospital in Hazaribagh.

The hospital gained a respected reputation for cleanliness, efficiency, and generally high standards. Maureen was the only Western staff member and on retirement the hospital was then completely staffed by Indians.

In 1990, Maureen was unwell, and she made her final trip back to Dublin. She stayed with her recently widowed niece there, and they had much in common. The house was warm and quiet. Maureen could be very good company. She had a good sense of humour, but she was a complex person, very shy and reserved. Some felt they could never understand her. Younger family members found it refreshing to be able to sit alongside her, and yet, not have to converse! One time, a great niece said, 'Auntie Maureen, I'll give you a drive to your friend's house.' She was so surprised. 'Why ever would you do that? I can catch a bus.' Grand-niece replied, 'I would do anything to help you.' Auntie Maureen sat in shock. She had not been aware of the great admiration and pride with which she was held by her relatives. And even they may not have then realised how she would inspire in the future.

Maureen died in the Adelaide Hospital on February 18, 1991. She was buried with her Cyril in the Rathcore Church graveyard. The inscription on their gravestone, which would have been chosen by them, reads:

'The strife is oe'r, the battle done.'

LETTER FROM DR. MAUREEN MURPHY
IN INDIA

Here in St. Columba's Hospital it is the season of the Eye Camps and so my mind is fixed very much on this side of our work. I have written so often about them in prose I thought I would try and describe the Camp from the point of view of the patient – in verse, this time.

Slowly we moved up the dusty road
Greeting the dawn as we passed along,
With the acrid smell of the cow-dung fire
And the joyful note of a bird in song.
Up to the gate we shuffled, and then
Hand in hand passed through th'open door,
Wondering, fearing, trembling with hope –
What would that long day hold in store?
People were there, muffled in shawls,
'Till the sun stole forth – touching with gold
First tree tops, then flowers, then red, red clay
Lighting up faces, banishing cold.
Joining the crowd we moved, step by step,
Shuffling, shambling, feeling our way,
Heard kindly voices, felt gentle hands,
Listening to all that we had to say.
Bright lights shining into our eyes,
Questions asked – "What is your name?"
"What can you see, Brother?" (Little, ah little,
Day and night almost the same.)
Silent we sit till the sunlight fades
Squatting together against the wall,
The "Come with me Brother, come, give me your arm."
And a young hand guides us into the hall.
With fear in our hearts we lie side by side
On firm narrow beds with mattress of straw.
Many are coming – women and men
Follow each other – a hundred or more.
And then, as we wait, a great silence falls–
Nurses are singing – how sweet is the sound!

Then a Padre steps forth and tells of a Man
Teacher, Physician – where healing is found.
Tells of one Jesus who came here to save,
One who will care for us, body and mind,
One who loves all and One who can give
Health to the sick and sight to the blind.
Dear Jesus, help us, who with eyes that are dark
Far from our jungle this journey have made
Seeking the light. Banish our fears,
Keep us in peace that we be not afraid.
Sleep comes at last enfolding us close
Wrapt in its web of repose,
Till the morn breaks forth and the great day dawns
And we join others – sitting in rows –
Waiting in turn for drops and for drugs.
White gowned, with hope shining bright,
Waiting the cut of the surgeon's knife
And the promise of new-found sight.
Sleeping and waking we pass the days
While nurses move here and there
Dispensing dressings and drugs and food
With infinite love and care.
Till the fifth day comes when, with bandages gone,
We gaze round that hall so vast
Faces are seen, food takes form,
Discomfort and pain are past!
As we gather together possessions and drugs,
Instructions and green eye-shades,
As with stick in hand we step from that room
To retreat the journey we made,
We see the sun, we see the grass
And the coolies bring their load,
And we see the rice fields, newly-cut,
On either side of the road.
And we think of that Jesus whose power to heal
Has shown us a world new-found.
And as we travel the sun-lit path,

Our hearts with joy abound,
Till we reach our jungle village once more
Where with loved ones the roads are lined.
There stands our house! There wait the fields!
Lo, we see, where once we were blind!

With greetings,

Yours sincerely,

MAUREEN MURPHY

28.
DEATH OF JAMES

Early in August 1918, when Trinity College professors were taking holiday time away from the university, James was at home, making the hay. The long grass out in the meadow was cut by scythe in mid-June, on a day when good weather was forecast. Spread out around the field to dry, for several days the cut grass was turned over and over with rakes. Unexpected rain or showers would cause trouble, for if left to lie damp, or if stored damp, the hay could go mouldy. After drying for several days, the hay was lifted up into hayricks by swinging pitchforks full of hay up onto the pile. Ropes with rocks tied to the ends were swung over the rick, to prevent it blowing apart. The sight of sweet-smelling yellow haystacks dotted around green fields is now a thing of the past.

Being the winter feed for stock, hay was gold to a farmer. By the end of July, the ricks were ready to bring into the barn, to store for winter use. For this job, farmers used flat carts with no sides, and the ricks were hauled up onto the cart to make the trip, one at a time, to the barn. The Rathcore farm was small, with a limited number of ricks, so it would take only a couple of men to throw up the hay onto a stack in the barn. The man standing on the top of the pile was a key player, as he had to keep each lifted forkful spread out to the sides, maintaining the top flat and level, ready for the next forkful. Building up a barn's stack is an art, and James would have had experience from helping his father in his youth.

Working with hay was dangerous, too, as the pile in the barn grew and the stack rose higher, men were now standing on the cart to swing up the hay. A well-built stack of hay makes a great playground, a slide from top to bottom is a thrill. But James took a wrong step, easily done, and lost his footing. He should have realised at sixty-eight he had no business being up there, in the first place. He skidded off the top of the stack in the barn, right down to the hard ground. Crashing onto his shoulder, he broke his collarbone.

Now confined to bed at home, he was cared for by his wife Emmeline Annie, a self-taught nurse of some repute. His son Dr Cyril Murphy directed care and provided medications. All autumn, James did well, the long healing process keeping him in bed, but shortly after Christmas 1918, he contracted pneumonia. James didn't have the strength to fight against this infection, his heart was failing, and although Dr Cyril could postpone the inevitable for a while, James died in Rathcore Rectory on April 7, 1919. His son Charlie was present at his death, and took care of all arrangements. Later, with the support of Rummer, Cyril organised the legal issues.

A huge funeral was held for James in Rathcore Church, the presiding clergy being Uncle Fred Lucas, assisted by two others, one of whom was the lifelong friend of James, the Rev John Quarry Day. James was buried in the cemetery surrounding Rathcore Church.

The gravestone of J. E. H. Murphy

*

The inscription on his gravestone, written in Irish:

Slán a Cara, agus codail ciuin.
Slán a Atair fa do dorus cung.
Slán a Sagairt is a Ollaim oll,
Is a Sair-fir fearda de Síol Murcuda.

which translates to:

Farewell Friend and sleep peacefully.
Farewell Father under your narrow door.[73]
Farewell Priest and distinguished Professor,
A gallant man of the Murphy clan.

Accounts of the funeral were written up in a number of newspapers, one of which reported, 'He was Professor of Irish, T.C.D., for quarter of a century.'

The parishioners rallied and purchased a lectern, still to be found in Rathcore Church. The plaque on the lectern reads:

To the
Glory of God
and memory of
The Reverend
JAMES EDWARD
HARNETT MURPHY
M. A.
Professor of Irish
Rector of Rathcore
from 1881 to his death 7 April 1919
This lectern was placed here
by his parishioners as a token
of their esteem and respect

Inscription on the Memorial Lectern in Rathcore Church

---

73   *Narrow door:* Possibly a reference to The Gospel of Luke, 13:24: "Make every effort to enter through the narrow door, because many, I tell you, will try to enter and will not be able to."

Dying prematurely, James left his work on manuscripts unfinished. This had been the same situation for former Professors of Irish at Trinity College before him. It is to be hoped James Murphy's name accompanies those of other scholars of Irish, so that his hard-earned achievements can be recognised and credited.

It is a long road to travel from an earthen-floored, stone-walled cottage in West Cork during the Great Famine to the hallowed halls of Trinity College, Dublin University, at the end of the Great War. That road had been opened up by opportunities provided by the Irish Education System. His whole life, James had determinedly travelled along his chosen route, intensely focused on the road ahead. He would never let family or society distract him from his set path or from his progress in any way.

The Murphy children said their father *made a god out of education*. He had worshipped education all his life.

FAMILY TREE OF SIBLINGS OF JAMES

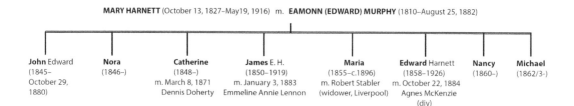

29.
SIBLINGS OF JAMES

John, Nora, Catherine, Maria, Edward, Nancy, and Michael

JOHN EDWARD

Also known as 'JOHNNIE'

John was born in 1845. It is very strange there is no record of his birth, or indeed of any part of his life, apart from his tombstone, near Lauragh in Kilmakillogue Cemetery.

John was *baptised a Catholic* as described below, on July 16, 1848. He was three.

IRE_PRS_MICROFILM 04282-04_0187

But we also know of him because a student notebook has come down through the generations:

This is a notebook signed as follows:

John Murphy

of

Droumard Ardgroom

Berehaven

Book held by great-grandson of James, James Royse Murphy.

Eva, eldest daughter of James, said to her own daughter:

> Your grandfather's brother [i.e,. **John**] was a merchant in the Merchant Navy. He died of a fever in Japan or China, dying before grandfather died. He didn't marry. He sent some things home, including an ornamental chest.

All information Eva left has proven with research 'to be true'. It is very unlikely she is incorrect here. We just have to find the record of the relative to whom she is referring. Perhaps John signed up? Researching the Merchant Navy records at UK National Archives, there was a John Murphy, born in the Cork area in 1846 (young lads lied about their age, and anything else, to increase their chances of being accepted). This lad signed up for ten years' service in 1871. He was a carpenter, and did very well until November 9, 1877, when he was invalided off-ship to an English hospital and later released.[74]

Another John Murphy, 'born in Bunnaugh, Kerry'[75] on April 1, 1844, signed up also as a carpenter for ten years starting on August 1, 1864.[76] He was in continuous service for ten years, serving as part of a carpenter crew. All the vessels he served on were hospital ships. It is understandable that his father Eamon recognised his son John had tuberculosis, rampant in every part of Ireland at that time. If John was on board Navy vessels, he would be exposed to the bracing, healing effect of fresh sea air, he would have been cared for by qualified doctors, and he would have been fed good food regularly. He would also have been removed from the Murphy cottage, no longer an infection risk for his young siblings.

This second John seems the most likely. His height was given as 5 feet 7 inches, he had a dark complexion, black hair, and hazel eyes. And surely he would have had mates here and there along the way, and one of those could have been working on board a ship that sailed to the Orient and then returned with the treasured chest, as described by Eva. The chest, about 1 foot high, was given to Rev James E. H. Murphy and Emmeline Annie as a wedding present from a brother of James, and has come down safely through the years.

---

74   *John Murphy I:* "Murphy, John, Official Number: 59960…" The National Archives, ADM 188/38/59960, Retrieved March 4, 2020, from http://discovery.nationalarchives.gov.uk/details/r/D6594095

75   *Bunnaugh, Kerry*: situated in the Tuosist area of the Beara Peninsula, also spelt as *Bunnaw* or *Bunau*.

76   *John Murphy II*: "Murphy, John Place of Birth: Bunaugh, Kerry, Ireland," The National Archives, ADM 188/38/59960, Retrieved March 4, 2020, from http://discovery.nationalarchives.gov.uk/details/r/D7919024

Murphy chest with open doors on R, which has come down through the generations

When he was about thirty, John went ashore, arriving back in Ardgroom, in 1874. Although now an experienced Navy sailor, full of stories, his health gradually deteriorated and he died when 35 years old, in 1880. He died before his father.

NORA

Nora was baptised in the Roman Catholic church in Lauragh on May 21, 1846. The Murphy family was living on Bere Island at the time, but baby Nora may have been born where Mary felt safe and cared for, perhaps even attended by a midwife, and perhaps in the house of her own mother. Mary's mother's name was Honora, and Mary's new baby was named after her.

However, we hear no further of Nora. She may not have been one hundred percent healthy, and her death may have been for the best, but we cannot be sure. The Famine had begun, and fevers and distress were on all sides. It seems wee Nora died, a heartbreak for her parents, however it happened. No record of her death has come to light.

CATHERINE

Born in the summer of 1848, Catherine was baptised on June 6, 1848, in the Church of Ireland, Reenavaude, Ardgroom, by Rev John Halahan, Curate. She was baptised a second time in the Roman Catholic church on Bere Island, where her family was living at the time, on July 16, 1848.

She was married in a Protestant church in Ardgroom or in Castletownbere on August 3, 1871, to Denis Doherty, a young farmer working his father's land in Capparoe, behind Templenoe.

Templenoe is on the northern coast of Kenmare Bay, almost straight across the water from the mouth of Ardgroom Harbour, on the southern coast of the Iveragh Peninsula. At that time, and for many years after, Ardgroom was renowned for its dances, held in a large workshop and later, in a dance hall. Admission price was 2 pence. The music was played on an accordion and a fiddle, and consisted mostly of old-time waltzes, sets, the stack of barley, the two-step, and the barn dance. People came from all over Beara and from across the water of Kenmare Bay, to these dances.[77]

As a young man, Denis would have rowed across the bay with friends to attend dances at Ardgroom, and surely that is how he met and fell in love with Catherine Murphy. There is a stony beach along the northern side of Kenmare Bay, at Templenoe, where a rowboat could have been readily pulled up for safekeeping. There was a main track which ran along the southern shore of the Iveragh Peninsula, and which today is paved and known as part of *The Ring of Kerry*. Across this roadway and up the hill, can be found the area known as Capparoe, where Denis was a farmer. Here, high up with a magnificent view looking south, out over the water towards Ardgroom, Denis and Catherine Doherty settled down together in a stone cottage and reared a family. They had nine children, possibly more, some dying young. All the remaining ones emigrated to the United States. Passenger lists held at UK National Archives at Kew, show the youngsters caught steamers from Dublin, and one by one emigrated across the Atlantic. But they needed an experienced family member to guide the emigrating traveller along, not only on board ship, but also across Ireland to Dublin and then finally, on arrival in New York or Boston. Mostly that guide was Emily, one of Catherine's daughters. Perhaps Emily was the healthiest, the strongest, perhaps she had a clear head and could speak her mind, but Emily travelled back and forth a number of times.

Meanwhile, Catherine was not well. Her eldest son Michael had settled in New York, but he became involved in a bar-room brawl, he slipped and fell, and badly knocked his head. He was never the same afterwards, and his siblings encouraged him to return home to the Old Country, which he did. He lived with his mother, Catherine, in the old Capparoe cottage, and together they farmed the land. Catherine died there, and was buried down in the Templenoe Graveyard right beside the waters

---

77   *History of Ardgroom* (Ardgroom: ICA Ardgroom, December 2008), 30.

of Kenmare Bay which had influenced so much of her life. It is only a step or two from her unmarked grave to the pebble beach where the rowing boats used to be pulled up for safety.

The neighbours remember 'the old Michael Doherty who lived on alone in the cottage before he eventually died there'. The cottage stands as a ruin today, a source of wonder to her modern-day relatives, who marvel at Catherine's strength and stamina in successfully rearing so many children in so tiny a space and under such harsh conditions!

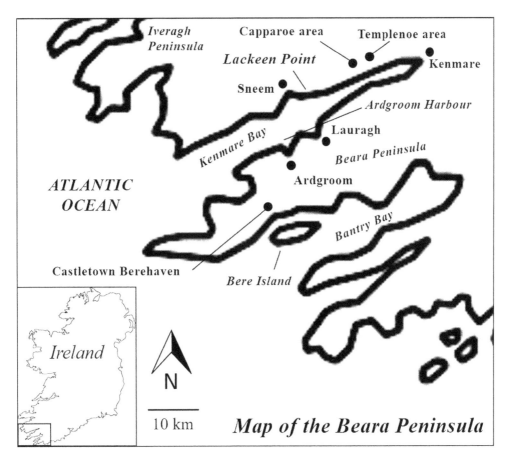

Map 8
Map to show positions of places mentioned in this chapter

MARIA

Also known as 'NANNIE' or 'NANNY'

Born January 23, 1855, in Droumard, Ardgroom. Baptised March 11, 1855, in Church of Ireland, Reenavaude, by the curate. Lived for a short while in Lackeen Point, Co. Kerry, and then in Liverpool.

Maria is recorded as 'Nanny', married February 14, 1879, in a Church of Ireland church, either at Reenavaude or in Castletownbere, to Robert Stabler, a widower and a coastguard, based in the Coastguard Station at Lackeen Point near Sneem, Co Kerry. Robert was the son of John Stabler, a cotton dyer, who may have lived in Derbyshire. Robert already had three children by his first wife: Mary Ellen, Fanny, and Robert.

Maria and Robert Stabler had five children. It is thought Maria Stabler fell down some stairs, about 1896, and was incapacitated until her death, on December 14, 1905, when she would have been fifty years old. Her brother, James Murphy, went over to Liverpool to attend his sister's funeral.

EDWARD HARNETT MURPHY

Also known as 'NED' or 'NEDDY'

Edward was born on December 12, 1858 in Ardgroom. Baptised in the Church of Ireland, he was taught at home by his father, who continued with instruction until Edward was fully literate in both English and Irish. Edward was four years old when his older brother James left for school in Bandon, and he saw his sister Catherine married and leave home when he was thirteen.

Once he turned eighteen, he had had enough of the crowded family life in the stone cottage. With his father's blessing, and determined to set out on his own, he likely walked to Cork where he boarded the *Queen of Nations* and on September 19, 1876, he arrived at Brisbane, Australia, still aged eighteen years.

Ned, as he was known locally, was employed on some of the huge sheep ranches, and he worked his way up to being a successful shearer. One of his arms and a hand had been damaged, but where or how this injury occurred is unknown. It is remarkable he could succeed at shearing with such a handicap.

On October 22, 1884, he married Agnes McKenzie at Roma, Queensland, where they lived for many years. They had five children.

On March 26, 1891, Edward was arrested at Roma for conspiracy, as one of the leaders of the 1891 Shearers' Strike. He had been valuable to his companion shearers because of his literacy. On May 20, 1891, a court case was held at Rockhampton and Edward was sentenced to three years hard labour at St. Helena Island. He was released from this prison on November 16, 1893.

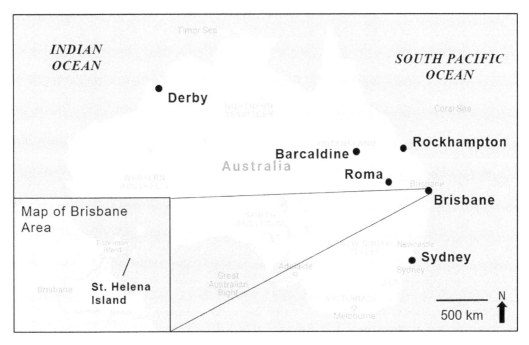

Map 9

When released, the men were blacklisted, and Edward could find work only as a labourer. Later, he obtained work as a boundary rider, when his duties entailed a regular tour on horseback of the outer perimeter, or boundary, of a sheep station, checking the condition of fences, collecting stock that may have escaped and ejecting strays that may have wandered onto the property.

Ned's marriage did not survive the stress of these years. His youngest son fought in World War I and was killed near Ypres on September 26, 1917, not far from where his first cousin, Leo Murphy, was second-in-command of a siege battery.

On April 22, 1926, Edward died in Derby, Western Australia, where he was buried. He was sixty-eight and his heart had given out.

The 1891 Shearer's Strike marks the founding of the Labour Movement in Australia, and those imprisoned for union activities are now revered for their actions. Edward is immortalised as one of the thirteen leaders sculpted on a commemorative bronze plaque in Barcaldine.

Sources: Jaclyn Hine (great-granddaughter). Brisbane
Kaylene Reynolds (Barcaldine Carrying Co.). Barcaldine
Richard Wormell and Pauline Lyle-Smith. London

Unionist prisoners sentenced May 1891, with their names engraved below. E H MURPHY

The following picture shows an information plaque at the Tree of Knowledge, in Barcaldine. In 2012, an event took place there, as recently described by Richard Wormell, great-grandson of James Murphy, brother of E. H. Murphy:

> My Australian wife, Pauline, and I went to the site with the Mayor of Barcaldine in 2012 as part of the Cook Society Commemorations. (The Cook Society was formed to reinforce the very special relationship between GB and Australia.) We were taken to the site so we could see the commemorative plaque for those who had fought for the shearers' rights. Everyone present was completely oblivious as to what was before us – namely, the brother of my great-grandfather was one of the 13 named shearers being honoured that day.

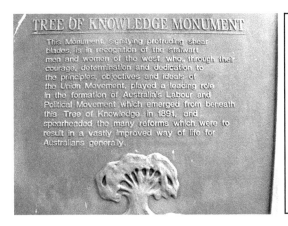

This monument, signifying protruding shear blades, is in recognition of the stalwart men and women of the west, who, through their courage, determination and dedication to the principle, objectives, and ideals of the Union Movement, played a leading role in the formation of Australia's Labour and Political Movement which emerged from beneath this Tree of Knowledge in 1891, and spearheaded the many reforms which were to result in a vastly improved way of life for Australians generally.

NANCY MURPHY AND MICHAEL MURPHY

We know so little about these two children. Only their baptism dates and birth places. Nancy was baptised on May 19, 1860, and Michael was baptised on February 16, 1862.

Their place of baptism is in Kilmichael, County Cork. It may be said, 'Oh, no, too far away.' Kilmichael is about 90 kilometres, 55 miles, from the Capparoe area.

However, the parents of each of these two were Mary Hartnett and Edward Murphy. By this time, Eamon was known as Edward. This record contains a most uncommon combination of names, Hartnett and Murphy, Mary and Edward. It is very likely Nancy and Michael were a part of this family.

There is a story which has been heard where a friend of one of the descendants of Mary and Edward was researching her roots, and was chatting to some local people in the Templenoe area. The conversation went something like this:

> *Local*: Is it your ancestors you're after?
>
> *Researcher*: Oh, it is indeed.
>
> *Local*: And what is the name ye have?
>
> *Researcher*: Catherine Doherty was the name.
>
> *Local*: Well now, isn't that amazing. Aren't I related to her, too? Yes, she was my family all right. We all come down from her.

But neither the **local descendant** nor the **visiting researcher** thought of asking any further questions. And it remains for us to wonder if the **Local** was a descendant of Nancy or of Michael, who might have settled in that area.

This is the gravestone of Edward Murphy, father of James and his siblings.

The apparent "ears" on either side of the top are in fact the ruins of a chapel above and behind.

This stone may be found in the Killmacanogue Graveyard, close to Lauragh, Co. Cork.

*Gravestone of Edward, or Eamon, father of James and his Siblings.
The inscription reads: ERECTED IN MEMORY OF JOHN MURPHY WHO DIED OCT 29 1880 AGED 35 YEARS AND OF EDWARD MURPHY WHO DIED AUGUST 25 1882 AGED 73 YEARS R.I.P.*

30.
A BICYCLE BUILT FOR TWO IN 2018

"But you'll look sweet, upon the seat, of a bicycle built for two"

Today, we would call the Murphy family of Rathcore Rectory, Enfield, Co. Meath, 'avid bicyclists'. Living in the early 1900s, cycling was their primary means of transport. When their grandfather brought them a present from England, a tandem bicycle, a two-wheeler built for two riders, they were ecstatic. The girls felt liberated, given the freedom to cycle 'up and away' with a boyfriend. Or, one of the Murphy brothers would take the big front seat with a crossbar and feel in control of the world. But to siblings Eva and Charlie Murphy, the bike became central to their quiet, rural lives. The two of them would hop on, cycle the 30 miles or so on unpaved roads, up to the latest show in the Gaiety Theatre in Dublin. They must have seen every play, every opera, every spectacle put on during those early years. Afterwards, they would pedal back home to Rathcore, passing the time on the ride by critiquing what they had seen and heard.

Eventually, Eva emigrated to Canada, and Charlie became the Secretary of the Irish Automobile Association. But Charlie had always kept a soft spot for the tandem. When his father died and his mother had to leave Rathcore Rectory, Charlie took charge of the tandem, carrying it off for safekeeping to his house, Auburn, in Malahide. Occasionally, Charlie's kids would take a spin together, but the trouble was, you always needed two for a ride! When Auburn was sold in the 1960s, naturally Charlie packed up the bike and drove it in his car to the home of one of Eva's daughters, Daphne Wormell, who had settled in South Dublin. Here the bike was suspended high up in the garage for about 10 years, and we kids used to play table tennis underneath it. Ping pong balls flew in and around the tandem's spokes! When the garage was converted to a granny flat, the bike was hung up in the henhouse, for a further 12 years.

In the 1970s, one of Eva's grandsons, Robin, began to take an interest. He painted the bicycle, and showed it to Joe Daly, a biking guru nearby in Dundrum who was well known to Dublin cycling enthusiasts as a skilled mechanic. Joe was enthralled, but he said he had no spare parts for such an extraordinary model. The trouble was, the sprocket for the chain on the back wheel kept breaking. One mechanic welded it back together, but even so, it continued to snap.

Word about this bike was getting around. At one time, a cycling enthusiast who collected rare bicycles and performed circus acts, visited the home, and Robin's father, Donald Wormell, Professor of Latin at TCD, took him to the henhouse for a viewing. The bike 'weighed a ton', was 'as heavy as a crate', and Dad could hardly move it. The enthusiast changed the back sprocket, but now the pedal kept moving whenever the back wheel rotated, even when supposed to be free-wheeling.

What to do about the lack of free-wheeling? We have a cousin living in London, John Leyland, who is a vintage car mechanic of the highest order. Robin pleaded, and John was persuaded 'to give it a go'. Robin, now based in London, took off the tandem's back wheel in Dublin and carried it over to London. For three days John worked his magic on wheel restoration, inserting new ball bearings and allowing the back wheel to rotate freely in an easy manner. Only John could have achieved such perfection!

Meanwhile, back in Dublin, as another house was sold, the bike was moved again, limping along one might say, and soon storage was found in Shankill, in a shed underneath a large, climbing wisteria. In 2002, the Shankill property was sold, and the tandem was carefully housed with friends and relatives, all of whom were very protective. The re-done back wheel remained in London. Finally, Robin heard of High Nelly Bike Centre in Tullabeg, Co. Limerick, who agreed to restore the front wheel, and the bike as a whole. They wrote:

> 'This tandem is an extraordinary bicycle. We will search three different continents to find in a scrapyard somewhere, anywhere, the required part for the damaged front sprocket. If we can't find it, we will make it.'

And that's what happened. High Nelly had no luck with their search, but they completely revamped the bike themselves. Today the bike with two perfect wheels is sparkling like new. A programme was broadcast not long ago on Ireland's *RTE Radio* about High Nelly, when the interviewee talked about 'the extraordinary bike we have been working on for a doctor in London.'

The Murphy tandem bicycle [photo credit: High Nelly Bike Centre, Co. Limerick. August, 2016]

Today, the tandem hangs in all its glory, pinned to a wall in the house of a friend who lives in Clondalkin. On June 16, 2018, at 11 a.m., the Murphy bike was at last returned to the streets, now all paved and smooth. It was ridden in the Bloomsday Bicycle Ride which ran from the Dalkey Garden Club to Mitchel's Winery. Robin himself was fully dressed in Edwardian gear, and 'felt like a million dollars' as the man in charge. He was accompanied by his nephew, James Wormell, from Bristol, and by his niece, Joanna Wormell from London, who 'felt liberated' on the back saddle, as her brother led the way. They, too, selected gorgeous period clothes, and Joanna was assured her petticoats and skirts would not catch in the back spokes, jamming up the spinning wheel, for the bike had been recently installed with specially developed, colourful, protective ribbons running out from each side of the back mudguard, like a fan.

This couple, Eva's great-grandson and Eva's great-granddaughter, rode along, each pedal push in memory of the great trips made to the Gaiety by Charlie and Eva a hundred and fifteen years ago, and in full appreciation of the care taken by all those who encouraged and kindly watched over a dusty antique, hoping someday it would have another moment in which to shine.

James Wormell and Joanna Wormell ready with tandem for Bloomsday Dalkey Ride, June 16, 2018

APPENDIX I

List of books sourced for Chapter 4

Ireland Before the Famine, 1798–1848, by Gearóid Ó Tuathaigh
The Gill History of Ireland
Gill and Macmillan, 1972 first published, 1982 reprint

The End of Outrage, Post-Famine Adjustment in Rural Ireland, by Breandán
Mac Suibhne
Oxford University Press, 2017

The Irish Quakers, A Short History of the Religious Society of Friends in Ireland
by Maurice J. Wigham
Historical Committee of the Religious Society of Friends in Ireland
Historical Committee, 1992

The Great Hunger, Ireland 1845–9, by Cecil Woodham-Smith
(First published 1962) N.E.L. edition, 1970

Achill Island, by Theresa McDonald
I.A.S. Publication (First published 1997) This edition, published 2006

Atlas of the Great Famine, 1845–1852
Editors: John Crowley, William J. Smyth, Mike Murphy
Cork University Press, 2012

*The Famine and The Illustrated London News – Illustrations as Evidence
Summary of Margaret Crawford, 'The Great Irish Famine 1845–9: Image
versus Reality, in Ireland. Art into History',* edited by Raymond Gillespie and
Brian Kennedy.
Town House, Dublin 1994, pp 75-88

Soupers and Jumpers by Miriam Moffitt
  History Press Ltd., 2008

Modern Ireland: 1600–1972 by Roy Foster
  Penguin Books; Reprint edition, 1990

The Way That I Went by Robert Lloyd Praeger
  The Collins Press; this edition 2014 (first published Hodges, Figgis and
  Co., 1937)

APPENDIX II

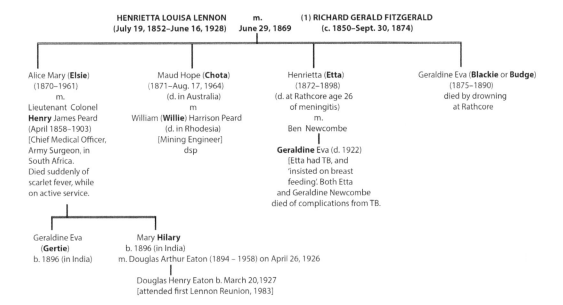

HENRIETTA LOUISA LENNON m. (1) RICHARD GERALD FITZGERALD
(July 19, 1852–June 16, 1928) June 29, 1869 (c. 1850–Sept. 30, 1874)

Alice Mary (**Elsie**)
(1870–1961)
m.
Lieutenant Colonel
Henry James Peard
(April 1858–1903)
[Chief Medical Officer,
Army Surgeon, in
South Africa.
Died suddenly of
scarlet fever, while
on active service.

Maud Hope (**Chota**)
(1871–Aug. 17, 1964)
(d. in Australia)
m
William (**Willie**) Harrison Peard
(d. in Rhodesia)
[Mining Engineer]
dsp

Henrietta (**Etta**)
(1872–1898)
(d. at Rathcore age 26
of meningitis)
m.
Ben Newcombe

Geraldine Eva (d. 1922)
[Etta had TB, and
'insisted on breast
feeding'. Both Etta
and Geraldine Newcombe
died of complications from TB.

Geraldine Eva (**Blackie** or **Budge**)
(1875–1890)
died by drowning
at Rathcore

Geraldine Eva
(**Gertie**)
b. 1896 (in India)

Mary **Hilary**
b. 1896 (in India)
m. Douglas Arthur Eaton (1894 – 1958) on April 26, 1926

Douglas Henry Eaton b. March 20,1927
[attended first Lennon Reunion, 1983]

Henrietta 'left' her four young girls in Rathcore Parish: Mary Lucas at Newcastle took Grandchildren Geraldine (Blackie) and Maud (Chota) and Grandmother Mary Fitzgerald took Etta and Elsie.

Two of Henrietta's children:
LEFT Henrietta, known as Etta, and RIGHT her sister Maud, known as Chota

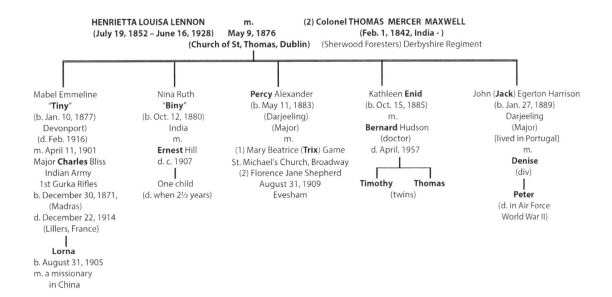

HENRIETTA LOUISA LENNON   m.   (2) Colonel THOMAS MERCER MAXWELL
(July 19, 1852 – June 16, 1928)   May 9, 1876   (Feb. 1, 1842, India -)
                              (Church of St, Thomas, Dublin)   (Sherwood Foresters) Derbyshire Regiment

Mabel Emmeline	Nina Ruth	Percy Alexander	Kathleen Enid	John (Jack) Egerton Harrison
"Tiny"	**"Biny"**	(b. May 11, 1883)	(b. Oct. 15, 1885)	(b. Jan. 27, 1889)
(b. Jan. 10, 1877)	(b. Oct. 12, 1880)	(Darjeeling)	m.	Darjeeling
Devonport)	India	(Major)	**Bernard** Hudson	(Major)
(d. Feb. 1916)	m.	m.	(doctor)	[lived in Portugal]
m. April 11, 1901	**Ernest** Hill	(1) Mary Beatrice (**Trix**) Game	d. April, 1957	m.
Major **Charles** Bliss	d. c. 1907	St. Michael's Church, Broadway		**Denise**
Indian Army		(2) Florence Jane Shepherd		(div)
1st Gurka Rifles	One child	August 31, 1909	Timothy Thomas	
b. December 30, 1871,	(d. when 2½ years)	Evesham	(twins)	**Peter**
(Madras)				(d. in Air Force
d. December 22, 1914				World War II)
(Lillers, France)				

Lorna
b. August 31, 1905
m. a missionary
   in China

NOTES: **Tiny** drowned when the ship she was travelling on, with her horse, hit a mine en route to Persia.

[May have been the *Lily Reaich,* which sank by a mine in the Adriatic Sea, on Feb. 26, 1916, OR the *Gavenwood,* which sank by a mine off Brindisi, on Feb. 20, 1916.]

APPENDIX III

A THANK YOU NOTE
and how were our US relatives found?

JULY 16, 2002

Julia Turner and her aunt, Valentine Urie, had been driving around the south and north shores of Kenmare Bay, seeking something, anything, about their Murphy ancestors. Val's grandfather had been born in the area mid-nineteenth century, and we had discovered one of his sisters had married a Doherty who was a farmer in the Capparoe area on the northern shore.

We thought, 'Maybe there are Doherty descendants, our cousins, living today in Capparoe?' We wondered, 'Will today's excursion be yet another dead end?'

This is a snapshot of that day's conversations, most of which took place over cups of tea:

Farmer: 'I've lived here all my life. I heard the name Doherty all right. They all disappeared. You can check at Capparoe. It's a mile from here, on the right-hand side. There's no things to see, only torn down farms and cattle. The house is a ruin.'[78]

A Lady: 'If I could remember, it was so long ago. There's a big white house on its own, near the forestry, and the Dohertys were up that way. I'm no use to talk to you, you see, I'm only married into the area, I'm not from here. Go to **Breda O'Sullivan**, but she may be away working this morning.'

Breda: 'Hello. How do you do? Right, sit down a moment. Now what I remember . . . I wouldn't know a bit, now, but I know of where I have heard of Dohertys living. The best thing I can do is take you up to meet another lady, **Teresa Brennan**. She is a bit older than me, she would have lived next door to these people and would know more about them than I would.'

---

78   The house, or cottage, is a stone-walled ruin, standing in a field overlooking the Bay of Kenmare and the southern shore with Ardgroom Harbour in the distance.

Breda very kindly put us in her car and drove us up to **Teresa**'s place, next door to what had been the Doherty property in Capparoe.

Teresa: 'I heard my father talking. I remember there was Mike Doherty. He died there, in his house, I believe. He wasn't married. The Dohertys, now, came back from Massachusetts but their friend, who was enquiring for them, wasn't a *Doherty.* She was *O'Brien,* and was staying over in Tuosist in a holiday home, and she drove up here to find me. First time, that was last year, someone directed her to me. But then, in the springtime, she returned with an American, who came here with this picture.'

Teresa had brought out a picture of three smiling American ladies, and also an address and an email address. She said, 'This is from her. The American. And the address there. You can take it if you like.' But this was the only copy, so we said to her, 'Well, we won't take it from you, then.'

Teresa said, 'It was only weeks ago that she came. And she left the picture with me in case someone should ever come along looking for Dohertys from Capparoe.'

A momentous visit, and following on, connections were made by email and telephone with the Massachusetts Dohertys and their descendants. But that day, a photograph was taken of **Breda and Teresa** holding the picture from the US and standing in the Capparoe area.

Here it is:

Breda and Teresa with US photograph and addresses

But, this story continues, for on January 9, 2019, Julia Turner received an email from Jan Veneto in Massachussets. It reads, in part:

'When I was in Ireland I left a copy of this picture with contact information at the farmhouse of Teresa Brennan who had the next farm up the hill from the old Doherty cottage. On a long shot, I thought maybe one day someone else in the family would come by looking for the trail of the Dohertys and would knock on Teresa's door for information.

'And it happened. Not long afterward Julia Turner and Val Urie did just that. And they called me from Vancouver!

'There are all kinds of little miracles once you start a genealogical search. And I consider that this is one of mine!

'God Bless,

'Jan'

A BIG THANK YOU TO YOU ALL

INDEX

(Most of the names listed here are arranged
alphabetically by first names)

R

Richard Fitzgerald
153, 247

Richard Wormell
135, 238

Robin Wormell
ix, 109, 176, 242

S

Sharman Ross
58, 118, 121, 122, 123, 127, 201

T

TBD
Richard Chenevix Fleury
159, 160, 161, 162, 163

V

Vera (Goligher) Murphy
189, 190, 191, 192, 193

Vera (Oliver) Murphy
173

Violet Murphy
139, 140, 141, 142, 154, 155, 210

W

Willie Murphy
Dr. Willie Murphy
ix, 109, 111, 116, 118, 220

Lightning Source UK Ltd.
Milton Keynes UK
UKHW032004101220
374897UK00011B/1160

9 781525 574054